WOMEN AND POLITICS

Women and
Culture Series

The Women and Culture Series is dedicated to books that illuminate the lives, roles, achievements, and status of women, past or present.

Fran Leeper Buss
Dignity: Lower Income Women Tell of Their Lives and Struggles

La Partera: Story of a Midwife

Valerie Kossew Pichanick
Harriet Martineau: The Woman and Her Work, 1802–76

Sandra Baxter and Marjorie Lansing
Women and Politics: The Visible Majority

Estelle B. Freedman
Their Sisters' Keepers: Women's Prison Reform in America, 1830–1930

Susan C. Bourque and Kay Barbara Warren
Women of the Andes: Patriarchy and Social Change in Two Peruvian Towns

Marion S. Goldman
Gold Diggers and Silver Miners: Prostitution and Social Life on the Comstock Lode

Page duBois
Centaurs and Amazons: Women and the Pre-History of the Great Chain of Being

Mary Kinnear
Daughters of Time: Women in the Western Tradition

Lynda K. Bundtzen
Plath's Incarnations: Woman and the Creative Process

Violet B. Haas and Carolyn C. Perrucci, editors
Women in Scientific and Engineering Professions

Sally Price
Co-wives and Calabashes

Patricia R. Hill
The World Their Household: The American Woman's Foreign Mission Movement and Cultural Transformation, 1870–1920

Diane Wood Middlebrook and Marilyn Yalom, editors
Coming to Light: American Women Poets in the Twentieth Century

WOMEN AND POLITICS

The Visible Majority

Revised Edition

SANDRA BAXTER

MARJORIE LANSING

Ann Arbor
The University of Michigan Press

Revised edition 1983
First paperback edition 1981
Copyright © by The University of Michigan 1980, 1983
All rights reserved
Published in the United States of America by
The University of Michigan Press and simultaneously
in Rexdale, Canada, by John Wiley & Sons Canada, Limited
Manufactured in the United States of America

1986   1985   5   4   3

Library of Congress Cataloging in Publication Data

Baxter, Sandra, 1945–
  Women and politics

  Bibliography: p.
  Includes index.
  1. Women in politics—United States.   2. Feminism
—United States.   3. Voting—United States.
4. Politics, Practical.   I. Lansing, Marjorie, 1916–
II. Title.
HQ1236.B28   1983   305.4'2   82-6555
ISBN 0-472-10043-2
ISBN 0-472-08043-1 (pbk.)

CONTENTS

TABLES

FIGURES

chapter one

THE STUDY OF WOMEN AND POLITICS

A major shift has occurred in the voting balance in the United States in the last decade: more women than men have gone to the polls to vote for president. Further, for the first time since receiving the right to vote in 1920, significant numbers of women have entered the world of politics as candidates, party workers, and lobbyists. This book explores changes in the political attitudes and behavior of women over the past twenty-five years and assesses the implications of these shifts as women move from an ineffective political minority to a more activist numerical majority in the 1980s.

An important development in the last decade or so has been the renaissance of a women's movement, dormant since 1920, which aggressively seeks to obtain for women the rights and responsibilities accorded men. Paralleling this change, and unrecognized by researchers and politicians alike, has been the growth of an invisible majority in the electorate which has coalesced at times to influence public policy. This book explores this underresearched area and locates a voting bloc among women which has been significant, in some instances, but unapparent. Whether the unity among women in the American electorate will remain invisible or will emerge as a powerful force in electoral politics is unknown. With gains in the socioeconomic status of women and the growing public support for a more egalitarian society, the opportunities for women to become full members of the polity, to become "co-signers of the social contract" (Chassler 1979) are now the greatest in sixty years. This book documents the political standing of American women in the last quarter-century and suggests what the future may hold.

Women outnumber men in the population, and the growing politicization of women is reflected in the fact that more women than men have gone to the polls since 1964, when women outvoted men by a million and three-quarters votes, a difference that more than doubled by the 1972 election. By mid-1970, women had nearly closed the 10 percent gap in voter turnout first documented in analyses of the 1952 and 1956 national elections and published in the classic *The American Voter* (Campbell et al. 1960). This increase ran counter to the general post-1900 decline in turnout in the United States, a decline which was initially accelerated by the entry of women into the electorate in 1920. In the midst of the decreasing turnout rate, several categories of women—particularly those in the work force and blacks—have voted in ever-increasing proportions. The social and economic environment surrounding the American electorate has changed considerably since *The American Voter* appeared, and this chapter offers a systematic update and explanation of how and why the turnout gap between women and men has been shrinking.

Another important development over the last twenty-five years has been the increasing political activism of women. It is argued in chapter 7 that women have had their principal impact on the American political system through voluntary organizations. The 1970s presented a new picture of increasing numbers of women working in political parties, standing as candidates, campaigning for others, and joining a host of new organizations and interest groups seeking changes in public policy. Since 1960, the federal government has mandated a Magna Charta for women through such legislation as the Equal Pay Act of 1963, Title VII of the 1964 Civil Rights Act, and the pending Equal Rights Amendment. Supreme Court decisions regarding abortion and salary and retirement equity have added further governmental sanction to women's demands for equal treatment under the law. These social policies have complex origins, but the lobbying by women themselves has clearly been an important factor in their achievement. Whether or not various pieces of "women's" legislation, such as the Equal Rights Amendment, become implemented by Congress and the state legislatures, the issues raised have served as lightning rods for a new generation of women. This book also updates documentation of the political participation of American women which takes place outside the voting booth.

A contradictory trend which runs through the years to be covered by this investigation is the failure of women to win elections themselves and to secure appointments to elite, decision-making posts. Despite the political strides made by women, the loci of power in this country have not shifted—powerful corporate structures, government agencies, labor unions, universities, and political parties remain male monopolies. Testimony from both the National Women's Political Caucus and the individual women candidates suggests that one of the major obstacles is a financial catch-22: women have more difficulty raising campaign funds than men do, a condition flowing from, and insuring, the perception that politics is a man's domain. If Congress and the state legislatures would enact legislation providing funds for candidates, one of the formidable barriers which now prevents the election of women candidates would be removed. A second barrier is the popular belief that women will not support women candidates. The book presents evidence showing that there have been tendencies for women to unite electorally on a range of political issues, a contention which has major implications for the future election of women to public office, for party alignments, and for policy outcomes in closely balanced electoral systems. Women have been assuming more responsible assignments in party and campaign organizations in the last decade, and they have gained the experience which qualifies them for appointment to public office and to judgeships. Their increased stature among political activists, however, has not resulted in commensurate increases in their political appointment. Several explanations for this situation are explored.

In every chapter, the analyses attempt to link the political behavior of American women to the profound cultural changes now taking place. The secondary status of women is deeply rooted in the interdependent structures of our political, economic, and social institutions. The institutional prejudice rests upon traditional attitudes and values regarding women's roles in society. But the major changes in the last twenty-five years in marital and family structure, the movement of significant numbers of women into the work force, women's greater access to education and training, and the amplification of these changes by the mass media, are challenging the stereotypes and forcing new definitions of roles for women more equal to those of men. As the persistent, de facto gap between the economic rewards given to women and to men closes, for example, there will be changes in the political status of women relative to that of men. The formal political status of women will not be changed only by Nora's stepping out of the doll house, contrary to the beliefs of many women's liberation theorists of the 1960s. Instead, the larger culture must also move toward new values and attitudes regarding gender roles before women reach visible positions of significant power in American politics. Women already form the invisible majority. For the first time in the sixty years since the granting of suffrage, we are witnessing again an American women's movement which is challenging the basic institutions of society and demanding full recognition. Our data extend from 1952 through 1976 and parallel the growth of this movement.

This book does not contain a thorough discussion of women's socialization nor the more specific topic of women's political socialization. Many books and articles have already been published with the sole purpose of documenting differences in the rearing patterns of female and male babies that produce girls and boys with different skills and interests and women and men with different life-styles. The conclusion reached in one recent synthesis of the lengthy literature is that there is greater variation in behavior and attitudes *within* each gender than there is *between* the "typical" woman and man (for a good summary see Maccoby and Jacklin 1974). This conclusion is supported in the coming chapters. The decision to omit a discussion of socialization should not be interpreted, however, as a discounting of the importance of socialization processes or outcomes. The significance of formative processes is apparent in the use of "gender differences" rather than "sex differences" when referring to women and men. Among social researchers, sex is understood to refer to biological differences between females and males, while gender refers to the socialized person with values and attitudes already inculcated (Walum 1977). The discussions here concern the political characteristics of women, and how those attitudes and behaviors differ from those of the other gender, men.

Socialization is also important in discussions of the political behavior of women because it provides the norms, values, and role definitions women and men carry into adulthood. These orientations are the bases on which people support, or challenge, the structures of society which continue to channel women and men into the social roles they play. In essence, socialization is assumed to be a significant shaping force in each woman's life; what is being tested here is the myth that women, because of their socialization, do not participate in or reflect upon politics in the same way as do men.

Even this statement, however, oversimplifies the importance of socialization. In chapter 7, the lack of women in visible positions of political power is documented. The scant number of women in high office is usually accounted for in two ways: by asserting that powerful men exclude women from high elective and appointive office, and by asserting that women do not aspire to such offices. Both explanations stem from the assumption that men and women are socialized into believing that men should hold the positions of real power in American society. There is evidence showing the belief to be widely held, particularly among certain subgroups in the population. Proof that the belief is inculcated during socialization lies in anthropological evidence from societies in which women are presumed to be the natural leaders.

Research on Women's Political Participation

The passage of the Nineteenth Amendment granting women the right to vote in 1920 generated extravagant predictions about the benefits and damage that suffrage would entail. Antisuffrage writers saw, of course, many harmful changes and titled their articles accordingly: "Women's Encroachment on Man's Domain" (Ludovici 1927) and "Evils of Woman's Revolt against the Old Stereotypes" (McMenamin 1927). Supporters of the amendment felt the need both to document improvement in society and apologize for the slow rate of "progress" (Catt 1927; Gilman 1927). Some social scientists marshalled the little data they could to gauge the amendment's impact.

One of the earliest quantitative studies of women's participation in politics by social scientists was the research of Rice and Willey (1924), which sought to determine whether the proportion of eligible women residing in the northern and western states who cast ballots in the 1920 election, the first following the enactment of the

Nineteenth Amendment, approached the proportion of men who voted. Their best estimate, reached after a complicated series of extrapolations, was that 3.66 million, or 34.7 percent of the eligible women had voted, which represented not only less than half of their potential voting strength, but was also markedly less than the corresponding figure for men. "The tradition that woman's place is anywhere but in the voting booth appears to persist," they concluded (1924, p. 643). This was predictably so, and a strong reminder that although women were then legally enfranchised, the social norms still discouraged their exercising it.

Another early attempt by a sociologist to gauge the impact of the Nineteenth Amendment was much less quantitative. Appearing in a 1930 issue of the *American Journal of Sociology*, the article was entitled "The Status of Women" (Woodhouse 1930). The short paragraph detailing women's status in the political field enumerated the number of women in Congress (eight), the number of states with women in the state houses (twenty-three), and asserted that with women state officials in a wide variety of offices, "progress must be reported."

The contemporary research on women's political participation is appearing at an ever-increasing rate. Most of what was widely known about the political attitudes and behavior of women was, until very recently, phrased in terms of the political characteristics of men. Consequently, women have been depicted as politically inadequate, unmotivated, naive, dependent upon the knowledge of men, and rightfully invisible.

Many social scientists have helped perpetuate the myth of apolitical woman, and not all of the researchers were men. It is easy to criticize the studies of thirty years ago for their limited samples, their simple analyses, and their readiness to reach certain conclusions. While most of the criticism is deserved, it is important to remember that empirical studies of political behavior were new and early conclusions carried more weight than they should have. Faulty analyses were perpetuated, and evidence counter to widely accepted explanations was difficult to get published. The scholarship is changing. In his 1965 book on political participation, Milbrath wrote:

The erosion of the sex difference in participation does not necessarily mean that women are becoming independent of men in choosing whom they will support; it means only that politics is less and less considered strictly a man's role. A good deal of solid evidence still suggests that wives follow their husband's lead in politics (sometimes vice versa), or at least that husband and wife tend to support the same parties and candidates. [P. 136]

In the revised edition issued twelve years later (Milbrath and Goel 1977), much of the original text on gender differences is retained, but the paragraph quoted above is absent.

A provocative criticism of the early political behavior research has been made by Bourque and Grossholtz (1974) who contend that assumptions and empirical distortions in the literature on gender roles in politics preclude women from ever being defined as full and equal participants in the political system. They classify the distortions in four categories: (1) "the assumption of male dominance" in the family which leads researchers to question neither the concentration of political power in men's hands nor the implications of such concentration for the functioning of society; (2) "masculinity as ideal political behavior" and as rational and normative, making the behavior of women appear as irrational, deviant, and deficient; (3) "commitment to the eternal feminine" which restricts women to nurturant roles of wives, mothers, and political helpmates, and finally (4) "fudging the footnotes" by citing material which does not substantiate the point being made but does support the image of apolitical woman conveyed by the first three distortions. This criticism has not been refuted.

Near the end of his influential book *Political Life* (1959), Lane considers suggestions for increasing the low participation of women.

Would it be wise to reinforce the feminist movement, emphasizing politics on the women's page along with the garden club and bridge club news, and making ward politics something like volunteer work for the Red Cross or the hospital auxiliary? No doubt something along this line could be done, but it is too seldom remembered in the American society that working girls and career women who insistently serve the community in volunteer capacities, and women with extra-curricular interests of an absorbing kind are often borrowing their time and attention and capacity for relaxed play and love from their children to whom it rightfully belongs. As Kardiner points out, the rise in juvenile delinquency (and he says, homosexuality) is partly to be attributed to the feminist movement and what it did to the American mother. [P. 355]

Not only is Lane's "commitment to the eternal feminine" apparent in the above quotation, but so is his belittlement of women's work in voluntary associations, an involvement of significant value both to the local community and to the woman herself, as is discussed in chapter 7.

The cross-cultural study of political attitudes conducted by Almond and Verba (1963) was the earliest well-known study to argue empirically that the levels of political interest and involvement are comparable between American women and men. Perhaps the small percentage differences found by earlier researchers in the activities of women and men would have been characterized as minimal, too, if comparable data from other cultures showing larger gender differences had been available to them. Without comparative data, it is difficult to decide when a numerical difference is negligible and when it is socially significant. Chapter 8 presents data from other nations showing how institutional and historical factors produce different levels of political participation by women.

Methodology

The argument in this book is that changes in women's social roles have led to changes in their political roles as well. To discuss change, researchers must rely upon data collected across many years and distinguish between long-term changes—trends which extend over many years—and short-term changes—fluctuations which disappear quickly. Data on political activity are particularly full of short-term changes because most studies are done during an election, and elections vary tremendously in the excitement and interest they generate among the public. In the tables that follow, data are presented from the election studies conducted at the time of the seven presidential elections held between 1952 and 1976. In chapters 2 and 7, data are drawn from the 1952, 1964, and 1976 studies; in chapters 3 through 6, the full set of seven elections studies is used. The chapters also vary in the depth of statistical analysis, depending upon the need to see trends in attitudes within subgroups of the samples or to see larger patterns among women in the electorate as a whole. Measures of statistical significance are reluctantly omitted due to the variety of comparisons implied in each table. Contrasts are drawn between the genders, across the elections, and across stratification variables and their categories. The inclusion of additional numbers in each table would clutter more than inform. The issues of statistical and social significance are critically important, however.

In some ways, the 1976 election is less than an ideal one for a study of changes in women's political roles over the last twenty-five years. The candidates and issues paramount in 1976 did not arouse the electorate and turnout was relatively low. Tables with data collected in 1952, 1964, and 1976 appear to herald a downward trend in the regard of Americans for the political system. The 1976 data reflect more short-term than long-term changes, the authors believe, and support is available in the many tables which contain data from the seven elections between 1952 and 1976. With information from the complete set of presidential elections during the twenty-five year period, short-term and long-term changes can be more easily disentangled.

The secondary analyses presented in the following chapters are based primarily upon survey data collected in connection with the presidential elections between 1952 and 1976. By looking carefully at the attitudes and actions of these samples of American adults drawn over the twenty-five year period, trends in how citizens regard the nation's political system and how they stand on the major issues of the day (and those issues change with the times) can be discerned. The primary focus is on the political behavior and attitudes of women, how these changed between 1952 and 1976, and how they compare with the actions and attitudes of men, who serve as a control group.

National surveys are common now and most people have a general idea of how they are conducted. Newspapers and television carry the results of the latest Harris, Roper, and Gallup surveys, and the image comes quickly to mind of an interviewer stopping pedestrians on a busy street corner or interrupting persons in their homes. In fact, the methodology of survey research is precise and complex, and the seeming simplicity of asking a number of people a series of questions in a well-designed survey hides a great deal of hard, systematic work. First, the respondents must be selected carefully so that they represent a much larger group—the adult population of a city or the population of college students in a state, for example—and secondly, the questions they are asked must be phrased so they can be understood by everyone without conveying the suggestion that one answer is better or more correct than another. Because the analyses to follow rely so heavily on surveys done at the time of the presidential elections, a fuller understanding of survey methodology is important.

The American National Election Surveys (from 1952 through 1976) used in this book were designed, executed, and analyzed by social scientists at the Center for Political Studies (CPS) at the University of Michigan's Institute for Social Research, Survey Research Center.[1] In each survey, interviews were held with a carefully selected group of adults whose characteristics—economic, social, and political—made them representative of the much larger set of adults living in the United States. The actual number of people interviewed varied from 1,899 in 1952 to 1,571 in 1964 and 2,248 in 1976, and each sample was designed to represent a national electorate which numbered approximately 98 million in 1952 and 135 million in 1976. Several small portions of the population were ignored in the sampling because of the difficulty in reaching them, and so the survey respondents do not represent military personnel and people in medical, mental, and penal institutions.

Interviews are held both before and after each election, allowing researchers to contrast the preferences and intentions of each respondent with the actual election outcomes. Did the respondent actually vote? Did her or his favorite candidate win? Did one's own political party make a good showing? As expected, a fair amount of rationalization is done, and respondents who in fact did not vote are prone to say they did, and party defeats can be portrayed as strong showings.

Social researchers have long known that the very act of interviewing someone can influence that person's answers. None of us has an opinion on every conceivable topic and few of us take consistent value positions across a variety of social issues. But when asked, the great majority has an opinion, and there is some tendency for that opinion to be socially acceptable as well. All of these pressures and tendencies which modify a person's "real" response are well known to researchers, as are techniques to combat them. The use of introductory phrases such as "People have a variety of opinions about issue X" and the explicit inclusion of "I don't know" and "I have no opinion" as valid response choices decrease the likelihood of instant opinions being voiced.

Although the methods of conducting reliable sample surveys are well known, not all survey efforts choose or are able to use them, so the responses collected in two different studies using a very similar question may vary considerably. One example of this familiar to political researchers is the difference in proportions of national samples reporting that they voted. Interviewers from Michigan's Center for Political Studies (producing what is referred to as the Michigan data) consistently generate voter turnout percentages that are higher than those produced by the federal government's Bureau of the Census. For example, 59 percent of the Census Bureau's United States adult sample reported voting in 1976 while 72 percent of the CPS-drawn adult sample did.

These variations complicate research, and are confusing to the reader. Traugott and Katosh (1979) investigated the source of the different voting rates produced by the two surveys, and concluded that among certain categories of the population there is a tendency to overreport voting. These researchers validated people's claim to have voted in the 1976 election and found that approximately 14 percent of the respondents in the Michigan study had not voted although they claimed to have done so.[2] The research design followed in the CPS studies, however, produces statistics which are misleading about the political behavior of the American population only in discussions of voting rates. For example, in 1976 the voting rate of women was reported to be 69 percent by the CPS and 59 percent by the Census Bureau. Voting rates are important indicators of political participation, however, and the discussion of them in chapter 2 follows a long tradition in the political behavior literature.

In the course of their investigation, Traugott and Katosh (1979) also checked whether repeated interviewing affected a person's trust in government and sense of power to influence the political system, two attitudes which are discussed more fully in chapters 3 and 6. They found that these political attitudes were not changed. In the pages ahead, there is heavy reliance on the Center for Political Studies election surveys and it is critical for the analyses made and the conclusions reached to know whether and how the CPS data are misleading.[3] Although not all of the attitudinal items used were subjected by Traugott and Katosh to the same scrutiny as the two mentioned above, their conclusion is that CPS data on political attitudes are accurate. Most of the other CPS variables used in this book are personal background characteristics, and it seems safe to conclude that repeated interviewing, which accounts for some misreporting of the vote, does not distort the accuracy of someone's response to questions on educational achievement, occupation, and age. Overall, the validity of survey methods in research on political behavior has been established over a quarter of a century.

In addition to the national election studies, some data are drawn from national surveys conducted by the United States Bureau of the Census in conjunction with the 1964 through 1976 presidential elections to provide larger samples for analyzing the vote of black citizens in chapters 5 and 6. Two other data sets are used in the chapter 8 cross-national analysis of women's participation. Stokes and Butler collected electoral information during the 1964 and 1970 parliamentary elections, and these are used to compare British and American women. The comparative chapter also draws on data known as Euro-Barometer 3: European Men and Women, a survey carried out by the European Omnibus Survey group in 1975.[4] All of the data sets used in the book were made available by the Inter-university Consortium for Political and Social Research at the University of Michigan.

Many social scientists believe that rigorous empirical research on topics such as women's political behavior is the best way to document and understand social phenomena. Too often, though, researchers are reluctant to conclude anything unless it is apparent in the patterning of numbers in a table. For readers without experience in interpreting tables (a brief lesson follows this discussion), even conclusions based on apparent statistical regularities must be taken on faith. This professional reluctance to generalize beyond one's data and to guess at factors producing a given attitude or action has the consequence of limiting both the types of questions and answers which good research can illuminate.

The lack of research on important, complicated issues will become apparent time and time again. For example, in chapter 7 figures are presented which show that a great majority of Americans say they would vote for a woman presidential candidate if one were nominated by their party. Yet no woman has ever been close to receiving the Democratic or Republican presidential nomination. Why? The answer is neither clear nor simple, and a full response would involve analyses of the role of women in the parties, campaign fund raising, the exclusion of women from the legal profession, perceptions and misperceptions of public support for women candidates, and a half dozen other topics. Few of these topics have been investigated in methodologically sound ways, and some researchers believe it is better to state nothing at all than to state something which may later be disproven.

The authors disagree, and causal relationships which cannot be documented are consciously and consistently discussed in this book. Only by moving beyond standard analyses of familiar data can the significant issues which intrigue us as political women and as social scientists be explored. And only by refusing to limit speculations can themes be raised which should be explored by the next round of research on women's political behavior.

A Brief Note on Reading Tables

The discussions on women's, and men's, political attitudes and behavior contained in the chapters ahead are empirical, i.e., they are based upon systematically gathered data, and are accompanied by tables which present those data in a relatively readable way. Most of the tables contain percentages rather than absolute numbers, because it is not the actual number of people who said one thing that is of interest, but the percentage of people giving a particular response out of all the people asked the question. The attitude or behavior under discussion is listed on the left of the table, and the categories of respondents (women, men, percentage of men minus percentage of women) are presented along the top. The discussion accompanying the table frequently mentions the patterning of percentages which supports the conclusion reached. The reader is encouraged to scrutinize the table and discover the patterning discussed, or perhaps even another one.

For those tables presenting the percentage of men minus the percentage of women, the argument concerns the similarity or dissimilarity in rates of action or attitude between women and men. The *actual percentages* of men and women reporting an activity or acknowledging an attitude is important as well as the gap between them. Because inclusion of those data would clutter the tables enormously, they have been collected in the Appendix which follows the last chapter. Thumb through those pages as well. Good tables raise more questions than they answer, and we have tried to present only good tables in the text and the Appendix.

Overview

The portrait of the American woman that emerged from *The American Voter* (1960) and numerous books and articles since then has depicted her as a generally apathetic citizen who left politics to the men in the family. This image is no longer conveyed by contemporary data on women's political participation, and an examination of statistics from 1952 to 1976 shows that women have emerged from political obscurity to constitute a numerical majority, but a majority still politically invisible.

In the following chapters, we raise and answer a series of questions concerning women's political roles. Do large gender differences in turnout and attitudes remain once socioeconomic and life-cycle differences between women and men in the electorate are considered? If fertility rates remain low, are women likely to become more politically involved in the years ahead? Do the younger women who were born shortly after the Second World War, who remember the assassination of President Kennedy, who grew up in an atmosphere of strife over civil rights, Vietnam, Watergate, and continuing crises concerning inflation, energy, and disarmament think and act any differently about politics than their mothers or grandmothers? Are women more or less interested than men in political campaigns? Do the genders have similar feelings of political efficacy? To what extent is there a bloc vote by women and how might it affect future elections? These questions are treated in chapters 2, 3, and 4.

In chapters 5 and 6, the question is raised whether the political behavior of minority women should be analyzed in terms of their racial identity, their gender, or both. In chapter 7, the participation of women is examined as it extends from grass roots voluntary organizations to the halls of Congress. If the definition of politics is expanded to include involvement in community organizations, do women still appear to be apathetic bystanders? How many women now belong to the ranks of the politically elite and what factors account for their ascendance? If women do achieve more clout in political decisions, will it make any difference, or do women who reach elite elective and appointive posts simply emulate their male colleagues? The portrait of the American woman citizen that emerges from answers to these questions is compared in chapter 8 with portraits of women in other social and cultural contexts in other countries. The book concludes with a discussion of the likelihood that American women will remain the invisible political majority on into the twenty-first century.

chapter two

THE AMERICAN WOMAN VOTER
From Minority to Majority

Karl Marx believed that universal suffrage would never be granted in capitalist nations, because it would result in a complete social upheaval in the interests of the proletariat. The women's movement of the early twentieth century in America had somewhat similar expectations: when women began to vote, a new era of social welfare legislation would dawn, and the government would turn away from war and corruption. Women's votes would transform society, the feminists claimed, and the politicians believed them and delayed congressional enactment of women's suffrage until 1919.

But once they gained the right to vote, relatively few women exercised it at first, and those who did supported candidates and held political opinions not very different from those of long-enfranchised men in similar social circumstances. Gradually, however, the participation of women in elections has increased. In their first national election in 1920, only about one-third of the eligible women voted, while approximately two-thirds of the eligible men did. The gap in voting rate has narrowed over the years since then due to large-scale changes in the social and economic roles of American women. Changes in the political involvement of women are the result of larger changes in their status. As gender role definitions have shifted, women have moved from a second-class political status to a position where their rate of participation resembles that of men. The exact differences between the voting rates of women and men fluctuate according to the significance of the election issues and the personal qualities of the candidates, but it is the changes in the gender difference over time that are of interest.

17

The emergence of women as the new political majority forms the theme of this chapter. In the first section, a brief overview of the women's suffrage movement is provided for historical perspective. Second, the presurvey era, 1920–48, is described with the minimal data which exist. Using data collected from 1952 through 1976, the similarity in the voting rates of women and men is examined. The greater this similarity, the less important gender becomes in under-standing political behavior. Other variables which serve to stratify society, such as education, income, and age, then become important for understanding how and why people relate to politics in the ways they do. The influence of gender relative to these other stratification variables is empirically tested at the end of this chapter.

The Struggle for Women's Suffrage

When the United States won its independence in the eighteenth century, the prevailing body of law governing the legal status of women was English common law. Common law barred women from voting, holding public office, or serving on juries, and denied them legal control of their children and property. Some historians ascribe the inferior legal status of women to the influence of the English jurist, Sir William Blackstone, who stated in his commentaries: "The husband and wife are one, and that one is the husband."

The legal prejudice against women was so great that few people during the nation's early decades sought to secure for women the basic democratic right of voting. Concern for the dignity and equality of women was the offshoot of concern for the dignity and equality of American blacks. The first movement for women's political rights is usually traced back to the 1840 World's Anti-Slavery Convention held in London. Having made the trip because of their beliefs in human equality, the American women abolitionists, and some of their male colleagues, were astonished to learn that the women were not to be seated on the convention floor but could voice their support for equality from the gallery (Kraditor 1965). Eight years later, a conference was organized by Elizabeth Cady Stanton and Lucretia Mott and held in Seneca Falls, New York, "to discuss the social, civil, and religious condition and rights of women" (Flexner 1959).

Three hundred women and several men attended, and one-third eventually signed a document patterned by Stanton after the Declaration of Independence and called the Declaration of Sentiments. The most controversial section of the document stated:

> Resolved, that it is the duty of the women of this country to secure to themselves their sacred right to the elected franchise.

Similar conventions in the years to follow brought the names Lucy Stone and Susan B. Anthony to public attention as well as to public ridicule.

During the 1860s, the suffrage energies were channeled into the Civil War. With that war's end, the abolitionist-feminists worked to ensure that the Republican party's gratitude for their war efforts would take the form of women's voting rights. Instead, party leaders saw the extension of the vote to black men to be more important. Women's suffrage slowly crept into state laws across the nation, however, beginning with the right to vote in school elections, and the territory of Wyoming in 1869 became the first member of the Union to grant full political equality as defined by law.

Suffrage strategists saw that national success would come only through state-level efforts, so during the next several decades state groups organized by the National American Woman Suffrage Association (NAWSA) demanded that the citizenry and the legislatures "remember the ladies." In 1915, Carrie Chapman Catt, who had come to suffrage from the temperance movement (Kraditor 1965), resumed the presidency of NAWSA and synchronized the state-level activities to the point where sufficient support was built up in Congress to secure the passage of the Nineteenth Amendment in June of 1919. By August of 1920, the required thirty-six states had ratified it and the final wording of the law was:

> The right of the citizens of the United States to vote shall not be denied or abridged by the United States or any state on the account of sex.

By this time, the suffrage movement involved millions of women and was devoted exclusively to obtaining the franchise. Thus, when the

Nineteenth Amendment passed, the feminist movement simply fell apart.

The prevailing view of social scientists in assessing the effects of women's suffrage is summarized by O'Neill in *Everyone Was Brave* (1969).

> It took seventy-two years for women to get the vote. Generations wore out their lives in pursuit of it. Some women went to jail, many picketed, marched, and protested their deprived state in other ways. In the last stages of the fight for equal suffrage, literally millions of women contributed something to the cause. Yet when the vote was gained it made little difference to the feminine condition. A few women were elected to office, political campaigning became more refined, and the sex lives of candidates were more rigorously policed. The ballot did not materially help women to advance their most urgent causes; even worse, it did not help women to better themselves or improve their status. The struggle for women's rights ended during the 1920's, leaving men in clear possession of the commanding places in American life. [P. 269]

Contrary to congressional fears, women did not clean up politics when they began to vote. Two University of Chicago professors, Charles Merriam and Harold Gosnell, pioneered in the study of voting by their analyses of the elections for mayor in Chicago in the twenties. They observed in their introduction:

> The first outstanding fact to notice is that nearly three-quarters of these non-registered adult citizens were women. Women were allowed to register for local elections in Chicago as early as 1913; yet ten years later not half of the adult female citizens of the city had established voting habits. [1924, p. ix]

The city of Chicago was one of the few political units which classified election statistics by sex, so the Merriam and Gosnell figures are more than estimates. In fact, the turnout of women throughout the nation for the 1920 election seems to have been quite low. One way of gaining an impression of the female turnout for voting in the early years of women's voting is to look at voter registration figures. Registration is a prerequisite to voting, so the actual percentages of women voting was undoubtedly lower than the figures in table 1 suggest.

The regional differences displayed in table 1 are also interesting, and show the beginnings of a pattern which persisted until 1976, as shown later in this chapter. The southern states consistently lagged in voting turnout among women. In Louisiana in 1920 only 18 percent of the registered voters were women, well below Chicago and Vermont. These figures may be attributed to regional differences in the role and status of women. They indicate that Elizabeth Cady Stanton was right: the real obstacle to equality was not the vote but the division of life-styles between men and women—and it was only as women became "self-supporting equal partners with men," as Stanton put it, that women began to exercise the hard-won right to vote in large numbers. The feminists of the early part of this century had it reversed: they believed that women playing an active role in politics would change society at its roots, but the opposite has occurred. Changes in the structure of society have brought about changes in the political role of women. As that role has evolved to the point where numerous women hold elected and appointed offices and pursue careers in the professions traditionally leading to politics, the likelihood of political equality becomes greater. But the primary impetus for the growth in the political participation of American women

Table 1. Trends in the Percentage of Registered Voters Who Were Women

Date	Louisiana	Vermont	Chicago
1920	18.2	41.0	37.8
1924	28.5	44.2	38.5
1928	30.5	47.3	43.2
1932	34.3	47.2	43.3
1936	—	47.6	46.3
1940	—	48.3	48.3

Source: "Report of the Secretary of State to his Excellency the Governor of Louisiana"; "Records of the Secretary of the State of Vermont"; "Records of the Board of Election Commissioners of the City of Chicago." The trends shown in table 1 are the most complete of those located either by us or by Gosnell (1948, p. 299).

from 1952 to the present has been their greater involvement in the social and economic (i.e., not explicitly political) spheres of society.

Voting Turnout in Presidential Elections

The measure of political participation used in this chapter is voting turnout for the presidential elections of 1952, 1964, and 1976. Voter registration and the actual casting of a ballot for the highest office in the land are not particularly demanding activities, given the ease of voter registration and the media buildup preceding such elections. Turnout, then, is a good baseline indicator of participation and for many years was the only indicator of political activity examined. Registration requirements can depress turnout, however, and historical comparisons of turnout across the American states (Kelley, Ayres, and Bowen 1967) and contemporary comparisons of voting rates across nations are complicated by differences in the electoral laws which facilitate or discourage registering and the casting of ballots. Activities such as contributing money to campaigns and attending political rallies are more demanding forms of electoral participation, and they are examined in chapter 7. In that same chapter the definition of political participation is broadened to include activities beyond those related to elections, such as involvement in community organizations. Under that definition, it is argued that women have had far greater political impact than usually credited them.

Out of the hundreds of published studies on political participation, surprisingly few discuss differences between women and men. A majority of studies, particularly the older ones, omit gender comparisons not only from their analyses but from the descriptions of their samples as well. Many of those studies which do look for differences in the participation rates of women and men use voting turnout as a measure of political involvement (Campbell et al. 1960; Lansing 1970; Verba and Nie 1972; Nie, Verba, and Petrocik 1976). These studies agree that men turn out in presidential elections at rates (*not* numbers) higher than do women.

When the turnout rates are plotted by gender for the 1952, 1964, and 1976 presidential elections, as is done in figure 1, the curve for

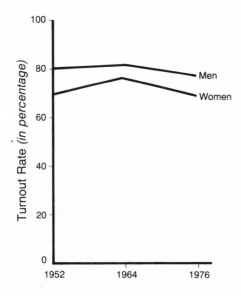

Fig. 1. Voter turnout rates of women and men, by election. *(Source of Data: Center for Political Studies, American National Election Studies, 1952–1976)*

men is higher than that for women. The difference between the genders has tended to decrease over the twenty-five years, but the change has not been a simple, linear one. The American electorate as a whole has voted at a lower rate in the presidential elections since 1964 than in that year and previous election years. The actual voting rates of women and men, and the difference between them, have varied considerably from election to election. Few of the differences are statistically significant, i.e., are of such magnitude as to be beyond chance occurrence. And compared to the gender difference in voting rates in other countries (see chap. 8), the voting gap between American women and men is small indeed.[1] The gap is real, however, and it is important to understand the demographic factors that account for both its current existence and its probable future disappearance.

The growing similarity in the voting rates of women and men has been occurring at the same time that the relative proportions of women and men in the United States population have changed. Prior to 1945, the number of men in this country was higher than the number of women. Males have been outnumbered in recent years, particularly in the older age groups. The increasing female voting rate and the larger number of women in the population produced a milestone in 1964: more women than men voted (nearly 1.8 million more) and in 1976, the margin more than doubled. In that year, there were 6.5 million more women than men over the age of eighteen, and by the year 2000 conservative estimates increase the difference to approximately 9 million (U.S., Bureau of the Census 1977, table 5). The increasing tendency for women to vote during elections and engage in other political activities at the same rates as men is producing a women's vote margin of growing size and political importance. These developments may accord women the political visibility they numerically deserve.

Some subgroups of women, however, vote at levels higher than those of the men plotted in figure 1, and it is the identity of those subgroups and the reasons for their heightened voting which are examined in the paragraphs to come. The simple curves in the first figure serve as baselines for our investigation of the ways in which social stratification factors combined with gender influence voter turnout.

Education and Turnout

Research on voting behavior has consistently found, from the first studies in Erie County, Ohio (1940), to the most recent, that an individual's educational level is the best predictor of politicization (Flanigan and Zingale 1979). Education has been found to make a slightly greater difference in the political behavior of women than of men: recent increases in the levels of education attained by women are closely associated with the increase in voting by women. Thus, change in the general educational levels of women is a good indicator of change in their overall role and status.

Education for women in the early nineteenth century was restricted to the daughters of the wealthy and was limited in scope. The theory that women have smaller brains than men was widely accepted: Elizabeth Cady Stanton writes of listening to a fellow traveler en route to the 1840 World Anti-Slavery Convention explain this theory of innate inferiority while she beat him at chess (Stanton and Blatch 1922, p. 69).

After the Civil War, primary education for both sexes became free, public, and almost universal. However, the doors of most colleges were closed to women. A few women's colleges were founded, beginning with Mount Holyoke in 1837, and three coeducational colleges existed before the Civil War. But college education remained for the most part a privilege for the sons of the family, while the daughters were groomed for marriage.

The picture changed dramatically in this century. Since 1900, women have been more likely to graduate from high school than men. There has been a steady increase in the level of education for both sexes; there has also been a steady rise in the level of education attained by women as compared with men. In terms of the median school year completed, adult women have been slightly better educated than men since 1920. Reliance on the median, however, obscures the fact that women are more likely than men to graduate from high school, but less likely to graduate from college.

However, women are also closing that gap. In 1900 only 18 percent of all bachelor's and first professional degrees were earned by women. By 1960, of all persons aged twenty-five and older who had been in college for four or more years, 39 percent were women. In 1975 the proportion had grown to 41 percent, and based on recent trends in enrollment it is projected to reach almost 45 percent by 1980. Clearly, the proportion of highly educated women in the population has greatly increased since the early years of this century. Young women as a group are much better educated than their mothers.

Education widens the world view of the individual and increases the sense of competence to live one's life as one wishes. Both of these consequences heighten the probability that the individual will perceive the pervasive influence the political system exerts on day-to-day life and will express her preferences by voting. When the turnout curve for women in figure 1 is decomposed into three curves, one each for those who attended college, those who only graduated from

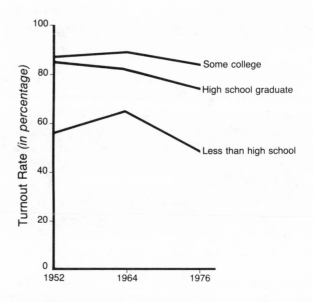

Fig. 2. Voter turnout rates of women, by education and election. (Source of Data: Center for Political Studies, American National Election Studies, 1952–1976)

high school, and those women who left school earlier, the influence of education on turnout stands clear (see fig. 2). The increasing educational attainment of women tends to push marriage and motherhood to later years, delaying the taking on of responsibilities and life-styles which tend to decrease turnout also. Figure 2 documents the well-known finding that persons with some college education are more likely to turn out during any given election than persons with less education.

The curves in figure 2 also reveal some interesting differences among the three education groups over time. In 1952, high school and college women voted at similarly high rates, compared to women without a high school diploma. In 1964, this last group increased their voting considerably, while college women increased slightly and high school women actually dropped a bit. In 1976, when fewer Americans went to the polls than they had in many elections, the turnout rate of college women dipped only slightly, but the other two education groups voted at considerably lower rates. Over the twenty-five year period, college women have voted at the highest rate and have shown only minor increases or decreases in particular elections, which suggests that the changing candidates and issues do not inspire or depress their participation in the same way that they do the involvement of other women.

Employment and Turnout

College-educated women are not the only women who have been voting in greater numbers in recent elections. Comparing the campaign participation of men, housewives, and working women from 1952 to 1972, Andersen (1975) found employed women had made the largest increase in involvement by far (a 32 percent increase versus 7 percent for men). All subgroups in the electorate voted at a lower rate in 1976, however.

One of the most significant changes in the status of women was the entry of large numbers of married women into the paid work force during the second World War. The majority of women without husbands had always worked, but until 1940 few married women were employed. As Chafe wrote in *The American Woman* (1972), the war broke up the traditional housewife-breadwinner division of labor when it became a national imperative that women join the labor force. Almost 7 million women went to work, three-quarters of them married. And they remained in the work force after the war. These women have been joined by others, with the percentage of married women in the labor force increasing from 34 percent in 1950 to 44 percent in 1972.

For women generally, the statistics on employment are striking. Over the past twenty-five years about half again as many women as men joined the paid work force. Today women represent 48 percent of the total working population, or some 12 percentage points more than in the early 1950s; by 1990, they will constitute more than half of the American labor force. Table 2 summarizes the percentage of women in the labor force from 1900 to 1980.

Table 2. Women in the Labor Force, 1900–1980

Year	Number (in thousands)	Percentage of total labor force	Percentage of all women of working age
1900	5,114	18	20
1910	7,889	21	25
1920	8,430	20	23
1930	10,679	22	24
1940	12,845	24	25
1945	19,270	30	36
1950	18,412	29	34
1955	20,584	30	36
1960	23,272	32	38
1965	26,232	34	39
1970	31,560	38	43
1975	37,087	41	46
1980 (projected)	47,900	48	53

Source of Data: U.S., Department of Commerce, Bureau of the Census, and U.S., Department of Labor, Bureau of Labor Statistics.

Paralleling this entry into the work force by women have been other developments affecting their status and role which relate to economic change. The trend away from early marriages, the lower birth rate, the increasing numbers of women entering colleges and professional schools, and the increasing proportions of married women in the labor force have altered women's life-styles.

Blood and Wolfe (1960) from their interviews of 900 city and farm women evaluate the extent of the entry into the work force by women, and locate generally when this exodus took place.

We are rapidly approaching an era of American history when almost all women will work at some time after marriage. There was a time when most American women did not work after marriage. But one must go back to World War I to find such a pattern. The big change seems to have occurred between the war and the depression. [P. 103]

The significance of women's entry into the labor force as a continuing major trend must be appreciated to evaluate its relationship to the political roles of women. Taeuber and Sweet (1976) point out that while there have been fluctuations in patterns of marriage and fertility during the twentieth century, with the rates falling and rising only to fall again, the proportion of women working was constantly rising. "Among women of working age, about one in five was in the labor force in 1900, about one in four in 1940, one in three in 1950, and nearly one in two in 1975" (p. 50). An analysis of the voting behavior of women who have left traditional home environments to take jobs provides an important test of the hypothesis that changes in women's role, while it includes changes in employment status, implies a change in political status as well.

It makes a difference whether one categorizes women by employment status (in the labor force versus housewife) or by occupation if she is working, because the relationship of the employment-occupation stratification variable to turnout is not a simple one. As shown in figure 3, professional and clerical working women voted in all three elections at rates higher than did housewives, and the turnout rate of housewives surpassed that of their blue collar, working sisters. The growing movement of women joining the labor force rather than being full-time housewives, and the expansion of job opportunities for women in professional and clerical fields means that the turnout level for women will necessarily rise in the years ahead, relative to the turnout level for men. Both men and women will continue to vote in some election years more than others, however, as the downturn in 1976 indicates, and among women, changes in voting rate will probably be similar across the four employment-occupation groups.

Income and Turnout

While women have been joining the labor force at increasingly higher rates in recent years, they still earn far less than men at all age and education levels and in all occupational groups. In 1971 women constituted about 30 percent of the full-time workers, but they accounted for only 7 percent of those with salaries of about $10,000 a

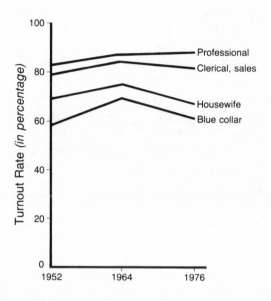

Fig. 3. Voter turnout rates of women, by occupation and election. *(Source of Data: Center for Political Studies, American National Election Studies, 1952–1976)*

year. While 73 percent of the men earned $7,000 or more a year, an almost equal proportion of women earned less than $7,000. Although the categories have increased in dollar value, the wage discrimination against women has not changed in 1980. Much of the salary differential is due to the concentration of women in low paying, low status occupations (Twentieth Century Fund 1975).

In addition to being strongly correlated with educational level and employment status, income level is independently related to political participation as well. This is especially true for women because income measures financial resources, such as the means to hire babysitters and household help, particularly conducive to their general social involvement. When the income distributions found in the 1952, 1964, and 1976 election surveys are divided into three equal portions (labeled low, medium, and high) and then graphed over the

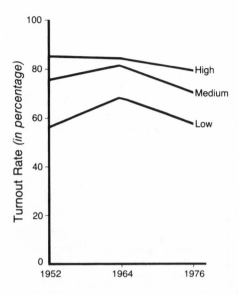

Fig. 4. Voter turnout rates for women, by income level and election. *(Source of Data: Center for Political Studies, American National Election Studies, 1952–1976)*

elections as in figure 4, the tendency for women with higher incomes to turn out at higher rates is apparent, as is their tendency to vote at a similar rate across different elections. Medium and low income women show a greater fluctuation from election to election.

Region and Turnout

It was shown in table 1 that the percentage of women registered to vote in the presidential elections following suffrage was considerably lower in Louisiana than in Vermont or the city of Chicago. The South is usually conceded to be the region where traditional values are more firmly held than any other area of the country, and these traditional values include the belief that the political arena is reserved for men (Scott 1970). When the turnout curve presented in figure 1

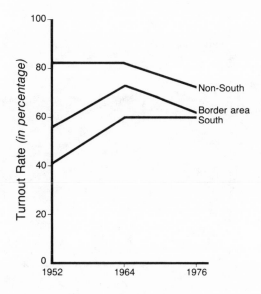

Fig. 5. Voter turnout rates of women, by region and election. *South:* Alabama, Arkansas, Florida, Georgia, Louisiana, Mississippi, North Carolina, South Carolina, Texas, Virginia. *Border area:* Kentucky, Maryland, Oklahoma, Tennessee. *(Source of Data: Center for Political Studies, American National Election Studies, 1952–1976)*

is decomposed into regional curves for women living in southern states, in states bordering on the southern states, and in states outside the South, the relative heights of the curves is as expected (see fig. 5). The southern women did vote in smaller proportions in the 1952, 1964, and 1976 elections than did women living in the border states; women in the border states, in turn, voted at a level lower than that of women in the rest of the country. But in 1976, the three curves show a striking convergence. Region is related to voter turnout for women because the strength of traditional beliefs about their proper political role varies from one geographical area to another, but as figure 5 indicates for 1976, those role definitions may be much more similar in the 1980s than ever before.

Age and Turnout

The final factor to be examined in the search for single characteristics influencing women's decisions to vote is age. As with education, income, employment status, and region, age is a basic feature of individuals which provides a clue to social scientists about how they will act. Kreps and Leaper (1976) found age to be the most important factor influencing married women's labor force participation. There are several alternative interpretations of how age makes behavior somewhat predictable, and these interpretations should be clearly differentiated. Some social scientists use age to indicate stage in the cycle of major life events. For women, the stages are particularly discrete and by knowing a woman's age, we can guess with some statistical certainty whether she's still in school, single and working, married and raising a family, or whether her child care responsibilities have ended. A second interpretation of the importance of age rests upon the notion that major *societal* events, such as world wars and economic depressions, traumatize all who experience them and that society can be usefully stratified into pre- and postevent subpopulations. By looking at major and minor societal events and the value systems which accompany them as jointly influential, age then becomes the basis for defining generations. This third interpretation views the commonality of social experience shared by persons born at approximately the same time, and passing through their life cycles at similar rates, as giving rise to groups distinctly different from the generations preceding and following them.

An analysis of American women by age is complicated by the fact that the proportions of women in any given age group has changed considerably since the turn of the century. These changes, which are shown in figure 6 (with 1980 values as predictions), are due to past fluctuations in birthrates as well as to recent medical advances which have increased the average life expectancy.

The concept of stage in the life cycle seems to be the most satisfactory interpretation of age here because of its emphasis upon the shifting life-styles and responsibilities of women (and men) as they move from young adulthood to retirement. The greater mobility of young people often keeps them from meeting local voter registration

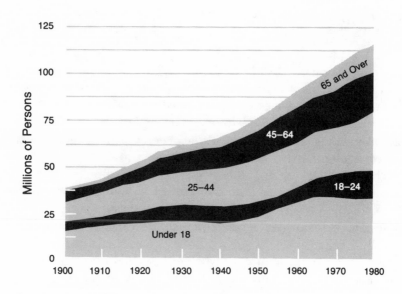

Fig. 6. Age distribution of women, 1900–1980. *(Courtesy of The Conference Board, 1973)*

requirements. Although federal electoral laws now allow citizens to transfer their registration from out of state to vote in presidential elections, they may not qualify for local elections and thus may be dissuaded from going to the polls. Younger people, except the college educated, are also less interested in campaign outcomes. Without a heavy stake in their local communities, the quality of the schools, and the size of the property tax burden, their incentives to vote are much weaker than those of older people (thirty-one to sixty) who have established community roots. A relatively low level of turnout and interest has been repeatedly documented for older people as well (Verba and Nie 1972; Milbrath and Goel 1977). Retirement from the labor force often means a withdrawal from other social routines, and the trip to the polls becomes more difficult as physical infirmities grow. As the five curves in figure 7 indicate, the age variable is related to voting in the predicted way across the twenty-five year period.

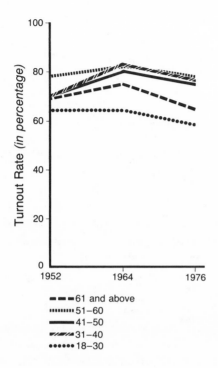

Fig. 7. Voter turnout rates of women, by age and election. *(Source of Data: Center for Political Studies, American National Election Studies, 1952–1976)*

The Multiple Correlates of Turnout

In the preceding pages, we have shown in very simple fashion how five basic sociodemographic variables serve to stratify society and how each produces subgroups among American women that have voted at different rates over the 1952–76 period. The political impact of these variables is not independent, however, because every woman has, simultaneously, educational and income levels, an employment status, a regional identification, and an age. Further, her standing on one variable is likely to influence her standing on one or more others. For example, a woman with a college education probably also has a relatively high family income and is likely to be employed. This is the multivariate patterning of variables which has emerged from the figures, tables, and discussion of factors predicting turnout. To summarize the analysis, the profiles of the women most likely, and least likely, to vote in a presidential election can be drawn.

The most likely woman voter has some college education, reports a family income in the upper third of the national distribution, practices a profession, lives outside the southern and border states, and is between thirty-one and sixty years old. Each of these characteristics has been shown to be related to voting in a simple bivariate way. When put into a multivariate equation, they predict a very high level of voting. The least likely woman voter, on the other hand, left school before completing the twelfth grade, has a family income in the lower third of the national distribution, is a housewife living in the South, and is younger than thirty or older than sixty-one. Again, these characteristics depress turnout more when combined in a multivariate formula than when treated separately.

A statistical technique called discriminant analysis recognizes the interrelatedness of social science variables and enables the researcher to discuss the relative importance of factors which are not completely independent of each other. Discriminant analysis statistically determines which variable from a set of variables serves to separate most distinctly a group of people already known to differ in some way (Nie et al. 1975). As used here, respondents in the 1952, 1964, and 1976 national election studies were classified as voters or nonvoters in those elections. The discriminant analyses were done to find out which variable of the six discussed in this chapter (gender, education, employment status, income, region, and age) was the most closely associated with voting or nonvoting and thus best distinguished between the two turnout groups. After the first variable was identified, the analysis then searched for the variable out of the remaining five which next best distinguished between the two groups. At the end of a discriminant analysis, the researcher can talk about the "best" and "worst" predictors of group differences.

In other words, the technique makes it possible to ask the following question: How useful is it in the prediction of voting to know whether an individual is a woman rather than a man, holds a professional degree rather than a high school certificate, makes $30,000 rather than $10,000 a year, is a white-collar worker rather than being unemployed, lives in Alaska rather than Alabama and was born in 1920 rather than 1940? If the prediction had to be made with information on only two or three of these variables, which ones would be most useful?

When the three discriminant analyses were run on the 1952, 1964, and 1976 data sets, education emerged each time as the most important predictor of voting.[2] Age was the second most important predictor in the 1964 and 1976 analyses and the fourth most powerful in 1952. In no election does gender appear as the most significant variable. The predictive utility of the gender variable was not consistent: it was the second most important variable in 1952, the fifth in 1964, and the third in 1976. Across the three studies, the ordering of the age, region, income, and gender variables differed considerably. The employment status variable was consistently the least important. Its value in the prediction of voting behavior in 1952 was so small that it was not treated as a discriminating variable at all. To estimate the probable turnout rate of a given group at election time, then, the researcher needs to know the proportions of people at different educational and age levels. The more college graduates and people aged thirty-one to sixty in the group, the higher the group's voting rate will be. Along with income and region, knowing the proportion of group members who are women will not increase the accuracy of the estimate very much.

Summary and Conclusions

Although women vote at a slightly lower rate than do men, women now constitute the numerical majority of the American electorate. The greater longevity of women partially accounts for their majority political status. More importantly, however, women are becoming better educated, are entering professional and white-collar occupations, and are earning more income—all characteristics associated with a high probability of voting. The analyses in this chapter have shown that in political behavior studies, women cannot be statistically treated as a homogeneous demographic group. Instead, we must look at the ways major stratifying variables in this society operate to produce subgroups of women (and of men, though figures on men are not presented) which are politically active to different degrees. The figures have shown that certain subgroups of women, for example those with college educations and in professional occupations, have been voting at high levels since 1952. Other subgroups, such as women from the southern states, have begun turning out at high levels only recently. The identity of these subgroups, plus an understanding of how their life experiences leads them to be more or less active in politics, enable us to better understand the demographic characteristics of women already voting in presidential elections, and the characteristics of women who remain to be recruited. As more and more women enter college and the professions, trends likely to continue, women will add to their majority in the electorate.

The most important message in this chapter is that voting behavior is best understood, and most accurately predicted, by a multivariate model. That is, simply looking at gender as *the* determinant of turnout is unwise. The discriminant analyses run on respondents to the 1952, 1964, and 1976 presidential election surveys did not find gender to be the most significant predictor of turnout. But the combination of gender with educational level, employment status and occupation, income level and region does lead to better understanding and more accurate predictions of voting. Further, combinations of the demographic characteristics are even more valuable analytically, and thus it was possible to specify the characteristics of the most likely woman voter and the least likely woman voter.

If an analysis of the political behavior and attitudes of women and men could not deal with the full set of voting predictors and their interrelationships, but had instead to rely upon only one demographic variable, that one should be education. The discriminant analyses found education consistently to be the most significant. In the following chapters, education will time and time again prove valuable in the understanding of political attitudes and behaviors other than voting.

Voting is only one form of political participation. Similarly, demographic characteristics are only one type of motivating factors that influence political participation. In the chapters ahead, we focus on other political activities, such as involvement in policy oriented community organizations and winning election to public office. Here, the participation rates of women are considerably different from those of men, and the difference is not simply a reflection of demographic variations. We must look, too, at the political attitudes of women and men and the political climate surrounding them. This first step has documented the fact that women have moved from being the numerical minority in the American electorate to constituting the majority. We will explore reasons why this movement has not been matched by their passage from political invisibility to prominence.

chapter three

ATTITUDES
What Do Women Believe About Politics?

From the time of the ancient Greeks, scholars have been interested in the degree to which citizens participate in their government and influence the quality of public life. In a sense, voting behavior studies have returned to this question in the effort to distinguish empirically types of participants and nonparticipants in political activities. Analytic interest in political attitudes comes from prior research which has documented high correlations between some political attitudes and voting and other forms of political behavior. In this chapter, the responses of women over the past twenty-five years to several attitude indicators traditionally used in political research are examined. Although these attitudes are usually regarded as antecedent to political participation, they often seem just as logically to follow from positive, negative or neutral experiences in politics. This quandary, whether attitudes are antecedent to or the consequence of behavior, lies at the heart of every social science effort to interpret a strong relationship between an attitude and behavior. Our goal is to explain how and why women differ on these measures from men. In chapter 4, we move from looking at attitudes as behavioral correlates to seeing them as evaluations of issues, candidates, and political parties, with an eye toward the possibility of women forming a powerful voting bloc in future elections.

In this chapter we will demonstrate that women are becoming more politicized across a considerable range of survey items measuring an individual's political outlook. We have selected three variables which Campbell and his associates (1960) found to have analytic and explanatory power in relation to voting behavior. They sought to measure an individual's psychological view of politics which they regarded in their theory as antecedent to political participation. For 1952 and 1956, they found that among other variables, interest in the campaign, concern for the outcome of the election, and sense of political efficacy showed high correlations with voting turnout. If it can be shown that women are increasing their levels on these three particular measures, it should follow that women are also becoming more politically involved, not only in voting, but in other forms of political activity as well.

It is important to note that public interest in political campaigns varies considerably by type of election, charisma of candidates, salience and significance of issues, extent of media coverage, and other factors. The elections for president, which are measured in our survey data, are regarded as "high stimulus" by Campbell (1966), compared to off-year congressional or state elections. This is simply due to the fact that the election for the highest office in the land generates more widespread interest.

Even in presidential election years, however, it has been a continuing assumption in American politics that women move in environments in which there are less stimuli than for men that encourage interest in political campaigns. We have shown in chapter 2 that women are entering educational and occupational environments full of political stimuli, and that women in these environments do indeed vote at higher rates than women in more traditional settings. It should be anticipated that their level of interest in and concern for political campaign outcome would increase as well. A partial explanation for this change may be found in the fact that these two variables, interest and concern, are strongly correlated with education level, and during the past twenty-five years the proportion of women pursuing higher education has been increasing. Furthermore, the women found at the lowest level of education are declining in proportions, simply due to the dying off of older generations. The third attitude measure is political efficacy, or the individual's sense of her own ability to participate effectively in the political system, and the sense of efficacy has strengthened among women as their psychological outlook toward the political process becomes more positive. We begin with data measuring interest in following campaigns in presidential election years.

Measuring Interest in Following Campaigns
in Presidential Years

In the early voting studies it was commonly reported that women had less interest than men in following election campaigns. From the first survey of the voters in Erie County, Ohio, 1940, Lazarsfeld et al. wrote:

> There is a prevailing belief that women are less interested in politics than men. This is corroborated by our data. In the May poll, 33 percent of the men but only 23 percent of the women professed great interest in the election." [1944, p. 45]

In the next study, done in Elmira, New York, in 1948, the finding was replicated, with women lagging 8 percentage points behind men (36 to 28 percent). The Elmira researchers wrote that on each interest level women were more likely than men to say they did not intend to vote (Berelson, Lazarsfeld, and McPhee 1954, p. 25).

Using those two election years as a baseline for comparison, a quick glance at measures of interest in political campaigns taken during the seven presidential elections held between 1952 and 1976 would lead to two conclusions. First, interest expressed by the electorate fluctuates between elections, as could be anticipated. For example, the second Eisenhower election (1956) saw a sizable drop in the level of campaign interest among both women and men voters, which was probably due to the popular consensus that the Republican incumbent would be reelected. President Eisenhower did in fact easily increase the margin of victory in his reelection. Since interest fluctuated for different elections, we have chosen to measure the gap between men and women for each election under study to monitor change over time.

Second, the personal characteristic which is most closely associated with interest in political campaigns is education. We noted in our analysis of voting in chapter 2 that persons with relatively high levels of education hold a broadened world view and a set of reasoning skills which increase the likelihood that they will understand and wish to influence their political environment by voting. For the same reasons, we should expect college graduates to be more interested in political campaigns than people with only a grade school education. There is no reason to expect that the larger world view produced by higher education is very different for women or men, nor are there many gender differences in their occupational and social experiences. Among people at lower educational levels, however, the strength of traditional gender roles define women as politically apathetic and produce considerable difference in political attitudes and behavior of women and men. (It is worth noting again, as in chapter 2, that a significant increase in number of college degrees and first-time college enrollees as a percentage of high school graduates has taken place among women, and not among men. From 1948 to 1965 the percent of male high school graduates going on to college did not change, while for women there was an increase from 32 to 46 percent. By 1975, more than half the population under 40 years of age had some college education, nearly half of them women.)

When the percentage of people saying they had high interest in the presidential campaign that year is broken down by education and gender simultaneously, as is shown in table 3, our expectations are largely met. The gap in interest between women and men shrinks with increases in education for the 1956, 1960, 1964, and 1976 elections; in the other three elections, the gap between the genders is

Table 3. The Relationship between Education and High Interest in Political Campaigns for Women and Men, by Election Year

Level of Education	Percentage Difference (men minus women)						
	1952	1956	1960	1964	1968	1972	1976
Grade school	9%	16%	22%	3%	6%	11%	10%
High school	4	8	9	8	2	6	4
College	7	0	0	−2	14	9	4

Source of Data: Center for Political Studies, American National Election Studies, 1952–1976.

Note: Respondents were classified according to the degree of their interest in the campaign from their responses to the following question: "Some people don't pay much attention to the political campaigns. How about you? Would you say that you have been very much interested, somewhat interested, or not much interested in following the political campaigns so far this year?" Table 3 reports respondents who stated they were "very much interested." A minus sign indicates that men scored less than women on this measure. (See table 58 in the Appendix for actual rates of men and women.)

greater at the college level than among high school graduates. A quick glance at the actual percentages underlying table 3, which are given in table 57 in the Appendix, shows that college-educated persons consistently showed the highest campaign interest across the seven elections. Education makes more difference in the interest among women than among men, as apparent in the greater range of scores among women than men respondents.

Women who had attended college expressed virtually the same level of high interest as similar men in four elections out of seven. The pattern is not so clear for women with less education. The greatest difference on this measurement is found at the grade school level when in 1956 and 1960 men and women were 16 and 22 percentage points apart. As we have indicated, there is a considerable fluctuation between elections in terms of individual interest.

Almond and Verba (1963) found in their cross-cultural study of political attitudes that the levels of political interest and involvement were comparable between American women and men. They found larger gender differences in Germany, Italy, and Mexico, and explained that in American, and British, families there was more integration of women into the political system.

We can look at this question in another way, and add supporting evidence from a similar question appearing for the first time in 1968 in the Bureau of Census study of the national electorate. When asked a reason for not registering to vote in the 1968 election, the respondents in table 4 reported they were "not interested." This question is not the same as in the Michigan data (CPS) but extends the measurement of differences between men and women on a very similar question. The negligible differences between men and women on this item are shown in table 4. Only at the thirty-five to forty-five age bracket were men and women as much as 2 percentage points apart. We updated this measurement in the 1976 Census data and found a similar pattern: that men and women at all age levels showed very little difference in reporting lack of interest as a reason for not registering to vote.

We are taking the position in this chapter that younger women today are responding differently from older women, and are replacing a politically less involved generation. In 1952, only 7 percent of the

Table 4. Percentage Differences between Women and Men Reporting "Not Interested" As Reason for Not Registering to Vote in 1968

Age	Percentage Reporting "Not Interested"		Percentage Difference (men minus women)
	Men	Women	
21–24	54%	53%	1%
25–34	55	54	1
35–44	54	53	2
45–54	56	55	1
55–64	55	55	0
65 and over	44	44	0

Source of Data: U.S., Department of Commerce, Bureau of the Census, Current Population Reports, Series P–20, no. 192 (December 2, 1969), p. 47.

electorate were under twenty-five years of age. This figure more than doubled (15 percent) by 1972, partly as a result of the voting age being lowered to eighteen. Because there are some political attitudes and actions which are especially frequent among people at certain ages (i.e., are age-related), changes in the American age distribution will affect electoral politics. Interest in political campaigns is not an age-related variable, however, and the lack of difference between women and men at all ages in following campaigns contrasts sharply with the myth of nonpolitical woman.

Measuring Concern Over the Outcome of the Election

Concern over the outcome of an election implies that some personal value is at stake, in contrast to interest in the campaigns. Concern has been used as an additional measure of the individual's psychological involvement in politics by the Michigan investigators. The CPS researchers found in their pioneering 1952 and 1956 studies that people with a high level of interest also had a strong concern about the outcome and were very likely to vote on election day. If we turn to table 5, it is clear that educational level of the individual again discriminates between levels of concern for election outcome. A comparison of table 5 with table 3 brings forth an interesting difference: women's concern for election outcome quite often equals or

Table 5. The Relationship between Education and High Level of Concern for Election Outcome for Women and Men, by Election Year

Level of Education	Percentage Difference (men minus women)						
	1952	1956	1960	1964	1968	1972	1976
Grade school	4%	4%	6%	1%	6%	0%	7%
High school	0	5	−3	0	1	−3	−4
College	6	0	−12	−6	0	7	1

Source of Data: Center for Political Studies, American National Election Studies, 1952–1976.
Note: Respondents were classified according to the degree of their concern over the election outcome from their response to the following question: "Generally speaking, would you say that you personally care a good deal which party wins the presidential election this fall, or that you don't care very much which party wins?" A minus sign indicates that men scored less than women on this measure. (See table 59 in the Appendix for the actual rates of men and women.)

surpasses that of men, while men are generally more interested in campaigns per se. Looking now just at table 5, after 1952 women of high school training and with college experience were slightly more concerned than their peer men in some years. Among college women and men the difference changes considerably over the years. The actual percentages underlying the table, given in table 59 in the Appendix, indicate again that in every election, college-educated men and women reported more concern than their grade school counterparts.

Measuring an Individual's Sense of Political Efficacy

One of the more revealing measures of political involvement and commitment is a psychological factor known as sense of political efficacy. By definition this is a feeling that individual political action does have, or can have, an impact upon the political process—that it is worthwhile for a citizen to perform civic duties. The notion of efficacy differs from concern and describes a more general orientation of the individual to the political system. Different interpretations of this concept have had wide use in electoral research. Janowitz and Marvick (1956, pp. 30–34) used a related concept under the label "political confidence." Kornhauser, Sheppard, and Mayer (1956, pp. 155–66) measured a "sense of political futility." Farris (1960, pp. 50–57) utilized a concept of "political anomie."

Although researchers' interpretations of political efficacy questions have shifted over the years, the significance of the concept remains in its continuing relationship to participation, particularly voting. For example, in the 1972 election there was a 26 percentage point vote differential between those expressing high and low efficacy.

This measure is also of particular interest because so much of the literature would indicate that women have low levels of political efficacy. In fact, the authors of *The American Voter* reported:

> It is the sense of political efficacy that, with factors like education, age, and region controlled, differs more sharply and consistently between men and women. Men are more likely than women to feel they can cope with the complexities of politics and to believe that their participation carries some weight in the political process. . .We conclude, then, that moralistic values about citizen participation in democratic government have been bred in women as in men; what has been less adequately transmitted to the women is a sense of some personal competence vis-à-vis the political world." [Campbell et al. 1960, p. 490]

The literature of the social sciences has provided more than adequate explanation for the low levels of political efficacy found among women in the early studies (1952–56). Psychologists looking generally at achievement motivation in American women have suggested that women are socialized into a sense of inferiority. Simone de Beauvoir wrote a classic analysis and summarized her perception of the status of woman in the title, *The Second Sex*. In describing the relation of the two sexes, de Beauvoir wrote that "she (woman) is defined and differentiated with reference to man and not he with reference to her; she is the incidental, and the inessential as opposed to the essential. He is the Subject, he is the Absolute—she is the Other" (1953, pp. 15–16). Janeway expressed the notion, "Women and girls do in fact have a greater problem than men in our society with feelings of worthlessness. That sense of worthlessness . . . explains why women attempting new roles will find a haunting challenge to value themselves and their experiences as seriously as they do those of men" (1973, p. 96). Horner, author of a well-known study in this area wrote, "a bright woman is caught in a double-bind. . . . In testing and other achievement-oriented situations she worries not only about failure but about success" (1969, p. 37). Horner reported:

> In light of the high and if anything increasing incidence of the motive to avoid success in our data it seems apparent that most otherwise achievement-motivated young white women when faced with a conflict between their feminine image and expressing their competences or developing their abilities and interests adjust their behaviors to their internalized sex role stereotypes. [1972, p. 67]

Bardwick has studied the psychology of women in considerable depth and made the following comments in a chapter dealing with the ego and self-esteem:

> A critical factor would seem to be the range of important motives a girl has developed, the diversity of her subidentities, and the extent to which she gratifies diverse aspects of her self-identity. Role conflict, or the frustration of aspects of the self, does not exist unless diverse and conflicting motives have evolved. Because role conflict is more likely to exist in women, in particular situations and in general women have lower self-esteem than men. [1971, p. 155]

Thus, psychological and sociological findings about female role stereotypes provide a theoretical foundation for *The American Voter*'s conclusions. Taking the analysis further, we may reasonably expect that as women change their psychological outlook, their political outlook, particularly their sense of political efficacy, will change accordingly.

We have made a comprehensive analysis of the differences between men and women on the efficacy scale from 1952 through 1976. Although we do not present all of those data in the next table, there is a clear increase in the sense of political efficacy among women in comparison to men. In 1952, 35 percent of men ranked as having high political efficacy, and only 20 percent of the women did. The gender difference dropped to 5 percent in 1960 and 1964; by

1976, women of all ages ranked very similarly to men of the same ages.

When the efficacy data are disaggregated by education and gender, however, as shown in table 6, a pattern quite different from what we have seen before emerges—the difference between women and men is *larger* among the college educated than among the less well educated. This is particularly stark in the 1952 data, and in fact once our analytical eyes move down the elections, the differences across education levels seem negligible. The 1952 figures remain puzzling. College-educated women were less numerous in 1952 than in the later years, so they did constitute a special subgroup in the electorate. Many college-educated women entered the labor force during the Second World War, and fewer of them (and their sisters with less education) stopped working at the war's end than is generally realized. Somewhere in the mix of postwar gender roles and attitudes regarding work, politics, and raising families, college women came to feel especially powerless to influence their government.

Table 6. Decline by Gender in Differentials on High Political Efficacy Scale in Relation to Level of Education, by Election Year

| Education | Percentage of Men Minus Women | | |
	1952	1964	1976
Grade school	7%	2%	5%
High school	16	5	2
College	22	6	5

Source of Data: Center for Political Studies, American National Election Studies, 1952–1976.

Note: The scale is the recorded sum of "efficacious" responses to the following items. The respondents are ranked in terms of the number of answers in which they "disagreed" with the statement. If a person agreed with three or four of the items, she would be measured as having "Low Efficacy." A person agreeing with two of the items would be ranked as having "Medium Efficacy," and a person agreeing with one or no items would be ranked as having "High Efficacy." The items were:

1. "People like me don't have any say about what the government does."
2. "Voting is the only way that people like me can have any say about how the government runs things."
3. "Sometimes politics and government seem so complicated that a person like me can't really understand what's going on."
4. "I don't think public officials care much what people like me think."

Social scientists argue today over the complexities of analyzing responses to the sense of efficacy items. It is clear, however, that women have an increased sense of self-esteem in political affairs today, but that their level does not quite match that of men. Instead of interpreting the difference as an inadequacy in women, we suggest that given the very limited number of issues that citizens can affect, the lower sense of political efficacy expressed by women may be a perceptive assessment of the political process. Men, on the other hand, express irrationally high rates of efficacy (Bourque and Grossholtz 1974).

Summary and Conclusions

What can we conclude from our demonstration that women have become more politicized in terms of their attitudes toward the political system over the past quarter of a century? We have suggested that structural changes in society which have influenced the social and economic status of women have also led to a redefinition of their political role. By examining the record of women over seven presidential elections we have found on standardized measures that many differences between men and women which were apparent in the 1950s have declined sharply. Specifically, we have analyzed measures generally described as antecedents of political behavior, that is, attitudes which show high correlations to voting performance. We have noted that there was very little difference in interest in the outcome of elections after 1952 between men and women of college experience. On this particular measure women with the lowest levels of education exhibited considerable fluctuation from election to election, as was also true for men who continued to express higher degrees of interest than women. By 1968, and continuing into 1976, women of all ages responded identically to men in admitting lack of interest as a reason for not registering. College women stated that they were equally or more concerned about the outcome of the election than peer men in five elections out of seven.

After 1952 college-educated women ranked similarly to men on a scale of political efficacy—a measure of the individual's self-esteem in relation to the political system. For women with less education the difference between men and women was smaller in 1952 but has fallen to approximately the same level. The educational level of the individuals made more difference for women than for men, and younger women showed more change than their elders. Significantly, higher education has increased more for women than for men in the last decade.

If we review these findings for their implication, the outlook for women is not altogether clear because the forces which dominate American politics are also undergoing fundamental change. However, if our traditional political institutions are becoming more open and tolerant of independent and unilateral action by candidates and organizations, then women have their best opportunity in fifty years to gain recognition. And women are increasingly likely to seek that recognition, as the data on interest in campaigns, concern for election outcome, and feelings of citizen efficacy presented in this chapter have suggested. In the next chapter, women's attitudes on public policy, their evaluation of candidates, and their views of the political parties are explored to illuminate further the invisible majority and its future role in American politics.

chapter four

HOW WOMEN VIEW PUBLIC POLICY, CANDIDATES, AND POLITICAL PARTIES

A tremendous change has occurred in American politics almost without notice: women now hold the balance of voting power. Whatever happens to the Equal Rights Amendment or feminist movement, plain statistics clearly show that the political opinions of women will count for more than those of men in the 1980s and decades beyond. By virtue of their numerical superiority, a superiority documented in chapter 2, women can provide the margin of victory or defeat in close elections. A difference of one vote per precinct in 1960 and 1968 would have elected a different man as president of the country; the 1976 election was almost as close. If women hold different views on public policy issues and candidates than do men, the fact that there are more women in the electorate and voting magnifies the importance of their opinions. In this chapter we will investigate the policy preferences of women and men, find out how women have evaluated candidates and the political parties, and draw some conclusions regarding the likelihood of a women's bloc vote in future elections.

The analysts who have looked at the question of a women's voting bloc have generally concluded that ideological differences and divisions along class, economic, or religious lines make the formation of a viable, recognized bloc among women extremely difficult. History is on the side of this argument. After the enactment of the Suffrage Amendment in 1920 feminism became a disorganized, localized phenomenon without effective leadership. Although the National Women's party beginning in 1923 introduced in Congress year after year a constitutional amendment to ban distinction in the legal rights of women and men, this measure was not approved by Congress until

1972, and then left to the states for ratification. After 1920, a few groups such as the League of Women Voters and the General Federation of Women's Clubs pursued the influence of public policy as part of their organizational goals. However, both of these groups emphasized their nonpartisan character, thus effectively destroying their capacity to lead a political women's movement which could cut across class or political party lines.

Another major reason for the decline of feminism after suffrage was secured in 1920 was the lack of an issue or ideology that would serve to hold together the diverse groups which had worked to attain suffrage. The successive development of the New Deal, the Fair Deal, the Great Society, and the New Frontier with their myriad social welfare programs focused the nation's attention on the needs of other subgroups within the population, and the few sparks of militancy among women for creating a women's vote or political party soon died. The women's movement remained quiescent until new forces, including the massive entry of women into the labor force during and after the Second World War, and the development of numerous women's civic, religious, and political organizations with common goals, consciousness-raising, and an elaborate communications network, brought renewed interest in the possibility of increasing feminine political influence.[1]

The issue of a women's bloc vote, or blocs among other subgroups in the electorate, was not very interesting to the early political researchers. They focused upon the weightier topic of whether the American electorate met the test of rationality as described in classical democratic theory. Social scientists accepted this proposition: that rationality of mind led to rational voting—a necessary ingredient for a democratic system of government. It was a disappointment in the early studies that this basic assumption in electoral research was not supported. The researchers were amazed to find in the Erie County study (1940), for example, that a person's socioeconomic status and "brand loyalty" to a political party had more influence on voting choice than public policy alternatives. No more than one-third of those surveyed in 1952 and 1956 were apparently aware of any of the sixteen major issues on which they were questioned. Roughly two-thirds of the individuals who were aware of one or more issues were frequently not personally concerned about those questions of public policy. Apparently, for the issue to have any weight·with the voter, the following conditions had to be met: the person had to be aware of the issue, the issue had to be of some personal concern and the person had to perceive one party as more nearly representing his position than the other. Thus, in those early voting studies (1952–56) the citizen's view of political issues was a relatively low predictor of the vote. Further, there was little evidence of attitude consistency or ideological coherence.

Social scientists differ somewhat in pinpointing when this picture changed, but the 1964 election often looms as a dividing line. In contrast to the bland years of the Eisenhower administration, the 1964 election seemed to pose strong issue alternatives. The Goldwater candidacy offered for the first time in three presidential elections a "choice not an echo." Among other reasons for the ascendance of issues, the 1960s were unlike the 1950s in many ways. Civil strife over race, a presidential assassination, urban unrest, and dramatic antiwar protests were highly visible. The conservative political majority did not materialize to support the Republican presidential candidacy of Barry Goldwater in 1964 but the issues were still alive in 1968, aggravated further by campus disorder, stronger antiwar protests, economic recession and inflation, and soaring crime rates. Democrats skirmished over forcing an incumbent president, Lyndon B. Johnson, not to stand for reelection and they held a national convention which was tarnished by violent protests. This contest in 1968 was further conflicted by the challenge of George Wallace who offered alternative policies to the voters on a number of key issues.

Like other analysts, Nie and Andersen wrote that in the elections of 1964, 1968, and 1972, "political atttitudes have come to be an increasingly significant force in determining the direction of the presidential vote, while the impact of partisan identification, once predominant, has become much less significant" (1974, pp. 540–91). Miller and Levitin wrote that "the election of 1972 was more heavily influenced by issue voting or voting on the basis of policy preferences than any election in the preceding two decades" (1976, p. 13).

Following the turbulence of the 1972 election, however, the contest in 1976 seemed to represent a decline in issue saliency. The

Michigan CPS researchers found that party identification turned out to be significantly more prominent as a cue to the voters than it had been in 1968 or 1972. It may well be that the type of election was also influential: two lackluster candidates, Gerald Ford and Jimmy Carter, competed to stand on the middle ground in 1976. Apparently economic issues, unemployment and inflation in particular, and the influence of party voting made the difference for the winner in the closest election in some years.

An important question to ask is why issues become prominent in some elections and not in others. This question has generated an avalanche of literature in voting studies with argument, counterargument, and revisionism questioning the original analyses done in the 1950s. It is still not clear whether the temper of the times, the choice of particular candidates, or the specific issues in the various elections moved the voter to be more interested in issues after 1964. Nor is it obvious the degree to which topical factors such as racial strife, international crises, increasing crime and inflation rates at home contributed to the change. One can speculate that population changes, such as an increasing number of black voters and lowering the voting age to eighteen, would have reduced the possibility that party identification would have carried more weight.

Our concern, however, is to determine the role of public policy issues as they have affected the politics of women. Since issues differ over the span of elections, it is difficult to identify absolute attitude change in one single attitude from one election to another. Our data are confined to observing the differences between men and women for particular elections. Moreover, we are interested in determining if there was a link between policy position and candidate or voting choice. From our look at the data on issues over seven presidential elections we present the following argument:

1. Women and men typically agree on a wide range of public policy questions. Other variables, such as income, class, region, race, education, religion, or occupation differentiate population subgroups more than gender does.

2. When, however, male-female differences appear on public policies, there is a pattern of consistency exhibited by women. Women seem to specialize in particular areas, often called humanitarian by

social scientists who have looked at their record. This pattern of consistency is especially obvious in the area of war and peace.
3. When the educational level of the individual is correlated with the direction of the attitude on issues, the effect in the more recent election years (1972 and 1976) appears to increase the percentage of liberal responses more so for women than for men.
4. When generational differences are compared on policy issues, younger women appear to be more liberal than their elders, and slightly more than young men.

We would expect to find women specializing in particular areas of public policy as a result of their socialization. We would also expect women to react more sensitively to issues which directly affect their own welfare, as for example, the Equal Rights Amendment, equal pay for equal work, and abortion. Although survey data found a majority of women favoring all of those issues by 1975, they have not been tested in presidential elections per se. For varied reasons, candidates have not chosen to make campaign issues of questions important to the women's movement. The fact that the majority of women were slow to support a controversial issue such as the Equal Rights Amendment may reinforce the failure of women to be recognized as a cohesive voting bloc at election time.

Having specified the generalizations about women and their views on public policy, we can extrapolate some evidence over the 1952–76 election years, looking primarily at three areas: foreign policy, racial strife, and socioeconomic questions.

Women differ from men most strongly on issues that pertain to war and peace. It is signficant that men and women have been more deeply divided on these issues than any others since the Second World War. Survey data abundantly describe women as being more opposed to militaristic measures than men.

A number of social scientists have commented on the pacifist position of women. Hero analyzed measures of political attitudes which spanned the years from the Second World War to 1968, looking at data from the major polling institutions (Gallup, Roper, Fortune, National Opinion Research Council, and the Survey Research Center). He summarized:

In the post-war period women have been slightly more likely to favor foreign non-military aid than have men especially with regard to its humanitarian objectives. Larger differences between the sexes have pertained to attitudes on the use of military force and the implementation of policies regarded as risking U.S. involvement in war. Females were more likely to view our entry into the two world wars and the Korean and Vietnam conflicts as a mistake than were males. Women have been more likely to support U.S. withdrawals from wars already entered into and to be less receptive to the idea of "peacetime" conscription. Support for the defense establishment, military aid, and collective security arrangements has been less as well among the fair sex. Women have likewise been less disposed to accord the U.N. the means and authority to use force. Fear of war and hatred of it have been stronger themes in the thought of women than men. [1968, pp. 52–54]

Another analyst interested in electoral studies investigated in some detail the 1968 and 1972 elections. He noted that from the beginning women were more opposed than men to American intervention in Southeast Asia (Pomper 1975). In 1968, over two-thirds of women regarded United States involvement as a mistake, compared to somewhat more than half of the men (1975, p. 78). "By 1972, more women consider the war as an important issue than men, and more women (49 percent to 44 percent) give first priority to ending the war" (1975, p. 79).

The field of foreign policy lends itself particularly to closer examination to document the observation that on some crucial issues in the past twenty-four years the range of differences in attitude between men and women has been considerable. In the 1952 Michigan survey almost half of the men (48 percent) felt that the United States "did the right thing in getting into fighting in Korea." In comparison, one-third of the women (32 percent) agreed with this position. The responses were reversed in relation to the position that "we should have stayed out" with 37 percent of the men favoring that position, and 45 percent of the women favoring "staying out."

A consistent pattern can be found in 1964 when 42 percent of the men felt that we did the "right thing" in Vietnam, compared to 30 percent of the women. Of more interest, on the question, "What should the U.S. do now?", 38 percent of the men felt we should take a "stronger stand, even if it means invading the North," compared to 21 percent of women who took that position.

Gallup asked people in 1969 to rank themselves as hawks or doves with this result:

	Hawks	*Doves*
Women	22%	64%
Men	38	48

Women were more opposed than men to the invasion of Cambodia in 1973. The range in these statistics is striking. Women's general tendency to oppose violence is reflected in their response to other social issues, such as gun control, capital punishment, and nuclear energy. In the aftermath of the Three Mile Island incident, Gallup found that 71 percent of the men compared to 59 percent women were opposed to shutting down all nuclear plants at that time (April 1979). One interpretation is that the risks of nuclear containment are seen to be greater by women than men.

A pattern stands clear over twenty-five years: women have been more opposed to the use of force and to the support of warlike policies. When these measures are correlated with level of education and age, the younger, more highly educated women take the more "dovish" position. One explanation of this trend sometimes voiced by feminist leaders and scholars relates to the biology of women. The simplest explanation is that women give birth and are thus more reluctant to destroy life. Furthermore, women are socialized into behavior patterns which are passive and nonviolent. But it is beyond the scope of this book to explain the durability of this attitude among the majority of American women. For whatever reason, nonviolent attitudes are more pervasive among women.

On the civil rights of racial minorities, the differences between men and women are not nearly so clear as on foreign policy. Although exceptions can be found, over the years there is sufficient difference to state that women have been more supportive of efforts to achieve racial equality than have men. Some examples to support the "sympathetic" position can be found in the Michigan data. We have tried to select the most controversial examples. In 1964, for example, 67 percent of the men reported at the time of the election that they felt people in the civil rights movement were pushing for change too fast, as compared to 58 percent of the women. In the same year, 25 percent of the women stated they would "go along" with busing. In that interview, 68 percent of the men declared they would try to change the busing decision. On the question of school integration, men and women responded more similarly. However, as is the case with many of these questions, if the responses are broken down by level of education, gender differences appear. Of those with grade school education, 10 percent more of the women than of the men supported school integration, and 15 percent more men than women opposed school integration. A similar question in the same survey found 5 percent more women than men at both the grade school and college levels agreeing that blacks have a right to live wherever they can afford to.

When we turn to the questions of social welfare there is evidence, again some of it contradictory, of male-female differences as well. Over three decades Hero found women "several percentage points more favorably disposed toward such programs as aid to dependent children, unemployment assistance, old age benefits, Medicare, anti-poverty programs and 'relief' generally" (1968, p. 53). Louis Harris found in 1972 that more men than women would oppose "Federal funds spent for housing, welfare, and other assistance" if this meant "reducing the United States to a second position behind the Soviet Union" (1972, p. 9). Fifty-six percent of the men opposed, and 27 percent supported such a policy, while only 47 percent of the women opposed and 31 percent supported it.

The significance of the gender differences on some issues is difficult to assess. Clearly women's attitudes on the war in Southeast Asia did not produce a national antiwar policy, but they were not totally disregarded either. We believe that women have influenced the strategy of managers of presidential campaigns on issues such as these, as we will show in looking at female support for particular candidates standing for election. The "women's vote," however, has not been recognized in presidential politics in, for example, the way the black vote was recognized as providing the margin for victory for Carter in 1976. Whether the impact of issues on women in future elections will energize a more articulate bloc vote remains to be seen.

Choice of Candidates

Do women choose candidates on the basis of their stand on policy issues, or for other reasons? For years social scientists have perpetuated the myth that women are more "irrational" than men, choosing candidates based on their good looks, personality, character, or style. Two women, Shabad and Andersen (1979) have recently set the record straight by drawing evidence from the CPS data which show that women evaluate candidates no less rationally than men, and are just as inclined to be issue oriented.

At times women have differed considerably from men in their responses to candidates. There is no single factor which explains voters' attitudes toward candidates, but a strong surmise is that when women have voted differently from men, they have been reacting to their perception of the candidate's position on policy alternatives. Three fairly obvious examples of gender differences can be found in the 1952, 1968, and 1972 elections.

This analysis is handicapped by the lack of longitudinal data in the Michigan archive which would reflect changes that take place in voter attitude during the course of an election. Michigan surveys studied here relied upon preelection and postelection interviews during an election year. Therefore, we will examine the Roper data in 1952 which included seven surveys, including a postelection survey jointly sponsored by two leading social scientists, Samuel Stouffer and Paul Lazarsfeld. They commented on the Roper surveys:

> Harris gives convincing evidence that in all social groups a larger proportion of women than men voted for Eisenhower. For a variety of reasons women have for several decades furnished somewhat larger supply of Republicans, but in 1952 the difference was especially great. [1954, p. xi]

Harris explained the upsurge of voting by women in 1952 as related to differences in patterns of thinking about issues. He cited female concern for the war in Korea, and its rippling effects also on price levels, wages, employment, and stock prices. By election day he found men lagging well over 10 points behind women in focusing attention on the fighting in Korea. He also found two other root issues, namely high prices and corruption of concern to women. Harris found in the Roper data in November, 1952, that women supported Eisenhower on election day at 58 percent compared to 52 percent by men, with a 7 point difference in male support for Stevenson (Harris 1954).

Harris commented on these voting differences:

> The implication of this new-found independence among women can have profound effect on the future of American politics. It raises the real possibility that in the future there will in fact be a 'woman's vote' quite separate from the men's. Politicians have often talked about women as a separate entity in political life, but for the most part, they have assumed that women in any election would get into 'line' with the men by election day. This is the stereotype of traditional thinking about women in politics, and is widely accepted by many political analysts. [1954, pp. 116–17]

A second example of gender differences in presidential voting is found in George Wallace's challenge to the two-party system in 1968. Half as many women (6 percent) voted for George Wallace as men (12 percent). Wallace captured 13.5 percent of the popular vote and won forty-six electoral votes in five states. In this closely balanced contest the Wallace vote very nearly denied Nixon the election. Nixon received 43.4 percent of the popular vote to Humphrey's 42.7—an electoral vote majority. Wallace's strong third-party challenge posed a threat to Nixon's or Humphrey's winning a majority of the Electoral College votes. In that case the decision would have rested with the House of Representatives where Wallace could have bargained on a state by state basis, with each state casting one vote. Wallace stated his objectives as desiring to win concessions on public policy, presumably more law and order, and less civil rights enforcement.

Women were consistent in the 1976 election in being less supportive than men of Wallace as a possible candidate. The Michigan data have measured response to a so-called feeling thermometer, which found women between the ages of twenty and fifty to be 5 to 10 percent more "cool" toward George Wallace than men. Only at the age of sixty and over were women less "cool" toward Wallace than men.

There is no hard evidence to explain why women were less supportive of George Wallace than men. There is speculation that can be
made based on George Gallup's comments that women are not inclined to support candidates who are perceived as being "extreme," a
description that would fit the former governor of Alabama. Since
women are inclined also to be less militaristic than men, they would
have perceived his views on ending the war in Southeast Asia differently from men. His vice-presidential candidate, General Curtis
LeMay, made speeches advocating heavy bombing.

The 1972 election, however, provides a better example of female
influence in a presidential campaign. It was at the nominating convention of the Democratic party where women came of political age
more so than in any other previous election. Kirkpatrick (1976) has
identified the party activists as *The New Presidential Elite*. It was also
true, however, that at the grass roots level women seemed to be given
slightly more notice. Dutton, who combined practical political experience with social science, wrote that the concern for the women's
vote in the 1972 election "affects our campaign organization, the
symbols that we signal, the issues we choose and the personality and
style of our candidate" (1972, p. 1512).

Dutton's candidate, George McGovern, however, lost in a landslide to Nixon. The women's support for McGovern dwindled over
the course of the campaign, but women still registered 7 percent less
support for Nixon than did men. Pomper reviewed the Michigan data
closely and explained:

> In contrast to the past, women in 1972 were more closely identified
> than men with a liberal party and voted in greater proportions for a
> liberal candidate. They were responding here not to biological neces-
> sity, but to policy issues of the time. [1975, p. 152]

Among other social scientists who have commented on a difference in attitude between men and women in relation to candidates
were Pool, Abelson, and Popkin, who reported in the fall of the 1960
presidential campaign on "the dramatic slippage of Kennedy behind
Nixon . . . and on the lag of Kennedy's popularity among women"
(1964–65, p. 23). It was their observation that a reason for Nixon's

greater support by women was that more women than men saw "avoiding war by negotiation with Russian leaders" as the most important issue (1964–65, p. 88). Women supported Kennedy on election day, however, in similar proportions as men.

What reasons do voters have for choosing one candidate over another? The literature of the social sciences creates an image of women as more dependent on personal than impersonal cues: "It was Eisenhower's personality or Kennedy's good looks that prompted greater appeal among women." This hypothesis overlooks the fact that candidates and issues are not disjunctive. We argue that men as well as women are impressed by the charisma and personality of candidates. We also argue that in the examples cited (women's preference for Eisenhower, and McGovern, early negative view of Kennedy, and lower vote for Wallace), the evidence also says that there were differences in policy positions which can explain the gender differences.

The real test of whether or not the women's vote would make a difference in the outcome of an election can be put this way. The reality of the close electoral balance between the two major political parties in the United States is a political fact of life. Nixon lost in 1960 by the equivalent of one vote in every precinct. A shift of one hundred thousand votes in four major states in 1968 would have defeated Nixon. A shift of two hundred thousand votes in 1976 would have defeated Carter. The mathematics of the electoral college also requires a consideration of the demographic distribution of women. More women than men live in metropolitan areas, which carry weight in the major states in relation to the electoral college formula which operates on a winner-take-all principle. The electoral vote in eleven major states can elect a president. Women in America began to outnumber men in 1950, and have outnumbered men by millions in actual numbers voting since 1964. As we noted earlier, women have a remarkable potential for influencing the outcome of presidential elections. Thus far, women have not been recognized for their vote on foreign policy. The opportunity, however, is there for the future as international issues more and more dominate politics.

Party Indentification

A surprising revelation of early voting studies was that the key determinant of voting was the party preference of the voter. The Michigan scholars demonstrated in their data that in 1952 and 1956, party identification as an independent variable accounted for a large proportion of the variance in the presidential vote (Campbell et al. 1960). Key and Munger described this attachment to a party as the standing decision of the voter (1959). Other scholars confirmed this view. Lane, for example, wrote that "Over the long run, party identification has more influence over a person's vote decision than any other single factor" (1959, p. 300). Party identification as described in *The American Voter* (1960) was measured by asking individuals to rank their partisan loyalties to political parties. The clear message in the early data that party identification was the main determinant of presidential choice led to voluminous research and disagreement among scholars. Converse (1964) developed from the 1952–56 data a so-called normal vote based on the distribution of voter allegiances to political parties, thus providing a statistical tool by which the outcome of elections could be more easily understood and accurately predicted. A wave of explanatory studies focused on the socialization of voters, with the early studies emphasizing the role of the family as an influencing factor—that, in a sense, a person was born into a political party preference.

A corollary of this central finding about the strength of party loyalty was simply that the voter was poorly informed about specific issues. Further, attitudes on public policy were not logically interrelated, and were not ideologically ordered.

By the 1970s a change occurred in electoral behavior with a marked decline in partisanship and an increase in issue voting in presidential elections. The decline in partisanship had several dimensions. There was a decline in the proportion of the electorate which identified with a particular party, and consequently an increase in the number placing themselves in the independent column—in some states, a third or more. There was a decline in what was called strength of party—the intensity of feeling directed toward a political party. Further, voters began a process called party switching, voting for one party on the presidential or federal election column and for the opposition party in state elections. Scholars vary in interpreting these defections from party voting, with Miller and Levitin (1976) arguing that these developments do not indicate a weakening of the general ties to the political parties. The growth of independents and ticket splitting are evidenced in the presidential vote, they argue; the congressional vote, which has maintained more stability, is a better reflection of the voter's partisanship. Converse and Markus (1979) have added to current scholarly dispute by comparing a 1956–60 panel study with a 1972–76 panel study in which the same respondents were reinterviewed. The preliminary analysis revealed nearly identical findings for both panels regarding party and issues.

The overall decline in partisanship has led to a more volatile presidential election scene and a continuing decline in the power of political parties. This development was expressed succinctly by the *Washington Post* columnist David Broder in the title of his influential 1972 book, *The Party Is Over*. These developments have profound implications for the women's movement. If factors other than the traditional political party become more prominent, it will be possible for women to make breakthroughs in a more open, competitive marketplace for votes to elect candidates and to influence policy outcome.

In view of the importance of the voter's identification with one party or another, it is analytically interesting to determine if there are gender differences in party preference. It should be noted that the correlation between an individual's statement of party identification and actual voting choice has varied over the twenty-five years under study. A voter can prefer one party and vote for another. With this caveat in mind we can look at the historical record, and update the findings with Michigan CPS data.

There was a prevailing impression in early voting research that women favored the Republican party more than men did. Berelson and Lazarsfeld (1945), Gallup (1952), and Harris (1954) have made that observation. The preference of women for the Republican party in the 1940s and 1950s is easily explained by Merriam and Gosnell (1924) in connection with their pioneering 1920 studies in the city of Chicago when women first began to vote. They found voting turnout to be higher in neighborhoods which reflected greater college experience, higher income, and generally higher social class. The higher socioeconomic class of men and women has traditionally supported the Republican party, leading some wags to comment that the Republican party is a class not a party.

If we search the Michigan data from 1952 to 1976 we find that there was a remarkable similarity among men and women stating their preference of political party. Table 7 documents the differences in the distribution of party identification and summarizes the percentage difference of men and women who were "strongly attached to either party." The differences are small. For purposes of this discussion the more important statistics are found in table 8 showing the decline of women of less 〔 〕cation who replied in terms of party identification that they were ╲political." Table 8 shows a greater decline of these women than 〔 〕men, and clearly substantiates the correlation between minimal educ 〔 〕on and an "apolitical" response. After 1960 this category of women di 〔 〕peared in significant numbers from the electorate. The dying off of ge 〔 〕rations and the replacement by a new electorate must also be inclu 〔 〕 in the change factor for women.

Table 7. Gender Differences in Party Identification, v Election Year

Party Identification	Percentage Difference (men x us women)						
	1952	1956	1960	1964	1968	1972	1976
Democratic	−2%	6%	2%	1%	−1%	%	−5%
Republican	−4	−7	−4	−1	3	−1	2
Independent	6	1	2	0	−2	7	3

Source of Data: Center for Political Studies, American National Election Studies, 1952–1976.
Note: See table 60 in the Appendix for the actual rates of men and women.

Summary and Conclusions

Women and men have been deeply divided on foreign policy issues since the Second World War. Women were more opposed than men to American involvement in Korea and Southeast Asia, and by 1972 more women than men still gave ending the war first priority. Our

Table 8. A Comparison of "Apoliticals" by Education, from Self-Classification of Party Identification

	Men	Women
1952		
Grade school	2.5%	9.6%
High school	0.8	1.6
College	0.5	0.4
1956		
Grade school	5.5	12.8
High school	0.3	3.1
College	0.6	0.4
1960		
Grade school	1.7	8.5
High school	0.6	2.9
College	—	1.1
1964		
Grade school	1.0	1.5
High school	1.7	1.8
College	—	—

Source of Data: Center for Political Studies, American National Election Studies, 1952–1964.
Note: This table measures respondents who reported they held an apolitical identification when asked: "Generally speaking, do you think of yourself as a Republican, a Democrat, an Independent, or what?"

examination of women's attitudes toward public policy questions revealed a clear pattern: they take a less violent and less warlike position than men. It is this dove-hawk difference which may propel the invisible majority of women voters into a cohesive voting bloc. Many men share the more peaceful orientation of women, and thus there may well be a pacifist bloc in the electorate as well. Men also join women in support of key feminist issues, such as ratification of the Equal Rights Amendment or prochoice legislation, so that another distinction should be made between a women's vote and a feminist vote.

Women have differed from men in supporting candidates, including Eisenhower, Nixon, Wallace, and McGovern. There is a remarkable similarity, however, between men and women in declaring their identification with political parties. The 10 percent of women who declared themselves "apolitical" in the 1950s has disappeared. This dying off of older women and their replacement by a generation with a new political outlook is a critical factor in electoral politics.

The political outlook for women is not clear because of the changes in American politics. If our political institutions are becoming more tolerant of independent and unilateral action by candidates and organizations, then women have a good opportunity to gain recognition. In the first place, the prevailing forces of change in recent decades have been rooted in providing opportunity for groups formerly underrepresented in the political system. In the 1980s, however, new forces are at work. What other changes in the political culture can benefit women?

The transformation in politics begins with the decline of political parties which have dominated electoral decisions since the beginning of the republic, and the rise of a more issue-oriented politics of special interest groups. In addition to party decline and more constituent concern for policy, other factors must be taken into account in describing the new political climate. The Supreme Court decisions prescribing more equitable apportionment of the House of Representatives and the legislative districts of state legislatures have encouraged more competitive elections. In a post-Vietnam and Watergate era there is an additional emphasis on ethics and disclosure by candidates and a subsequent use of sunshine laws to conduct the public's business in full view. New campaign techniques with the advent of professional managers, survey analysts, and media experts also make it possible for newcomers to break through the barriers formerly dominated by male political figures and their interests who held entrenched positions. A dramatic change in the electoral process itself, with the broad expansion of the use of primaries in presidential elections, also works against traditional interests. And the use of federal financing of presidential elections in 1976 has opened the door to the possibility of public financing of other offices, federal as well as state. These shifts in the political environment have already had their effects with far more turnover and a changing membership in state legislatures and the halls of Congress. The new politics is also changing the old rules which have governed these halls for more than a century, meaning that if women do succeed in voting their candidates into office, the opportunities are more open for achieving success also in policy formation. Obvious evidence of political change which favors new-comers is found in the 1976 presidential election of an obscure governor of Georgia who defied conventional wisdom and tradition by winning the state primaries and the general election.

How do these changes in the political environment relate to the changing attitudes of women, who by 1976 had caught up with men in voting and attitude from a lag going back to their enfranchisement in 1920? The opportunities for women would seem to lie in the rise of the influence of issue-oriented politics, brought about by lobbying groups coming into greater prominence from all socioeconomic groups, spanning the concerns from Common Cause to the National Rifle Association. It may well be that women will not in the immediate future move in the direction of a cohesive voting bloc, recognized as representing the women in the electorate. But women are experienced in bypassing the traditional, official political parties, and other entrenched political power. If these establishment institutions are now challenged by political change leading to a more open system of independent action by candidates or organizations, women may find better opportunities. Women since 1920 have chosen the back door to politics, working for change through organizational channels and as volunteers. Whatever their mark has been politically, it may well be said that women have thus far achieved their greatest gains in effecting change in public policy through volunteer efforts.

From a movement rooted in an economic and educational elite in the 1960s, the women's movement has developed support for its goals—a broadening in the past several years to include the majority of men and women. While women were slower than men to support issues on sex role equality, by the end of the 1970s there was a clear majority of men and women favoring more egalitarianism in sex roles, equal pay for equal work, abortion legislation, child care centers, and other issues of particular interest to women.

Furthermore, women have at various times provided a hidden majority in electoral politics and differed from men on some candidates and issues. The minority model of political behavior, as presented by ethnic, religious, or racial groups does not fit the minority status of women, but it is highly conceivable that women will unite on single issues and form a cohesive voting bloc that may or may not be visible, but still it can be influential. The outlook, however, is also clouded by new worldwide developments of shortages of energy and other scarce resources. This recent turn in events does not favor upgrading the political status of women.

The direction of the trends favoring a women's collective vote will also depend on the authority of the leadership of women's groups. Thus far there has been no strong sentiment among the leadership to articulate and organize a movement for women's bloc vote. However, all of the elements are in place to move in that direction. The leadership has been exemplary over the past two decades in raising the consciousness of women and men to accept more egalitarian sex roles. Further, the rate of change in attitude across a broad spectrum has been dramatic. An innovator in the leadership is Martha Griffiths, former member of Congress who led the fight for Title VII adding the word "sex" to the Civil Rights Act of 1964, and who steered the Equal Rights Amendment through the House. She has been an innovator in the past in the women's movement, and has recently issued a call to arms, at a conference of leaders who were looking at the 1980s. She stated:

Women have the right to vote. They must learn to use it for themselves rather than being distracted by highly idealistic slogans such as "peace in our time," "food for the hungry world" or other equally worthy pleas; to vote for those men and women who propose a course of action that will promote the equality of women and to vote against those who do not support such equality. A woman voter, for a while at least, will need to let her party line count less, and the candidate's position on the rights of women more, than any other single issue. [1976, pp. 145–47]

chapter five

THE BLACK WOMAN VOTER
An Enigma

The voting patterns of American black women over the last two decades present a puzzling picture to the analyst of political behavior. All the statistics on their disadvantaged status when compared either to white men and women or black men, lead us to expect extremely low political involvement among black women. The data, however, do not bear this out.

The evidence supporting their low socioeconomic status is quite clear. Of the four gender-race groups black women have the lowest median income: in 1970 white women earned about 30 percent more, black men earned 57 percent more, and white men earned 150 percent more than black women. Black women are likely to be located in the most menial jobs and have a higher rate of unemployment than the other three groups. Although in the past they attended college at higher rates than black men, this situation has changed. By 1973 the proportion of black women aged eighteen to twenty-four enrolled in college was 14 percent, while the rate for black men was 19 percent, both rates being considerably lower than those for white men and women. At the same time, one-third of black women, compared to one-fourth of the white, are heads of household, with black women more often finding it necessary to work even when their children are young (U.S., Bureau of Census, Series P-23, no. 50, 1974).[1]

Their demographic profile in terms of low income, education, social class, and employment would suggest that the typical black women would be found among the least likely voters, as described in chapter 2. The data, however, point in a different direction. Since

1952, black women have increased their rate of voting faster than have black men, and more than either white men or women from whom turnout has been declining. These increases in voter participation for black women are all the more remarkable because black women had the longest way to go to show an increase. From the most reliable data we have, we estimate that only one-quarter (28 percent) of black women voted in 1952 and 1956, with black men voting 11 percent higher (39 percent). The rate for black women more than doubled by 1968, and in 1976, 50 percent of the eligible black women voted—some 3 percentage points more than black men (47 percent). Black women, when compared to white women, have gone from a deficit of 46 percentage points in voting rate in 1952, to a difference of only 11 percentage points in 1976 (Lansing 1977). As a result, although blacks continue to show a lag of 8 to 15 percentage points behind whites in recent elections, the black minority is voting at rates much closer to the majority group than ever before. And, significantly, blacks have joined other minority ethnic and religious groups who have tended to vote in blocs. There is a fascinating story in American history of the Irish vote, the Italian vote, the Catholic vote, and the Jewish vote, among others. Following that tradition black leaders in America have organized a solidarity among their followers which has resulted in their sending a growing representation to state legislatures and to Congress. Their clout has also led to the election of black mayors in a number of major cities, including Atlanta and Detroit. Their influence, however, reached its high water mark in the 1976 election when their vote provided the margin for victory for Carter. Gerald Pomper looked at the demography of that vote and wrote: "In a close election any sizeable group can claim to be critical, but in 1976 this claim can be most deservedly made by blacks" (1977, p. 62). There is an obvious lesson that the leadership of the women's movement could learn from the model of voting provided by black voters. However, feminists have not generally used the minority concept in the struggle for political gains. The only interesting exception has come from sociologists such as Hacker (1951) and Rossi (1964) who have described women as an economic minority because of their lack of resources.

Our purpose in this chapter is to examine the voting patterns of the

American electorate by gender and race subgroups and to document the magnitude of the increased vote by black women over time. In chapter 6, we will examine a number of theories or conjectures as possible explanations for our findings. Published research on black women is scarce and often contradictory. Further, a white researcher explores variations in gender roles in the black race with some trepidation and caution. Nevertheless, the voting history of black women is a dramatic success story and invites scholarly investigation.

The Dual Factors of Race and Gender: An Overview

Several interesting features of the voting behavior of black women suggest the dual effects of race and gender. Later in this chapter we will examine each of these in greater detail and attempt to tie them together theoretically; for now, we will simply list a few:

1. Young black women are now voting at higher rates than young black men.
2. The gap in voting between black men and women is less than that of whites, especially for women with only an elementary education.
3. Black women in the white-collar and manual occupations voted at slightly higher rates than black men until 1976 when their rates became similar. Men in farm occupations voted at higher rates. Black professional women voted at higher rates than black men of comparable status.
4. Some black women, at the low and high ends of the economic scale, appear to have a life-style with egalitarian sex roles which encourage assertive behavior by women, including voting.
5. In 1972, survey data on the attitudes of black women showed a distinct pattern regarding the quality of life and the problems facing the federal government. These attitudes were often the reverse of the attitudes of whites, and were far distant from those of black men, suggesting an attitude-set of self-interest in seeking rewards from the political system.
6. Black women who were classified as feminists on a nine-item test voted at higher rates than women classified as nonfeminists.

Certainly the increased politicization of black women can be linked to the removal of legal and other intimidating restraints on voting.

The participation of black women of all classes and ages in the protests of the 1960s led to a political resocialization which has, apparently, resulted in a pattern of increased voting. But there is more. We will also demonstrate that increased voting by female blacks is related to their rising expectations for change in their status and role as women. A review of their voting history is basic to this analysis.

Voting History

Before the 1960s probably no more than one-third of black women, not only in the South but in the country as a whole, voted in presidential elections. A black woman reared in the South who was sixty years old in 1972 probably was not allowed to vote until she was in her thirties, and quite possibly not until she was over fifty. Voting figures for these early years are difficult to find and accept, but it has been estimated that before 1940, only 12 percent of the black population voted (U.S., Commission on Civil Rights, 1959, 1961). Ralph Bunche, researching the problem for Gunnar Myrdal's *An American Dilemma* (1962), estimated that only two hundred fifty thousand blacks voted in the South in 1940. The Commission on Civil Rights estimated that the total number of black voters in the South was double that figure by 1955, and that by 1964 the number had climbed to slightly more than 2 million (*New York Times*, November 22, 1964, p. 34L).

As the black population was no more than 11 percent of the total population in the 1950s, the small number of black individuals included in survey samples which reflected that percentage did not permit extensive cross-tabulation. Therefore, we have chosen to use the data of the Bureau of the Census, which has the largest samples of the survey institutions, and which since 1964 has collected voting data in federal elections. However, to demonstrate the significance of the increase in voting by black women, it is essential to establish a baseline for prior voting. The Michigan data found that roughly one-quarter of the eligible black women voted in the 1950s (28 percent in 1952 and 29 percent in 1956 compared to 39 percent in 1952 for black men and 46 percent in 1956). These survey data, however, are based on small numbers and can only be regarded as approximations. A second basis for comparison drawn from the same data is found in table 9 which notes that in measuring people who had never voted, 87 percent of black women in the South were in that category in 1952 and 70 percent in 1956. In the non-South 11 percent of black women in 1952 and 32 percent in 1956 reported that they had never voted.

A third source which provides a baseline is found in the surveys of Matthews and Prothro. They made detailed studies in four counties chosen to represent the eleven states of the old Confederacy, and collected aggregate information on all biracial southern counties.[2] They reported that in 1961, in the four counties:

> in terms of voting alone, 47 percent of Negro males and 38 percent of Negro females would qualify as participants (including voting) . . . . At every level of education, and for all forms of participation, more Negro men than women are active. [1966, pp. 67–68]

Within their larger definition of political participation which included voting, campaigning, holding political office or membership in a political group, 63 percent of the black males and 47 percent of the black females were active in the politics of the South. Matthews and Prothro commented on the extremely low rate of participation among black women, concluding that "Negro women tend to be frozen out of southern politics" (1966, p. 68).

The major change did not come until the passage of the Voting Rights Act in 1965 which provided direct federal assistance in registration and voting. The act is generally seen as the most significant step since the Fifteenth Amendment in opening opportunities for black citizens to register and vote. The abolition of the poll tax and literacy requirements were also beneficial.

If a black woman did vote before 1964, she probably had moved north or west to a state where blacks had experienced greater opportunity to vote prior to that year. The years between 1940 and 1966 witnessed the massive migration from the South of 3.5 million blacks, according to Census Bureau reports. By 1973 only 53 percent of the original number remained in the South (*Newsweek*, February, 1973,

Table 9. Men and Women by Race and Region Who Have Never Voted

	1952		1956		1960		1964		1968		1972		1976	
	White	*Black*	*White*	*Black*	*White*	*Black*	*White*	*Black*	*White*	*Black*	*White*	*Black*	*White*	*Black*
South[a]														
Men	12%	65%	14%	60%	8%	33%	5%	26%	9%	25%	13%	12%	14%	23%
Women	33	87	27	70	17	63	14	39	26	31	20	25	18	28
Non-South														
Men	6	17	6	17	6	11	7	10	9	0[b]	8	7	8	5
Women	7	11	10	32	7	28	7	18	7	17	8	9	10	25

Source of Data: Center for Political Studies, American National Election Studies, 1952–1976.

a. Includes Alabama, Arkansas, Florida, Georgia, Kentucky, Louisiana, Maryland, Mississippi, North Carolina, Oklahoma, South Carolina, Tennessee, Texas, Virginia, West Virginia.

b. Sampling problem.

p. 33). By 1979 the trend was reversing. Thus, older blacks, male and female, especially those from the southern states of the old Confederacy, have generally only begun to vote late in life—if they vote at all. It is our contention that in the process of political resocialization heralded by the fall of legal barriers, the younger black women have adapted more easily than their mothers and grandmothers.

Generational Differences

We have already seen that in the 1950s and 1960s black women lagged behind black men in all forms of political participation, including voting. Table 10 shows voting rates for black and white men and women for the 1964, 1968, and 1976 presidential elections, and makes clear that black women have made great progress in catching up to, and in the younger age groups surpassing, the voting record of black men. In the 1964 and 1968 elections black women up to the age of fifty-four voted at rates comparable to or higher than those of black men. In the youngest cohort, aged twenty-one to twenty-four, 10 percent more women than men voted in 1964, and 6 percent more in 1968. Voting was about the same for the three middle cohorts aged twenty-four to fifty-four of both sexes, while for people born before 1909—the oldest cohorts—black men voted at progressively higher rates than black women: 5 percent more in the fifty-five to sixty-four age group and 19 percent more in the oldest group in 1968.

From the 1976 election statistics a similar pattern emerges. Up to the age of sixty-four, the same number or more black women than black men voted, and even among the sixty-five to seventy-four cohort the pattern is similar, with only 2 percent more men voting in this age group. Thus, while young black women continued to exceed the voting rate of their male peers, the older women made a great deal of progress over the twelve-year span represented here: women who were in the forty-five to fifty-four group in 1964 were in the next older group by 1976, while the oldest women in the earlier election—those who voted a great deal less than their male peers—have disappeared from the statistics for the most recent election. Another source of evidence about the increasing politicization of young black

Table 10. Comparison by Gender, Age, and Race of Persons Voting for President in 1964 and 1968 and 1976

				1964		
	White			Black		
Age	Men	Women	Men Minus Women	Men	Women	Men Minus Women
21–24	53%	52%	1%	39%	49%	−10%
25–34	66	65	1	58	62	−4
35–44	76	73	3	64	62	2
45–54	80	75	5	65	66	−1
55–64	80	74	6	65	60	5
65–74	79	51	28	57	48	9

				1968		
	White			Black		
Age	Men	Women	Men Minus Women	Men	Women	Men Minus Women
21–24	53%	53%	0%	36%	42%	−6%
25–34	64	63	1	56	57	−1
35–44	73	71	2	65	65	0
45–54	77	75	2	66	66	0
55–64	79	69	10	65	60	5
65–74	68	51	17	51	32	19

				1976		
	White			Black		
Age	Men	Women	Men Minus Women	Men	Women	Men Minus Women
18–20	39%	42%	−3%	22%	24%	−2%
21–24	47	49	−2	32	33	−1
25–29	54	56	−2	40	46	−6
30–34	60	61	−1	47	51	−4
35–44	64	66	−2	52	57	−5
45–54	69	69	0	58	63	−5
55–64	73	69	4	65	65	0
65–74	73	64	9	58	56	2

Source of Data: U.S., Department of Commerce, Bureau of the Census, Current Population Reports, Population Characteristics, Series P-20, no. 143 (October 25, 1965), no. 192 (December 2, 1969), and no. 322 (March 1978).

Note: The primary percent entries represent a simple subtraction of the proportion of women within the category voting for president from the same proportion among men. Negative percentages indicate that women voted at a higher rate than men.

women is Matthews and Prothro's study of the civil rights movement. They found no large gap between males and females in rates of participation in student protests. Demonstrations against segregation in 1960 and 1961 included almost as many young women as men: 48 percent of the participants were female. Matthews and Prothro found that 42 percent of the men in their sample were in the two most active levels of involvement when respondents were classified by degree of participation; this figure was nearly matched by the women, of whom 38 percent were in the two most active groups. Well over half (57 percent) of the blacks enrolled in predominantly black institutions at the height of the sit-ins were women. Matthews and Prothro suggest that this fact reflects the special position of women in black culture (1966, p. 417).

The pattern does not appear to be the same for white voters. In the first two elections shown here, white men voted at the same or higher rates than white women in every age group, though only among the oldest cohorts was this difference a large one. In the 1976 election, however, the pattern for white voters is closer to that for blacks: up to the age of fifty-four, women voted at rates greater than or equal to those of men, while among the two oldest cohorts men still had an edge. In other words, it could be said that white women have been moving in the same direction as black women—but several years later—in terms of their voting rates relative to those of their respective men. To put it more simply: white women have taken longer than black women to reach voting rates comparable to those of their respective men.

It should be noted that the voting rates for all groups went down between 1972 and 1976. Though both races showed a similar amount of decrease, the men in both races showed a somewhat greater decline than the women. According to the Bureau of the Census report for 1976, the overall voting rates by race in that election were 49 percent for blacks and 61 percent for whites. However, most of this difference is attributable to differences in the age, education, and income distributions of the black and white populations. When rates are standardized by education and age, the voting rates for blacks and whites become much closer—56 and 60 percent, respectively. Similarly, standardizing for age and family income produces black and white voting rates that also differ by only about two points. When both education and income are standardized, the turnout difference between the races is reduced to the same negligible level (U.S., Bureau of the Census, March 1978, p. 3). Any basic discussion of the black vote must also take regional characteristics into account, however.

Black Voting in Relation to the South and the Non-South

As we saw in our discussion of black voting patterns before 1964, very few blacks voted in the South until after that year, and this was particularly true for black women. Until very recently, southern blacks lagged far behind northern blacks in terms of voter participation—for well-documented historical reasons. Verba and Nie concluded from their 1967 survey data that

> blacks voted almost as regularly as whites in the North, much less regularly in the South. And when one takes out the effects of social class one finds that in the North blacks are more active in voting than their class would predict, whereas in the South they are less active than their class would predict. Clearly this reflects the fact that historical legal discriminations against black voting in the South still make a difference. [1972, p. 171]

Data from the 1976 election, shown in table 11, reveal that the influence of region on the black vote has been declining. In that year

Table 11. A Comparison by Race, Gender, and Region of Voting in the 1976 Presidential Election

	Northeast		North Central		South		West	
	White	Black	White	Black	White	Black	White	Black
Men	62%	46%	66%	55%	58%	44%	59%	48%
Women	60	49	66	59	56	47	60	52
Both Sexes	61	48	66	57	57	46	59	50

Source of Data: U.S., Department of Commerce, Bureau of the Census, Current Population Reports, Population Characteristics, Series P-20, no. 322 (March 1978).

region no longer had a marked effect on the voting rates of black people. Although the black voting rate was lower in the South than in the other three regions, the difference was negligible: blacks in the South voted only 2 percentage points behind those in the Northeast, and four points behind those in the West. When compared to whites, blacks voted about the same number of percentage points lower in all four regions. In other words, the interaction of the effects of race and region which existed previously has weakened in the 1976 data.

It is interesting to note that black women voted at higher rates than black men in all regions, including the South. Thus the picture presented by the early Michigan CPS data, which showed roughly one-quarter of black women voting (1952–56) and by Matthews and Prothro (1966) which showed that black women in the South had extremely low rates of political involvement, is clearly no longer accurate in the 1970s.

This conclusion receives added support from the figures in table 9 presented earlier. In 1952 about half of the eligible citizens who stated in surveys that they never voted lived in the South; more than two-thirds were women. Still, nonvoting had declined in the South from 38 percent of the electorate in 1952 to 15 percent in 1968. In 1952, fully 87 percent of southern black women had never voted—a remarkably high figure which, however, has decreased steadily, so that by 1976 only 28 percent of adult black women in the South had never cast a presidential ballot. Black men in the South, though not starting at such a disadvantage, have made similar, if less spectacular, gains. By 1976, although the percentage of nonvoters was still higher in the South than in the North for all groups, the differences between blacks and whites were relatively small.

A host of changes in the South in recent years are partially responsible for the increased rates in political participation in that region. The decisions of the Supreme Court and state courts, the acts of Congress and state legislatures, and the orders of chief executives of federal and state governments have had their differential effects on the southern region. For example, voting rights statutes were applied to such an extent following the Voting Rights Act of 1964 that the number of blacks registered to vote in sixteen southern states jumped from less than 1.5 million to 3.5 million as of 1976. There were almost four thousand black officeholders in the nation, tripling the number since 1969, with more than half, 57 percent, in the sixteen southern states. Economic and demographic changes apparently led to a reverse migration so that by 1977 the previous trend of black migration to the North had been reversed. Although recent increases in the economic growth and prosperity of the South as a region are not generally shared by black people, the breakdown of overt racism has meant greater opportunities for unionization and integration into the labor force—a development which encourages voting. The movement of southern rural blacks to urban centers of the South with continuing pressures from organizations, including the powerful pressures provided by the churches, aided the abetted political action. Another change in the position of blacks is apparent in statistics on educational achievement.

The Relationship of Education to Voting by Blacks

In 1950, black people in America received an average of seven years of schooling; by 1970, this figure had jumped to eleven years. The number of blacks aged sixteen and seventeen who were attending high school increased from 77 percent in 1960 to 86 percent in 1970, and in that year 16 percent of young black people were attending college. Although in the 1950s and 1960s black women received more years of education at all levels than black men, that trend has been reversed in the 1970s: more black men than women were attending college by 1973 (U.S., Bureau of the Census, Series P-23, no. 50, 1974).

How are these facts reflected in the voting patterns of black women and men? Table 12, which shows voting rates by level of education for black and white men and women in 1968 and 1976, reveals that, for both races, men outvote women at the lower education levels, while women tend to outvote men at the higher levels. In 1968, black women of elementary education voted at rates slightly higher than white women of comparable education—7 percentage points higher with zero to four years of schooling and 8 percentage points higher with five to seven years of school—and in 1976 this trend was stronger, continuing up through the eighth year of school. In the

Table 12. A Comparison by Gender, Race, and Education of Eligible Persons Voting for President in 1968 and 1976

	1968					
	White			Black		
Years of Education	Men	Women	Men Minus Women	Men	Women	Men Minus Women
Elementary						
0–4	45%	32%	13%	43%	39%	4%
5–7	60	45	15	54	53	1
8	68	59	9	56	54	2
High School						
1–3	65	60	5	57	56	1
4	73	73	0	67	65	2
College						
1–3	78	80	−2	73	74	−1
4	84	83	1	79	80	−1
5 or more	86	88	−2	87	91	−4
	1976					
	White			Black		
Years of Education	Men	Women	Men Minus Women	Men	Women	Men Minus Women
Elementary						
0–4	30%	23%	7%	42%	34%	8%
5–7	47	36	11	47	46	1
8	57	47	10	49	52	−3
High School						
1–3	49	48	1	42	44	−2
4	59	63	−4	44	49	−5
College						
1–3	68	72	−4	56	58	−2
4	79	82	−3	70	79	−9
5 or more	84	84	0	81	83	−2

Source of Data: U.S., Department of Commerce, Bureau of the Census, Current Population Reports, Population Characteristics, Series P–20, no. 192 (December 2, 1969), and no. 322 (March 1978).

Note: The primary percent entries represent a simple subtraction of the proportion of women within the category voting for president from the same proportion among men. Negative percentages indicate that women voted at a higher rate than men.

most recent election, black men also made gains on white men at the elementary levels, compared to the 1968 voting rates. At both the lowest and highest levels of education, black citizens tend to vote as frequently, or more frequently, than whites with the same level of schooling, while in the middle ranges of this variable, whites show a marked advantage.

It should also be noted that the gap between men and women is smaller for blacks than for whites. As with the data on age, however, the gap has been narrowing among the white electorate, while black women have been moving ahead of black men in the two election years presented here. In 1968, black women at the lowest level of education voted 4 percentage points less than comparable black men; white women at the lowest level voted 13 percentage points less than comparable white men. At the same time blacks of both sexes who had more than four years of elementary school voted at similar rates, while white women remained behind white men up to four years of high school. In 1976, black women voted at higher rates than black men for all education levels above seven years, while white women surpassed white men only at the high school graduate level and above. Interestingly, at the lowest education level—zero to four years of school—blacks of both sexes voted at higher rates than whites of either sex, and it is not until the high school level is reached that whites, as a group, show rates much higher than blacks.

Thus, education level has less of an influence on black than on white voters, in that black voters show much less increase in voting rates from the elementary to high school levels, having already started at a relatively high rate of voting—compared to white voters—even at the lowest education levels. We may conclude that, in general, black women tend to vote in percentages slightly higher than their levels of education would predict—if the prediction is based on the performance of white women. We can turn now to investigate other criteria, and see the effects of participation in the paid work force.

Labor Force

Data on the voting rates of black and white men and women according to occupational group also reveal a pattern for black women which differs from that for white females. As shown in table 13, black women in white-collar and manual occupations slightly exceeded the voting rates of similarly employed black men in the 1964 and 1968 elections. In 1976, gender differences for blacks remained negligible in manual and white-collar, and professional and technical occupations. However, in the white-collar category the managerial/administrative group of black women voted at a much higher rate (77 percent as opposed to 65 percent for the men). (This breakdown is not shown to simplify the data array.) In other words, black women in the highest occupational groups have tended to vote at slightly higher rates than black men in the same groups in recent elections. This overall pattern exhibited by black women does not hold for white women, who have not outvoted men in these occupational categories.

The data on occupational groups presented above provide some evidence, albeit limited, of a greater degree of political participation by black women in manual and white-collar trades than could be expected on the basis of their occupational level alone. It would be anticipated, however, that women of managerial and administrative rank would vote at high rates. One explanation is that women at the high end of the economic continuum are in a unique position and that this is particularly true of black women. Although there are few black women in the ranks of lawyers, doctors, and business executives, their numbers are proportionately greater than for white women

Table 13. A Comparison by Gender and Occupation of Eligible Black Persons Voting for President in 1964, 1968, and 1976

	1964		1968		1976	
Occupation	*Men*	*Women*	*Men*	*Women*	*Men*	*Women*
White collar workers	77%	82%	77%	82%	68%	66%
Manual workers	61	68	58	63	45	50
Service workers	68	60	62	61	52	52
Farm workers	34	24	44	a	35	a

Source of Data: U.S., Department of Commerce, Bureau of the Census, Current Population Reports, Population Characteristics, Series P–20, no. 192 (December 2, 1969), and no. 322 (March 1976).

a. Base less than 75,000, so percentage not reliable.

(when each group of women is compared to its respective group of men). Epstein (1973) concluded from a survey of thirty-one black female professionals that the double prejudices of racism and sexism can work to the advantage of the few select women at the top. She wrote that black women are less likely to arouse traditional sexist hostilities in the primarily white, male professional world than are white women. Even among black male professionals, sexism is less prevalent because black men are more accustomed to the image of working women.

A more extensive analysis of the status of black women by Burlew in 1977 points to the underrepresentation of black females in those careers that are nontraditional for women, and noted that "actually black women are typically at the bottom of the occupational pyramid" (1977, p. 89). Stone extended this argument, noting that the erosion of racial barriers in employment is working more to the advantage of black men than black women, thus contradicting the commonly held view that the black woman fares better in American society than the black man (1978, p. 581). Burlew and Stone are not calling into question the findings of Epstein, but pointing out that black women have never held high status professional jobs in any great numbers—that the high status fields of law, medicine, and dentistry, for example, are as much male fields among blacks as among whites. Their observations underscore the fact that in terms of actual numbers, relatively few black professional women exist.

So far, our examination of the voting behavior of black women has provided evidence of patterns of political involvement which cannot easily be fit into the theoretical framework we have developed for explaining the political behavior of white women. Age, region, educational level, and employment status have been presented as independent variables which may have an effect on the dependent variable—voting rate—but the reasons why these variables operate differently among the black population, and particularly among black women, are not easily explained.

The increasing voting rate of black women might be explained as due entirely to the removal of illegal barriers to voting by blacks, and the transfer of black power objectives to mainstream politics. These facts account for the overall increase in voting rates among blacks, but fail to account for the fact that black women are increasing their rate of voting faster than black men. It is important to point out that white women have also increased their voting rates over the same interval at higher rates than white men (chapter 2).

Our thesis is that black women are becoming more active at the polls because of the combined effects of racial and gender discrimination—described by the congressional leader Shirley Chisholm as "the double whammy." The relative importance of these two types of discrimination has not yet been determined, and there has been considerable argument among social scientists as to their proper weight. It is difficult in the first place to define the questions, and virtually impossible to find systematic evidence to generate conclusions. Nevertheless, it is instructive to examine a number of factors unique to the situation of black women in America which might shed some light on this neglected area of political behavior, and we do so in the following chapter.

Summary and Conclusions

In 1964, 1968, and 1972, black women in America were voting for president at the same rates as black men; in 1976, they voted at slightly higher rates. Using 1952 as a baseline for comparison, we have noted that less than one-third of black women voted in that year, and that this rate was doubled by 1968 and 1972. While some 28 percent of black women voted in 1956, 46 percent of black men voted. Thus in the 1960s black women increased their rate of voting at rates higher than either white sex, for whom turnout has been declining since 1960. This is true despite the fact that, of all four race-gender groups, black women can expect to attain the lowest income and educational levels and the highest unemployment levels—variables usually closely correlated with low voting rates.

Using census data for 1964, 1968, and 1976, we noted that the youngest black female cohort voted at slightly higher rates than their male counterparts (black women, 10 percent more than men in 1964, and 6 percent more in 1968). The middle-aged female cohorts voted at about the same rates as black men. Only at ages fifty-five and over was there a sharp increase in voting rates by black men as compared to black women (black men, 5 percent more in the fifty-five to sixty-four age group, and 19 percent more in the sixty-five to seventy-four age group in 1968). In 1976, black women voted at slightly higher rates than black men in all age categories until age fifty-five, and even in the highest age groups black men had only a very slight edge.

Besides age, variables such as region, educational level, and occupational group were shown to have an effect on the voting rates of black women. By 1976, region no longer had the powerful effect on black voting rates it had previously exhibited, and even in the South black women were now voting at higher rates than black men. In terms of education level, we saw that the gap between the sexes by education is smaller for blacks than for whites at lower levels, and at these levels blacks tend to vote at higher rates than whites. Thus, black women of elementary education voted at rates ranging from 5 to 11 percentage points higher than similar white women in 1976. Turning to the effects of occupational choice on voting rates, we reported that black women in the white-collar and manual occupations—and especially those in the area of management and administration—voted at slightly higher rates than black men in those occupations until 1976, when men and women voted similarly. Black men voted at slightly higher rates in the service and farm categories.

In the next chapter, we move beyond documenting the patterns of increase in voting rates among black women in the past twenty-five years. We will attempt to find explanations for the contradiction between the classical pattern of socioeconomic status leading to voting, and the status and political behavior of black women.

chapter six

THE DOUBLE WHAMMY FOR BLACK WOMEN
Toward an Understanding of Their Increasing Vote

The voting pattern described in the previous chapter becomes even more puzzling when we turn to measures of political estrangement, citizen efficacy, and sex discrimination. Our data show that black women, when compared to black men and to white men and women, have the lowest levels of trust in the federal government, the lowest feelings of political efficacy, and the highest sense of discrimination in the area of employment. On the assumption that these variables are measures of alienation, and that alienation is correlated with nonvoting, black women would be expected to go to the polls at very low rates.[1]

As we have already seen, black women have been increasing their voting rates in the past twenty years. In the face of a declining voter turnout by white Americans since 1960, black women have moved ahead to voting levels comparable with those of black men. By 1968 and 1972, black women voted at the same rates as black men, and in 1976 they voted at higher rates. The actual increases in income, education, and occupation, where they have occurred, have not been enough to explain the continuing increase in black women's voting rate. And the gains of the civil rights movement and the removal of numerous legal barriers—though important factors in the increase in voting by black men and women—are also insufficient to explain the paradox: black women are voting at the same or higher rates than black men, while their confidence in the federal government and their sense of political efficacy are declining. Thus if black women present a contradiction to the conventional association of

91

socioeconomic and educational levels with voting rates, they offer a similar contradiction to the canons of voting behavior research which have long found an association between patterns of political alienation and low levels of voting.

Underlying this discussion are broader questions about the general significance of nonparticipation: How much nonparticipation can a democratic system tolerate while still remaining a democracy? What is the significance to a democratic society of a vocal minority group with a strong sense of distrust and alienation from the political institutions of that society? Why do blacks in general, and black women in particular, continue to participate—and increase their rates of participation—in the electoral system despite their general lack of confidence in elected officials and the mechanisms of the political system? These major theoretical questions are beyond the scope of this analysis but belong on the agenda for future research. We can, however, document the levels of alienation found in survey data reported by black women and comment on its apparent effects.

Alienation and Nonparticipation

Many contemporary political analyses have focused upon citizen distrust and the rejection of political leadership and institutions. A general conclusion has been that citizen rejection has increased in intensity since the days of Vietnam and Watergate and as crises related to inflation, energy, and international affairs continue to occur. This conclusion is controversial, however, with major survey analysts such as Warren E. Miller and Patrick Caddell finding different evidence in their data. When used in systematic empirical analysis, the theme of alienation serves as a useful tool with which to examine various types of citizen estrangement from the political system. Our interest is to examine the attitudes of black women as measured by the traditional indicators of political alienation, one of them already discussed in chapter 3, and to see how alienation is related to voting. We will argue that their sense of alienation, compounded by the effects of the double whammy, instead of paralyzing them politically, leads them to vote at a higher rate than black men in order to derive tangible rewards from government. A closer look at measures found in survey data reveals that black women have a unique outlook on the political world.

Miller, Brown, and Raine in comparing levels of political estrangement from 1958 to 1972, found that "black women who feel discriminated against because they are women are substantially less supportive of the government than black women who are not aware of sex discrimination. This was also true of white women, but the relationship was not nearly as strong" (1973, pp. 41, 43). Miller et al. found also a sharp decline in trust in the government by blacks of both sexes in 1972. They commented that it was "surprising" that "a minority group (black) traditionally discriminated against and economically deprived was as trusting of the government in 1958 as was the white majority that controlled it" (1976, p. 12). They pointed out that the data from the Center for Political Studies reflects an all-time high in black optimism in 1964 (at the height of the civil rights movement) with 73 percent of the respondents at the "most trusting" end of a scale of cynicism. It was their view that the trust continued into 1966, and that the decline since then can be explained as the outcome of a clash between quickly rising expectations and the reality of slow-moving system changes. Other authors have also provided evidence for this decline. Finifter (1972), for example, found that blacks demonstrated a higher degree of normlessness (that is, political distrust) than whites. Miller and Miller (1977) extended the analysis to the 1976 election and found a continuing pattern of lack of trust in government by black citizens of both sexes. It was their conclusion, however, that "despite the attention given to the issue of trust during the campaign, it had relatively little direct impact on the vote (1977, p. 46). People most cynical about politics were more supportive of Carter (55 percent voted for him) than were trusting individuals (40 percent voted Democratic). This was especially true of the black voters in 1976, both men and women, who voted heavily for Carter.

We are supplementing the Miller findings with two items from the Center for Political Studies 1972 survey, the first question dealing with trust in Congress and the second concerning trust in political parties. As table 14 shows, black women and men agreed at rates almost 20 percent higher than white men and women that "those we elect to Congress in Washington lose touch with the people pretty

Table 14. Responses by Race and Gender to Questions on Trust in Congress and in Political Parties, 1972

Question: *Generally speaking, those we elect to Congress in Washington lose touch with the people pretty quickly.*		
	Agree	Disagree
Black Women	85%	15%
Black Men	79	21
White Women	65	35
White Men	67	33

Question: *Parties are only interested in people's votes, but not in their opinions.*		
	Agree	Disagree
Black Women	82%	18%
Black Men	72	28
White Women	57	43
White Men	58	43

Source of Data: Center for Political Studies, American National Election Studies, 1952–1976.

quickly"; black women were somewhat less trusting than black men on this measure. The next question reveals that 82 percent of black women respondents felt little trust in political parties, agreeing with this statement at a rate 10 percentage points higher than white women and men, who gave similar responses to this question. Thus on both measures black women showed considerably less trust in the political process than whites, and slightly less trust than black men. This finding lends added support to our contention that the political attitudes of black women are polarized from those of white people, and also to a lesser extent from those of black men, giving an overall picture of high levels of distrust in government.

We turn now to the scale of political efficacy, designed as a measure of subjective sense of involvement by an individual in the political system, as discussed at some length in chapter 3. The main significance of the scale is that a high sense of political efficacy has been shown to be correlated with voting.

Table 15 provides evidence that from 1956 to 1968 there was a shift from low efficacy among black women toward higher efficacy

Table 15. A Comparison by Gender and Race on a Scale of Political Efficacy

	Low (0–1)	Medium (2)	High (3–4)
Black Women			
1956	59%	30%	11%
1968 (weighted)	51	28	20
1972	67	25	9
1976 (weighted)	75	12	13
Black Men			
1956	64%	20%	16%
1968 (weighted)	44	35	22
1972	58	21	22
1976 (weighted)	66	31	4
White Women			
1956	35%	28%	37%
1968 (weighted)	47	25	28
1972	49	21	31
1976 (weighted)	55	18	27
White Men			
1956	27%	24%	49%
1968 (weighted)	41	27	32
1972	40	23	37
1976 (weighted)	54	15	31

Source of Data: Center for Political Studies, American National Election Studies, 1952–1976.

scores. Black men showed the same shift. However, this shift is reversed in the 1972 and 1976 data for both black sexes. It is clear from these figures that in general blacks show lower efficacy scores than whites, but that there has been a trend for this gap to decrease in the years shown here. Thus while all groups have shown a general decrease in efficacy—which correlates with recent decreases in voting rates in national elections—black men have shown the least decrease and white men the greatest, with black women and white women falling in between. In addition, these figures reveal that efficacy fluctuates from election to election for all four gender-race groups, and the pattern of fluctuation shown by blacks differs from that of whites.

If we compare low efficacy scores for black women with other related measures in 1972, the efficacy scores are consistent with their low scores on trust in the federal government, their level of cynicism on governmental policy, and with their perception of sex discrimination (to be discussed in a later section). These findings also suggest that measures developed in the 1950s to be applied to predominantly middle-class, white Americans have a poor fit for black citizens whose socialization and life-style have been very different from white America.

In interpreting the data in tables 16 and 17, having to do with interest in the campaign and its outcome, it should be remembered that the 1956 election was not a close contest, and therefore may not have been particularly interesting. There does seem to be more interest in the campaign among black women in 1968 than in 1956, which is consistent with the rise in efficacy scores in 1968 discussed above. While in 1956, black female respondents were about evenly split in caring/not caring about which party won, in 1968 approximately three out of four black women respondents cared very much

Table 16. The Interest of Black Women in Following Political Campaigns in 1956, 1968, 1972

Year	Low	Medium	High
1956	48%	33%	19%
1968	25	46	30
1972	37	35	28

Source of Data: Center for Political Studies, American National Election Studies, 1952–1976.

Table 17. The Degree to Which Black Women Cared Which Party Would Win the Elections in 1956, 1968, 1972

Year	Care Little or None	Medium Care	Care a Great Deal
1956	47%	1%	52%
1968	25	1	74
1972[a]	34	66	

Source of Data: Center for Political Studies, American National Election Studies, 1952–1976.
[a] Only two response choices in 1972.

or pretty much which party won, and only one in four cared little or not at all. Two explanations are possible: (1) Partisan loyalties were stronger in 1968, perhaps as a result of twelve years of exposure to the performance of the parties on civil rights; (2) The party differences on civil rights issues were clearer in 1968 than in 1956. Note that both these explanations make the following assumptions: party identification was a major determinant of the vote of black women in both 1956 and 1968; black women were cognizant of party stands on civil rights issues; and civil rights issues were salient to black women. In any case, this rise in concern fits with other evidence for the increase in political involvement by black women during this period.

In 1972, black women indicated about the same percent (28) as in 1968 in reporting high interest in the campaign. There was a slight decline in the number of black women "caring very much" about party outcome in 1972. Since the measure was recoded in 1972, the comparison may not be completely valid. Still, since these three questions all reveal a similar pattern of change for black women in the years shown, their validity appears reasonably strong.

We turn now to investigate data on the life-styles and attitudes of black women. As a part of the growing research effort to monitor changes in the social climate, the survey of the national election of the Center for Political Studies in 1972 included several "social indicators" which sought to discover the respondents' perceptions of life and their evaluations of its quality. We can compare black women and provide evidence that they were polarized in a set of attitudes different from those of black men and whites. We will comment on the relationship of these attitudes to their politicization in the latter half of the chapter.

Table 18 describes the responses to the question, "In general, how satisfactory do you find the way you're spending your life these days?" The percentage scores for women of the two races are almost reversed: the percent of black women with unsatisfactory lives and the percent of white women completely satisfied are close. The scores of the men were fairly close to those of the women in the same racial group.

The second question measures whether or not the respondent feels that "planning ahead in life" is worthwhile. Here, black women

Table 18. Responses by Race and Gender to Three Social Indicator Questions, 1972

Question: *In general, how satisfactory do you find the way you're spending your life these days?*

	Completely Satisfactory	Pretty Satisfactory	Not Very Satisfactory
Black Women	12%	61%	28%
Black Men	11	64	25
White Women	24	65	11
White Men	22	69	9

Question: *Do you think it's better to plan your life a good way ahead, or would you say life is too much a matter of luck to plan ahead very far?*

	Plan Ahead	Too Much Luck to Plan
Black Women	58%	42%
Black men	67	33
White Women	66	34
White Men	74	26

Question: *When you make plans ahead, do you usually get to carry out things the way you expected, or do things usually come up to make you change your plans?*

	Things Work Out As Expected	Have to Change Plans
Black Women	30%	70%
Black Men	34	66
White Women	51	49
White Men	50	50

Source of Data: Center for Political Studies, American National Election Studies, 1952–1976.

indicated less of a tendency to plan their lives "a good way ahead" than any other group. Black men responded nearly the same as white women on this question, while white men showed the greatest trust in planning ahead. Forty-two percent of black women, 33 percent of black men, and 34 percent of white women felt that "life is too much a matter of luck to plan very far ahead," a response which indicates a sense of powerlessness and lack of control over their lives.

The third question complements the second by measuring whether the respondent feels that "things work out as expected." Of black women, 30 percent responded that "things work out as expected"; for black men the scores are very similar: 34 percent reported "things work out as expected," and 66 percent "have to change plans." White men and women responded nearly identically to this question, revealing that for some 20 percent more whites than blacks, "things work out as expected."

These responses to social indicator questions—in which black women systematically describe unsatisfying and insecure lives—suggest the roots of the disaffection of black women from the political system, a disaffection expressed elsewhere in our data as low feelings of efficacy and low trust in government.

Another study, conducted by Louis Harris and Associates, Inc., tapped the attitudes of three thousand women in 1972. Responses to this questionnaire reinforce the above data on the quality of life, obtained in the same period of time. Table 19 shows the percentages of black and white women who felt that the eleven social and economic problems named were "very serious." Clearly, the black women evidence much greater concern for these economic and social welfare issues than white women do. None of the problems was considered "very serious" by even half of the white women (though four received scores of close to 50 percent), whereas only one of the problems was *not* rated "very serious" by more than half of the black women.

In a 1976 study, Campbell, Converse, and Rodgers found that black women were more "negative" than either black men or white men or women in terms of both their overall sense of well-being and their satisfaction with specific domains of life. In addition, black women more often reported experiencing feelings of stress than did black men, whereas white women were similar to white men on this measure. Moreover, black women expressed slightly weaker feelings of personal competence than black men. Their data support the theory of the "double whammy," as the authors' conclusion suggests:

> The quality of life of the black female appears less positive than that of any of the other segments of the population in question. It is ironic

Table 19. A Comparison of Black and White Women on Seriousness of Problems Facing America in 1972

Problem	Black	White
	"Very Serious"	
Providing more help for poverty-stricken people	74%	49%
Helping older people	68	49
Providing health care for everyone	71	47
Improving public education	58	46
Providing more low income housing	65	31
Taking steps to achieve racial balance in housing	48	26
	"More Good"	
Are President Nixon's economic policies doing more good than harm?	16	50
	"Reasonable"	
Are taxes in the U.S. reasonable?	9	23
	"Too Fast"	
Speed at which blacks in America are trying to move	15	55
	"Are Justified"	
Are blacks justified in their demands?	67	36
Favor busing children to achieve racial desegregation	43	13

Source: Louis Harris and Associates, Inc., *The 1972 Virginia Slims American Women's Opinion Poll: A Survey of the Attitudes of Women on Their Roles in Politics and the Economy*, pp. 72–73.

that some elements of the black leadership in this country have taken the position that women's liberation is not an appropriate cause for black women. The present study implies that the black woman's need for liberation is as great or greater than that of the white women, and a recent Institute for Social Research survey (1973) demonstrates that a national cross-section of black women are even more approving of the women's liberation movement than white women. [1976, p. 465]

Thus, by looking at measures of political alienation and social indicators which describe the quality of life, we have provided evidence that black women in comparison to whites, and also to black men, are more estranged over the years under review and are less satisfied with their lives. We turn now to investigate other aspects of their life-style to suggest the relationship of this estrangement to politics and to attempt to explain their increasing political participation.

A search of the literature and informal interviewing do not lead us to simple conclusions. In fact, the published research on the role and status of women lead to more questions than answers, and in some instances the questions are almost taboo. When the question has been raised: Why do black women vote at higher rates than would be expected, considering their socioeconomic status? the answer given most generally has been that the black church has been responsible. It is not possible, however, to relate this question to systematic survey data. The best answer that was published came from Pauline Terralonge Stone who wrote:

> For whatever reason, it is significant that the church is the most important social institution in the black community and the one in which the black women (in contrast to black men) spend most of their time and energy. This dedication undoubtedly has contributed in no small part to the black female's passive acceptance of her subservient societal role. [1979, p. 581]

This answer, however, does not describe political involvement. But the question of the relationship of religion to the political behavior of women is a research frontier not only for blacks, but for women worldwide. Survey data from various institutions have mostly measured political participation in relation to church attendance, which does not get us very far. Religion undoubtedly has had major effects on women in regard to their political role. In our chapter comparing women in Western Europe the data are clear that women living in countries with Catholic traditions have a different political history than do women found in Protestant countries.

If we search the literature dealing with black women we are confronted with observations time after time which make clear that their role and status in society differs markedly from the position of white women in America. Thus we proceed to elaborate on our thesis of the double whammy which we describe as casting black women in a unique role. Almquist states this notion very well.

It is possible that the interaction of race and sex produces further disadvantages than those which accrue from the sum of the variables taken individually. If interaction effects are strong, then black women appear as a unique group whose interests are solely allied with neither black men nor white women. [1975, p. 130]

This unique group can be described further by social scientists who have made a close study of their role and status. The complexity of this question is stated by Lerner.

I learned in studying the history of black women and the black family that relatively high status for women within the family does not signify "matriarchy" or power for women, since black women are not only members of families, but persons functioning in a larger society. The status of persons is determined not in one area of their functioning, such as within the family, but in several. The decisive historical fact about women is that the areas of their functioning, not only their status *within* those areas has been determined by men . . . this is one of the decisive aspects of their history. Any analysis which does not take this complexity into consideration must be inadequate. [1975, p. 9]

In this section we will try to relate the complexities of the unique position of black women to our findings about their political involvement. We will start with the hypothesis that the forces of economic survival have generated a relationship between black women and men which differs from that existing between white women and men. Ladner provides a statement of this difference in roles.

Women in American society are held to be the passive sex, but the majority of black women have perhaps never fit this model, and have been liberated from many of the constraints that society has traditionally imposed on women. Although this emerged from forced circumstances, it nevertheless allowed black women the kind of emotional well-being that Women's Liberation groups are calling for. [1972, p. 39]

A great many black families simply could never afford the luxury of an unemployed wife. Chafe, in his history of the roles of American women since 1920, described the economic position of black women before the Second World War, documenting what Ladner referred to as "forced circumstances."

> In the years preceding the war [Second World War] black women were twice as likely to be employed as whites, but their economic horizons were severely limited. Over 70 percent worked as domestic servants in private homes, and another 20 percent toiled in the fields, picking crops and hoeing gardens on small farms. For them the war represented in some ways a second emancipation. The man-power shortage broke down rigid employment barriers and gave them an unparalleled opportunity to advance. [1972, pp. 142–43]

We are interested in discovering whether a connection can be traced between black women's active roles and their political participation. Studies on the effects of social role on voting behavior date from the Merriam and Gosnell surveys done in Chicago in the 1920s, which found that nearly three-fourths of the adult citizens who weren't registered to vote were women. Merriam and Gosnell concluded from these findings that voting appeared to be "inappropriate" behavior for the women in their sample, which was principally white (1924, p. ix). The hypothesis we wish to test is that black women who head households vote at higher rates than black women who hold roles as wife of heads of households. The hypothesis would suggest that black females who head households should have higher voting rates than black women who were wives of heads. This relationship should not hold in the white culture, in which the role of female head of household is both more rare and less socially acceptable than in the black culture.

Matthews and Prothro looked at this question in their survey in the South in 1961. From their general finding that for all forms of political participation more black men than women were active, they went on:

> The idea that responsibility for acting as head of the household might carry over into political activity receives uneven support. Negro women who are heads of their households exceed Negro housewives in political activity by only a very small margin. . . . Being head of the house does not necessarily increase the probability that Negro

women will become politically active, but the combination of such responsibility with outside employment does seem to lead to a modest increase in political participation. [1966, p. 69]

There is, however, a contradiction in our hypothesis: black female household heads include some of the most disadvantaged people in America. In 1976, 28 percent of all black families had incomes below the poverty level, compared to only 7 percent of white families; some 40 percent of black children are being raised in poverty. (Bressler and McKenny 1968). At the same time, approximately half of the children in families with incomes below poverty level were in female-headed households. Furthermore, the question takes on significance because one-third of all adult black women head households by 1980. Therefore, on the basis of the general findings in voter behavior studies which show low correlations between low socioeconomic position and voting, the expectation would be that black female heads of households would not be very likely to vote. This conflicts with the notion that because black female household heads tend to be more assertive and independent than white women in comparable positions, the black women heads would vote at higher rates.

As table 20 reveals, the evidence on this question gives clear-cut support to neither hypothesis. Still, it is suggestive to note that in two of the three elections presented here, black female household heads voted at slightly higher rates than black wives of heads, while in all three elections white female household heads lagged behind white

Table 20. A Comparison of Female Heads of Household and Wives of Head of Household by Race Voting for President, 1968, 1972, and 1976

| Year | Black | | White | |
	Female Head of Household	Wife of Head of Household	Female Head of Household	Wife of Head of Household
1968	63%	61%	74%	78%
1972	68	63	65	75
1976	56	60	66	74

Source of Data: Center for Political Studies, American National Election Studies, 1952–1976.

wives of heads in voting rates. In every case, the independent variable in question—head of household or wife of household head—made more of a difference for the white than for the black women in this sample. This could be because the role of household head is more easily integrated into the cluster of roles common to many black women, whereas for white women it is a more unfamiliar and uncommon role. While these data do not, then, lead to any clear-cut answer to the question of role and political participation among black women, they do offer indirect support for the notion that black women, of whom one-third are heads of households, have higher voting rates than their presumably low socioeconomic levels would predict. Until data controlling for the variables of income, education, social class, and occupation become available, we cannot venture much beyond this admittedly tentative generalization.

Before moving away from the topic of black women's roles as they relate to political participation, we will look briefly at findings from several different areas which may help illuminate the nature of these roles further. In particular, we will be interested in seeing how the dual effects of racism and sexism interact in the arena of changing sex roles for black women.

Although black women do not in general occupy higher status positions than black men in terms of education and employment levels, there is some evidence that they may have a more positive self-image, especially in relation to success. Horner, in studies using black samples, found that imagery indicating a fear of success was more common to black men than to black women—the reverse of the pattern shown by whites. Thus when race role and gender role were both studied, a reversal in attitudes toward achievement appeared, resulting in a pattern of fear-of-success imagery as follows:

White men	10%	Black men	67%
White women	64	Black women	29

The author goes on to say:

It has become quite clear from the various samples tested that one's disposition to accept success as a truly positive experience, enhancing self-esteem is by and large a function of how consistent this success is with one's internalized standards and expectations, one's stereotypes, of appropriate sex and/or race role identity and behavior. [1972, pp. 63]

In this discussion the main themes have centered on the uniqueness of black women's role in comparison to black men and to white men and women. This role has given them an independence which has made political participation entirely appropriate, in contrast to an earlier era for white women when politics was seen as a man's world. The economic survival and kinship patterns of black women, coupled with a more egalitarian role relationship with black men, may also have intensified their interest in black power objectives finding their solution in the ballot box. Economic survival is more often than not given as a reason for political participation by both black men and women, and should be noted. Verba and Nie offered this explanation in 1972:

> If blacks participate more than one would expect of a group with a similar socio-economic status, the explanation may lie in the fact that they have over time, developed an awareness of their own status as a deprived group, and this self-consciousness has led them to be more politically active than members of the society who have similar socio-economic levels but do not share the group identity. [1972, p. 157]

But for our purposes the previous discussion is only half of the double whammy. We argue that black women are increasing their vote also because of their concern for sex discrimination.

Feminism in Relation to Voting

During the 1960s, the early years of the women's movement, black women did not participate in significant numbers, nor appear to support it in principle. Nathan and Julia Hare expressed the common explanation: that the objectives of white women and black women are somewhat reversed.

> Even those black women who share the goals of the Women's Liberation are reluctant to participate . . . it appears to some that white and black women are in a race to change places. [1970, pp. 65–68]

Stone (1978) has identified five factors which have hindered the development of a black feminist consciousness: (1) sexism has been viewed as a racially divisive issue, (2) black females have tended to view all whites regardless of sex as sharing a racist ideology, (3) the message that emerged in the black social movement of the 1960s was that the liberation of the black man was more important than female liberation, (4) the idea of the black matriarchy suppressed the development of feminist consciousness among black women, and (5) Patriarchal views have persisted in black churches (basically Christian).

There is, however, as described earlier, evidence that in recent years black women have become increasingly supportive of the goals of the women's liberation movement. The Louis Harris survey of women in 1971 found black women to show the greatest sympathy with women's liberation of four race-gender groups. Of the black women, 67 percent reported being sympathetic—nearly twice as many as the 35 percent of white women giving this response. About half of the black men, and 41 percent of the white men, gave positive responses to this question. Neither black sex increased their sympathetic responses from the 1971 to the 1972 survey; however, both white sexes increased their affirmation of efforts to strengthen or change women's status in society today.

Lewis, among others, adds an additional insight to this puzzle in commenting that:

A trend toward a greater acceptance of feminism may be due to a change in black women's perception of oppression, which in turn reflects changes in the social order. In the 1960's, the black liberation movement began to generate important structural shifts in the relationship between blacks and whites in America. Blacks began to participate more fully in public activities previously reserved for whites. In such domains they encountered patterns of sexual discrimination. As the bulk of the higher-status, authoritative positions meted to blacks went to black men, a number of black women, particularly in the middle class, became more sensitive to the obstacle of sexism and to the relevance of the women's movement. [1977, pp. 339–61]

Thus there is clear support for the idea that black women perceive themselves to be affected by sexual discrimination. This also indicates that some role conflict does exist between black men and women, and that whatever egalitarian gender roles may exist in the black community, they are not such as to do away with sexism. On the other hand, combatting racial discrimination has long been seen as of more primary importance than fighting sexual discrimination, partly because feminism has been regarded by some people as a racially divisive influence which could be a source of conflict between black men and women, as Stone pointed out.

The picture that emerges from this complex network of factors relating to the sexual role and identity of black women is one that is generally consistent with their increasing levels of political participation. Black women are more economically independent than white women, and more likely to be supporting their families than white women are. They are generally sympathetic to the goals of the women's liberation movement, which advocates independence and self-determination for women. Undoubtedly, recent decades have seen rapid changes in the gender-role norms of black men and women, as they have for whites. Though it is difficult to pinpoint the exact relationship between these changes and the rising levels of political participation among black women, it seems likely that a more egalitarian relationship exists.

We suggest that the hypothesis that black women have come to see themselves as a special interest group fighting to overcome the twin barriers of racial and sexual discrimination appears to be the one which best explains these trends. According to this hypothesis, increased awareness of discrimination should be associated with higher voting rates among black women. This is the prediction we will now test, using a scale of questions reported in the 1972 elections survey of the Center for Political Studies.

We have classified the responses to each question as feminist or nonfeminist, as shown in table 21. For example, for the first statement, "Men are born with more drive to be ambitious," disagreement was considered the feminist position and agreement, the nonfeminist position. Of course, a respondent's choice of what we call a feminist position does not mean that she considers herself a feminist, or even that all feminists would agree with the categorization of answers as feminist or nonfeminist.

Table 21. A Comparison of Black Women Voters in Relation to Feminism in 1972

Test Item and Feminist Response	Percentage of Black Women Who Voted		
	Feminist Position	Nonfeminist Position	Feminist Minus Nonfeminist
Men are born with more drive to be ambitious and successful than women. (Disagree)	69%	60%	+9%
Women have less opportunity than men to get the education for top jobs. (Agree)	59	68	−9
Women are usually less reliable on the job than men, because they tend to be absent more and quit more often. (Disagree)	65	63	2
Our schools teach women to want the less important jobs. (Agree)	66	64	2
By nature women are happiest when they are making a home and caring for children. (Disagree)	69	61	8
Many qualified women can't get good jobs; men with the same skills have much less trouble. (Agree)	67	59	8
In general, men are more qualified than women for jobs that have great responsibility. (Disagree)	69	58	11
Our society discriminates against women. (Agree)	69	60	9
Women have just as much chance to get big and important jobs; they just aren't interested. (Disagree)	71	55	16

Source of Data: Center for Political Studies, American National Election Studies, 1952–1976.

Note: The question was: "In general, women in our society have not been as successful as men—in business, politics, the leadership positions in our country." The respondent agreed or disagreed. This table combines "agree a great deal," and "agree somewhat"; and "disagree somewhat" and "disagree a great deal," and presents a conversion to feminist position or nonfeminist position.

We cross-tabulated feminist position and nonfeminist position with the 1972 presidential vote, as shown in the table. On eight of the nine questions, black women taking the feminist position voted at higher rates than black women holding the nonfeminist position. This margin ranged from 2 percentage points to 16 percentage points higher for those giving a feminist response. On only one item, "Women have less opportunity than men to get the education for top jobs," did the nonfeminists vote at a higher rate than the feminists. This discrepancy is easily explained: females in the black community have in the past received more education than males, so the question is actually inapplicable for black respondents. (Our classification of this question is in line with the original conception of the research designers.)

Black females taking the feminist position on economic issues voted at the highest rates. On the question, "Men are more qualified than women," 11 percent more feminist black females voted than nonfeminists. On the last item, "Women are less interested in good jobs," the discrepancy was 16 percent, feminists voting at a rate of 71 percent, and nonfeminists voting at 55 percent.

This table summarizes all black females found in the survey sample. Unfortunately, further breakdown of the table by variables such as income, education, age, or region was not possible because of the size of the samples. Nevertheless this overall measure has described a relationship between voting and the perception of sex discrimination which lends added support to our previous findings. A more intensive analysis would provide a fascinating indication of which black women tend to perceive sex discrimination. Harris (1972) found strong support for feminism among young, single, black city-dwellers, among college-educated women, and among poor women.

Summary and Conclusions

What, then, can we conclude about the political participation of black women? Overall, the data presented in this chapter make it clear that there is no explanatory theory which totally accounts for the unique voting record of black women and their recent political activism. Verba and Nie concluded that socio-economic differences explain a good deal of the difference in the participation rates of blacks and whites. If there is any impact on participation associated more directly with race, it is one that gives some boost to black citizens—particularly if they have a sense of group consciousness. [1972, p. 173]

Their analysis, however, does not address the effects of gender in particular.

We have drawn from the work of other scholars the suggestion that the political behavior of black women is heavily influenced by their activities in the black church. We found support for the double whammy thesis that black women are voting at higher rates than their socioeconomic status would predict, and voting recently at higher rates than black men as a response to the dual discrimination forced on them by racism and sexism. We examined attitudes, noting that, in general, black women show less trust in government, less satisfaction with the control over the quality of their lives, lower levels of political efficacy, and greater sympathy for the goals of the women's liberation movement than black men or either white sex.

It may well be that the "rational voter" model is a more useful explanatory concept for black women. According to this model, voters select candidates and choose to vote according to the expected benefits that will accrue from that choice. Downs has applied to voting behavior a concept used in economic analysis, namely, that the voter acts out of a rational calculation of self-interest. This cost analysis states that

> The total return each citizen receives from voting depends upon (1) the benefit he gets from democracy, (2) how much he wants a particular party to win, (3) how close he thinks the election will be, and (4) how many other citizens he thinks will vote. These variables insure a relatively wide range of possible returns similar to the range of voting costs and returns, some vote and others abstain [1957, p. 274]

The critical problem regarding black women is simply the absence of research on their participation: any analysis at this point is based on weak evidence. Ladner (1972) has suggested that black women have filled roles almost the reverse of those held by white women.

And, as Lerner (1975) has pointed out, black women derived a unique status from their relationship to black men. Still, black women—especially young, well-educated, well-employed, black women—are becoming increasingly aware of the fact that they suffer from dual discrimination by virtue of both their race and their sex, and have begun to join together in an effort to promote their own interests in a political system which, in the past, has excluded them almost entirely. In the face of these rapid and dramatic changes, we can do little more than take note of them as they occur, and wait for sociology, psychology, and political science to produce evidence to explain definitively the increasing rates of political participation among black women in recent years.

chapter seven

PARTICIPATORY POLITICS
Women at the Grass Roots and Elite Levels

Citizens participate in their political systems in many more ways than just voting. The discussions in the previous chapters have used voter turnout as the measure of political participation because it requires some intentionality, but very little. In this chapter we explore the routes outside the voting booth that women and men have chosen to influence public policy.

The data sets substantiating the arguments so far were generated through interviews with randomly selected members of the American electorate both before and after presidential elections. Most of the measures of participation included in the surveys are based on activities relevant to a political campaign, such as trying to persuade others about the way to vote, contributing money, and attending a political meeting or rally. As the figures in table 22 show, the proportion of women and men engaging in these activities has remained small since 1952, and the differences between the genders have been negligible. The only exception to the pattern of low involvement is in persuasion efforts, and here 44 percent of the men and 32 percent of the women interviewed in 1976 said that they had tried to influence someone's vote that year. Giving financial support to a campaign is the next most popular form of election involvement, and only 7 percent of the women and 11 percent of the men did so in 1976. If the definition of "political participation" is expanded to include persuasion efforts directed to public officials, probably at nonelection times, then the American citizenry appears to be more concerned about politics than the electoral measures would indicate. Almost one-third of the men and one-quarter of the women surveyed in 1976

113

Table 22. Political Activities of Men and Women, by Election

	1952			1964			1976		
	Men	Women	Men Minus Women	Men	Women	Men Minus Women	Men	Women	Men Minus Women
Electoral Activities									
Try to influence the votes of others	33%	22%	11%	30%	26%	4%	44%	32%	12%
Attend political meetings or rallies	7	6	1	10	8	2	6	7	−1
Work for a party or candidate	4	2	2	5	5	0	4	4	0
Give money to a party or candidate	6	3	3	12	8	4	11	7	4
Nonelectoral Activities[a]									
Write a letter to a public official	—	—	—	18	16	2	31	25	6
Write a political letter to an editor	—	—	—	4	3	1	9	7	2
Voter Status									
Registered to vote	81	73	8	87	82	5	78	75	3
Voted in the election	80	69	11	80	76	4	77	68	9

Source of Data: Center for Political Studies, American National Election Studies, 1952–1976.

a. These two questions were not asked in the 1952 study.

said that they had written to a public official at some time, percentages considerably higher than those calculated in 1964. As with voting, the gender differences in these other forms of political participation are small. The fact that the differences are commonly believed to be much larger attests to the invisibility of women in political analyses.

The continuing importance of education in predicting nonelectoral forms of political participation, as well as electoral, is apparent for women in table 23. As the level of education increases, the percentage of women reporting that they tried to influence the voting decisions of others, attended a political meeting, and wrote to a public official also increases. The figures suggest that the bulk of political participation in this country is done by relatively well-educated people.

A quick reading of the nation's newspapers makes it clear that less well-educated persons are politically active too, but perhaps not in the ways customarily measured by election researchers. If the term "political" is taken to mean efforts to keep current on and perhaps

Table 23. Selected Political Activities of Women, by Education and Election

	1952	1964	1976
Tried to Influence the Vote of Others			
Grade school	15%	17%	19%
High school	29	28	31
College	37	46	45
Attended a Political Meeting or Rally			
Grade school	5	9	2
High school	6	16	6
College	13	26	13
Wrote a Letter to a Public Official			
Grade school	—	7	10
High school	—	18	26
College	—	34	40

Source of Data: Center for Political Studies, American National Election Studies, 1952–1976.

influence public policy, then some of the ordinary activity in community groups, such as parent-teacher organizations, church groups, and business associations, is political. By raising the possibility that local voluntary associations which are not explicitly linked with political parties are in fact political organizations, we have opened up an entirely new avenue for exploring issues of political participation. The same realization is voiced by Verba and Nie.

> We wish to look beyond the vote as a means of activity and beyond the electoral system. Nor do we consider participation a unidimensional phenomenon. In short, the citizenry is not divided simply into more or less active citizens. Rather there are many types of activists engaging in different acts, with different motives, and different consequences. [1972, p. 45]

An examination of political activity outside the voting booth is particularly appropriate in a book on women and politics because historically, women have had their greatest impact on public policy at the local, grass roots level.

Women in Grass Roots Politics

Given the political system today, the only ways researchers can study women political elites is through purposive sampling or through an expansion of the definition of the political arena to include grass roots voluntary organizations where many more women are in leadership positions, as did McCourt (1977) and Kruschke (1963). These two studies, in addition to those by Wells and Smeal (1974) and Baxter (1977), provide the best evidence available on the political participation of women at the grass roots level.

Kruschke (1963) sought to study the community political leadership activity of women but realized he could best do so if he also had a sample of women who were not politically involved. He identified three issue areas which were of great concern in Madison, Wisconsin, in the early 1960s and then used the reputational approach to generate a sample of forty-six "Politicals," women deeply involved in the issue areas selected. The "Apoliticals" were chosen at random from the mailing list of the University of Wisconsin alumni association and were matched on marital status and some college education. The guiding supposition was that

> the female Politicals would be characterized by political and other attitudes different from those of the female Apoliticals, and that these attitudes may partially serve to account for their acceptance, or non-acceptance, of political leadership roles. [1963, p. 147]

Kruschke tested the ability of a wide range of variables to distinguish between the two samples. The Politicals had significantly higher family incomes than the Apoliticals, but the two groups were similar in age and the number of memberships in voluntary organizations. Successfully involved in activities outside their homes, the Politicals were found to be more liberal and to have a stronger sense of political efficacy than their Apolitical sisters.

In sum, Kruschke found fewer differences between his samples of Political and Apolitical women than he hypothesized, and those he did find served to distinguish the active sample from the inactive in much the same manner as political elites have been shown to differ from nonelites and, to a lesser extent, the general political participation of men to differ from that of women.

In another study, Wells and Smeal (1974) contrasted the support for women in politics given by a sample of registered women voters in Pittsburgh with the support of a sample of local Democratic and Republican party committeewomen in the same town. The researchers found no significant differences between the samples and assumed the reasoning of the committeewomen to be as follows: the low status of women in politics is a constant source of personal insecurity, and an improvement in that status would enhance our own power. The Pittsburgh committeewomen did not appear to be queen bees, described later in this chapter as women who feel they reached high position on their own merit without benefit of affirmative action (Staines, Tavris, and Jayaratne 1973). In fact, they preferred a woman candidate if an equally qualified woman and man were running for the same office, at a rate significantly above that of the registered voters.

To test whether women involved in assertive community organizations in southwest Chicago differed from their inactive women neighbors, McCourt (1977) interviewed twenty-three women active in direct action community organizations and seventeen inactive women. Because both samples came from the same white, predominantly working-class neighborhoods, only a few background differences were hypothesized. As expected, smaller proportions of the actives worked or had small children, freeing their time for community action. But surprisingly, the active women were not more integrated into and attached to their neighborhoods than the inactives, as measured by length of residence and proximity to relatives, though they did express stronger intentions to remain there. The actives scored higher on sense of political efficacy and they favored more heavily the idea that neighborhood problems could be resolved through collective action. McCourt expected the active women to voice nontraditional attitudes about marriage, child rearing, and the rights of women because their political activism defied the working class dictum about women's proper roles. In fact, support for nontraditional attitudes on the family and women's roles was voiced more by the inactive women. The study suggests that women newly engaged in community groups challenging the political system may experience considerable role conflict which they diminish by voicing very traditional attitudes about the social roles of women.

Further evidence regarding the differences and similarities among women participating in grass roots politics to different degrees comes from Baxter's (1977) study of women in southeastern Michigan. She selected three samples for study: (1) women registered voters, whose political participation usually begins and ends at the ballot box; (2) women whose political activism finds expression within the nonpartisan voluntary organization known as the League of Women Voters; and (3) women whose activism leads them to low-level elected positions within the Democratic and Republican parties. These samples reflect a division within the women's movement that was apparent at the time suffrage was won.

At the March, 1919, Jubilee Convention of the National American Woman Suffrage Association (NAWSA), called to celebrate the fiftieth anniversary of Wyoming's grant of suffrage, Carrie Chapman Catt called for the creation of a permanent, nonpartisan organization to "finish the fight and to aid in the reconstruction of the Nation." The League of Women Voters was born. Its goals were lofty—to win final enfranchisement at home and abroad, end all legal discrimination against women, and bolster the spread of democracy throughout the world (Sanders 1956; Adams 1967). These goals were thought achievable in five years. At the following year's convention, Catt urged the delegates to join the political parties, run for office, and help formulate public policy. Another portion of the NAWSA membership, led by Jane Addams, argued that women's attention and newly won political power should be directed to the social reconstruction of their communities. The convention comprised and assigned to the National League of Women Voters the political but nonpartisan tasks of reforming the electorate, educating women for citizenship, and training them for assumption of full positions in the parties and the government (Lemons 1973).

By 1921, therefore, both the political parties and the League of Women Voters were viewed by most suffragists as appropriate arenas for women interested in politics, but the roles women could play were seen to be qualitatively different. The league, by restricting its membership to the newly enfranchised women and its mission to educating the electorate, was necessarily on the periphery of a political system dominated by the long-established parties (Gilman 1927). Women who joined the Democratic and Republican parties were members of the premier political organizations but were relegated minor roles in them (Blair 1929), probably due to both their new legal standing and the view that politics had always been men's business. However small the political power these league and party women wielded, though, it surpassed the influence of women who merely cast ballots during elections, and their effect, in turn, surpassed that of women who chose not to participate in politics at all.

As shown in table 21, women (and men) low in political involvement are simple to find; they predominate in virtually any national or local sample. In the 1976 presidential election, over two-thirds of adult American women were registered and voted; only about one-third reported that they attempted to persuade others how to vote. Seeking a sample of low as opposed to nonactivists, that is, women for whom politics is salient, the first sample included women who fulfilled the traditional minimal role of good citizens by being registered and ballot-casting voters.

The second sample was to consist of women participating more than minimally in politics. As mentioned earlier, a portion of the women who became deeply involved in politics following the passage of the Nineteenth Amendment chose the nonpartisan League of Women Voters as their organizational affiliation rather than the Democratic or Republican parties. The league today is a highly visible but relatively unstudied political organization. Still nonpartisan by charter, women and men members lobby for good government legislation and on behalf of issue positions they have thoroughly researched. The organization scrupulously avoids appearing to favor one party over the other and declines to make candidate endorsements; its self-appointed tasks are to inform voters about issues and candidate qualifications and to lobby at all levels of government for legislation considered socially beneficial. However intensely league members embrace politics, the impacts of their efforts are necessarily blunted because they choose not to participate in the selection, campaign, or advisement of individual candidates, and it is these successful candidates and their appointees who hold the bulk of formal political power in this country.

The league sees itself as a training ground where members become knowledgeable about current events and the form and function of government. Individuals may not only work for parties and candidates while maintaining their league membership, being careful to distinguish between their activities as league members and as citizens, but they are urged to move from their political apprenticeship in the organization to the world of partisan politics. Yet the league repeatedly has been criticized for the sheltered view of political life it offers its members (Sanders 1956, for example), who are mostly civic-minded housewives with limited time and energy for politics.

Each local league has a board of directors, members of which are prohibited in the national bylaws from engaging in partisan political activity during their term of office, although the interpretation of this restriction has been shown to vary (League of Women Voters 1956–58). These women are the most interesting to research: sophisticated political activists by virtue of their years in the league, they probably realize most fully the limits on the influence of their organization due to its refusal to support individual candidates. League board members, then, provided an ideal sample of women who have chosen to become politically active but in a nonpartisan fashion.

For the third sample, the search was for women who had chosen to participate in politics as partisans and whose strong commitment had led them to formal positions within the Democratic and Republican parties. Lower-level party offices were scanned and the position of elected delegate to the party county convention was selected. Michigan county delegates are elected by precinct within party, and they traditionally handle the tasks of taking censuses of their constituents, conducting candidates for public office on door-to-door campaigns, and distributing candidate and issue literature, in addition to attending county conventions. There is precedence for focusing upon precinct workers as the party functionaries at the grass roots level. Forthal entitled her study of precinct captains in the Chicago political machine *Cogwheels of Democracy* (1946). Although called county committeemen, the party activists in Manhattan studied by Hirschfield, Swanson, and Blank (1962) are comparable to precinct delegates.

Although not identical empirically, three of Verba and Nie's (1972) subsamples are strikingly similar conceptually to the three samples of women in Baxter's (1977) grass roots study. The group labeled "voting specialists" vote regularly in local and national elections, but neither participate in campaigns nor contact public officials individually or as members of a group (1972, p. 79). This group is similar to the sample of registered women voters.

The women league members are very similar to Verba and Nie's category of "communalists." Persons in this group engage in cooperative political activities which tend to have collective rather than personal rewards and to shy away from campaign participation in favor of less conflictive politics. The local leagues are by definition formal, cooperative organizations seeking political policies which they perceive as beneficial to their communities, and their nonpartisan stance necessarily screens them from some of the conflict in the formal political system. Another of Verba and Nie's groups, referred to as both the "campaigners" and the "partisan activists," is very close conceptually to the Democratic and Republican party women sample. These women, like the "campaigners," devote most of their political activity to the waging of campaigns. Although the only responsibility the Michigan party women assumed upon their election as precinct delegates is to attend their party's county convention, they experience considerable informal pressure to perform campaign activities as well.

In the pages and tables that follow, the differences among these three samples of women politically active in varying degrees in their local communities—the registered voters, the League of Women Voters board members, and the Democratic and Republican precinct delegates—are examined. Do they come from the same backgrounds? Do they perceive women's roles in politics in the same way? These issues are of interest in themselves, given that so much of women's political participation takes place at the grass roots level, but the issues serve also to introduce a later discussion of how women members of state and national politically elite groups differ from their women constituents, and from their male colleagues.

It was shown in chapter 2 that women and men with higher levels of education vote at higher rates than people with less education. Education is a primary determinant of political attitudes as well, as the tables and discussion in chapters 3 and 4 made clear. When our attention is turned to differences between people participating in local politics to varying degrees, the expectation that well-educated women would be more active at the grass roots level is confirmed. As the data in table 24 indicate, the league and party women were heavily drawn from the ranks of the college educated (87 and 70 percent, respectively), while only 51 percent of the registered voters had been to college. Education is just one indicator traditionally used by social scientists to measure socioeconomic status. Along with income and occupation, educational achievement is a reliable sign of life-style and life experiences, and a useful predictor of a range of attitudes. The fact that the more activist league and party women also had higher family incomes in 1971 should be no surprise. Indeed, the generalization that individuals of higher social and economic status participate more in politics, which "holds true whether one uses level of education, income, or occupation as the measure" (Verba and Nie 1972, p. 125), is supported by these data.

Table 24. Personal Characteristics of Grass Roots Women, by Sample

Characteristic	Registered Voters (n = 194)	League of Women Voters (n = 47)	Party Officials (n = 34)
Educational Achievement			
Less than high school	12%	0%	3%
High school graduate	37	13	27
Some college	39	55	43
Graduate school	12	32	27
Family Income in 1972			
Less than $10,000	22	0	6
$10,000 to $19,999	55	51	36
$20,000 to $29,999	16	18	19
$30,000 and more	7	31	39
Age			
18–30	31	13	19
31–40	26	42	16
41–50	19	25	37
51–59	13	18	19
60 and older	11	2	9
Membership in Voluntary Organizations			
Civic groups	46	68	79
Professional groups	25	19	21
Party organizations	1	4	100
League of Women Voters	1	100	18
Social groups	30	45	29

Source: Baxter 1977.

The curvilinear relationship between age and turnout shown in figure 7 in the first chapter suggests that the political participation rates of younger and older women are surpassed by the rate of their sisters aged thirty-one to sixty. This pattern holds true when we look in table 24 at involvement in partisan and nonpartisan community organizations. Only 15 percent of the league members and 25 percent of the party women were relatively young or old, but 42 percent of the registered voters fell into those categories. Further evidence that political participation changes with age is available in many studies (Verba and Nie 1972; Milbrath and Goel 1977).

The final characteristic useful in understanding differences among the voters and the more activist grass roots women is membership in voluntary organizations. The percentages shown in table 24 for this variable do not sum to 100 because they indicate the proportion of each sample who reported belonging to one or more organizations of each type. The league and party women were clearly more involved in groups, aside from those which served as the basis for their inclusion in the study. Most people who participate in politics beyond voting have a wide range of other organizational ties, some to local volunteer groups and some to state or perhaps national organizations. The link between political involvement and more general social involvement is well established in the research literature (Erbe 1964). Further, the tendency for activists to come disproportionately from higher status backgrounds, found by Baxter, is just a reflection of the more basic relationship between status and social participation of any kind (Hodge and Treiman 1968).

Because the relatively active league and party women come from wealthier and more highly educated backgrounds, it is possible that their perceptions of the roles women can and should play in politics may differ from the perceptions of registered women voters. A set of items was included in Baxter's study dealing with attitudes toward politics in general and women's participation in particular. The items tested the importance of several assumed explanations for the lack of women in politically responsible positions. A biological explanation was implied in the item "Women by nature are unsuited to politics." Explanations relying more heavily on socialization pressures were captured in three items: "More women would become active in politics if they didn't have to compete with men"; "Family responsibilities have kept more women from participating in politics"; and "Women are taught not to want to be active in politics." The league and party women were expected to view participation as a natural behavior for women, and to be less sympathetic to the biologically based explanation than the women voters. A perception that the political system is necessarily conflictual, "Politics too often turns into no-holds-barred fights," was one of two items mentioning characteristics of the political system itself. A second item contends that women do have political clout but the system hides it: "While women hold few public offices, they work behind the scenes and have more influence than they're given credit for." The greater familiarity of the league and party women with everyday politics was expected to lead them to see less conflict and to report less often than the voters that women do hold power "behind the scenes." The figures in table 25 show that the *only* item which effectively distinguishes the activists from the voters is the socialization item that "women are taught" that politics is not appropriate for them. Similar percentages of activists and voters reject the ideas that women fear competition with men or are biologically unsuited to participate in politics.

Table 25. Comparison of Grass Roots Samples on Women and Politics Items

	Percentage Who Agree		
Item	Registered Voters (*n* = 194)	League of Women Voters (*n* = 147)	Party Officials (*n* = 34)
Women by nature are unsuited to politics.	20%	11%	21%
More women would become active in politics if they didn't have to compete with men.	33	22	31
Family responsibilities have kept more women from participating in politics.	79	81	65
Women are taught not to want to be active in politics.	42	61	61
Politics too often turns into no-holds-barred fights.	79	74	50
While women hold few public offices, they work behind the scenes and have more influence than they're given credit for.	86	85	85

Source: Baxter 1977.

Women as Members of the Political Elite

The bulk of the research on women political elites has consisted of comparisons on the background characteristics and attitudes of women and men officeholders. The value of these studies has depended to some extent on the proportions of their samples which are women. If the percentage of women is small, say less than one-quarter, we should wonder how stable the characteristics are and how the recruitment and election processes operate to keep the proportion of successful women candidates so much less than the proportion of women in the electorate. For example, in Pisciotti and Hjelm's (1968) profile of Colorado state legislators, we are told that over the past ten years, only 8 percent of the legislators were women. In learning about the few women, we also learn about the Colorado political system, but an explicit examination of candidate selection and support procedures, formal and informal, would shed more light on the unequal representation.

The definition of an elite varies from study to study, and includes congressional legislators (Werner 1966; Bullock and Heys 1972), state legislators (Diamond 1977; Johnson and Stanwick 1976; Johnson and Carroll 1978), national nominating convention delegates (Jennings and Thomas 1968; Farah and Jennings 1977), officers throughout state and local government (Sigelman 1976), and school board members (Bers 1978). It is important to know whether women (and men) who participate in the American political system to different degrees come from dissimilar backgrounds and hold contrasting attitudes. Do political elites reflect the values of their constituents, or do they take on a concern with "the general welfare" that sometimes is at odds with the folks back home? Because there are so few women elites, it is important to know what their attitudes are regarding women's proper roles in the political system and society more generally, and whether their values and behaviors differ from those of their male colleagues. In other words, does the election of women appear to make a difference in public policy? If not, then one argument supporting the demand for more women in public office—that women will produce more humanitarian legislation—must be seriously questioned.

Women as Convention Delegates

A group of political elites which enjoys some power to influence American life without holding public office is the set of people elected by their state political parties as delegates to the national nominating conventions. These individuals have the responsibility to elect their party's candidates for the presidency and vice-presidency of the country, and thus their decisions fundamentally limit the electoral choices of the American voters. Selection as a national delegate is a recognition of one's current political status and it also may help later in an individual's run for public office.

We have argued that access to positions of power has been severely limited for women at the top levels of the American political system, but that an increasing proportion of important system roles are being played by women as we look "down" the list of public and party offices. Since selection as a national convention delegate is less prestigious than election to Congress and carries no formal political power, women could be expected to constitute a larger proportion of delegates than congressional members. And since convention delegates serve as "gatekeepers" for aspirants to high national office, it is important to know about their personal characteristics and their attitudes toward women's roles in politics.

The data used in this analysis of convention delegates were collected by mail questionnaires sent to delegates before they attended the 1972 Democratic and Republican national conventions and by personal interviews conducted afterward. Like the national election studies of 1952 through 1976, this data set was also generated by researchers at the University of Michigan's Center for Political Studies and it is the empirical basis of Kirkpatrick's discussion of *The New Presidential Elite* (1976).

People elected as convention delegates in 1972 were very different from their predecessors. During the mid-1960s, a number of budding social movements, including the protest against American involvement in Vietnam, the struggle for the rights of blacks and poor people, and the growing militancy of feminists, came into full bloom. Their supporters converged on Chicago in 1968 and their anger erupted inside and outside the doors of the Democratic

National Convention and in full view of the nation's media. Another protest met the Republicans when they convened weeks later. One of the major tasks facing planners for the national party conventions in 1972 was to regain the loyalty of those they had alienated four years earlier. Both before and during the conventions, efforts were made to liberalize the delegate selection procedures and to include women's planks in the party platforms. When the Democrats gathered in Miami in July of 1972, there were four times as many women among the delegates as there had been four years earlier (Johnson 1972) as well as many more blacks, Spanish-speaking, younger, and older persons. When the Republicans convened in Miami the following month, 30 percent of the delegates were women, almost double the figure for 1968 (Quinn 1972). Further, the delegates to both conventions adopted rules covering the selection of delegates to the 1976 conventions which would give greater representation to women and to the aged and ethnic groups historically underrepresented.

The party platforms of the two conventions reflected a new awareness that many women voters might base their electoral choices on which party better addressed their concerns. The Republican platform contained a strong plank on federal support of child care services and promised that the party would work for ratification of the Equal Rights Amendment (Kilberg 1972). Attempts to secure a pro-abortion plank were defeated, however. The Democratic platform contained a fifteen-point women's rights plank, more comprehensive but less specific than that passed by the Republicans (Quinn 1972).

The new faces and new platform planks were heavily covered by the media and widely regarded by the American citizenry. The research department of the National Broadcasting Company projected, on the basis of viewers of the first two nights of the Democrats' proceedings, that approximately 120 million people would see some portion of that convention, 15 million more than saw the 1968 convention (Aarons 1972). Combined with the additional viewers of the Republican convention and the radio and press audiences, well over half of the American population was expected to follow the political parties in action. A national poll taken one month after the Democratic convention indicated that the new faces and the public airing of disputes over delegations and planks had made a significant, positive impression.

> By 52 to 25 percent, a majority of the American people had a highly positive reaction to the Democratic National Convention. . . . The most widely remembered parts of the Democratic conclave were the openness of the convention . . . . and the representation of the young, minorities, and women. All of these aspects of the Democratic convention were followed and recalled by between 59 and 70 percent of the electorate. [Harris 1972, p. A–7]

The conventions were significant events for women political activists, whether in the parties or in partisan or nonpartisan voluntary organizations, because the proceedings provided a new set of successful women role models and a new legitimacy to their political aspirations. The summer of 1972 was an important time for women in the wider electorate also, for they saw, heard, or read that politics was not exclusively a man's realm.

Several personal characteristics of the 1972 convention delegates are shown in table 26. How do these women compare with other women at various levels of political involvement? In chapter 2, we saw that the most likely woman voter has some education beyond high school, is in the top third of the national distribution in terms of family income, practices a profession, and is middle-aged. A look at table 26 reveals that this is a fairly apt description of the typical woman delegate, at least in terms of educational achievement, family income, and age. Of course, a picture of the "average" woman citizen would show her to be younger, less well educated, and with a lower income than the women who attended the 1972 convention as delegates.

At the other end of the spectrum is the small and elite group of women who have served in Congress, women who are likely to be somewhat older and of higher socioeconomic status, as measured by education and income, than the convention delegates. Statistics compiled by the Center for the American Woman and Politics in 1975 bear this out: in their survey of women in national, state and local office they found that all nineteen of the women serving in the

Table 26. Personal Characteristics of 1972 National Convention Delegates

Characteristic	Women (*n* = 659)	Men (*n* = 677)
Educational Achievement		
Less than high school	3%	4%
High school graduate	17	10
Some college	54	38
Graduate school	26	47
Family Income in 1971		
Less than $10,000	14	8
$10,000 to $19,999	32	27
$20,000 to $29,999	28	26
$30,000 and more	23	35
Age		
18–29	18	17
30–39	20	21
40–49	30	30
50–59	19	19
60 and older	13	13
Membership in Voluntary Organizations		
Civic groups	27	18
Professional groups	16	25
Unions	3	8
Party organizations	44	37
League of Women Voters	10	1
Number of Political Campaigns Worked In		
None	7	6
One	5	2
Two or three	19	12
Four or five	18	13
Six or more	45	58

Source of Data: Center for Political Studies, Convention Delegate Study.

United States House of Representatives in that year had at least some college, while nearly half (nine) had attended graduate school. Most of these women (78 percent) were over forty years of age, and none was under thirty. In terms of family income, the nine Representatives for whom this information was available all reported family incomes of over $30,000 annually, with seven in the $50,000 and over range (Johnson and Stanwick 1976). Thus, the women convention delegates in the Center for Political Studies survey seem to be somewhere in between the "average" woman voter and the woman United States representative in terms of age, education, and income. Since these factors tend to be strongly correlated with political participation, this finding is not surprising.

Another way to characterize the women who served as national convention delegates in 1972 is to compare them with the men in the same group. To a large extent, the women and men delegates come from similar backgrounds. In age distribution they are practically identical, as shown in table 26. But while 80 percent of the women delegates and 85 percent of the men have attended some college, a higher proportion of the men have received graduate educations— most likely indicating a higher proportion of the men in professional fields, which have traditionally been a foundation on which to build a political career. The men in the 1972 delegations also slightly exceeded the women in family income, with 35 percent of the men, as compared to 23 percent of the women, in the $30,000 and over group, and a greater proportion of the women in the less than $10,000 range. In general, the female delegates have been more active in voluntary organizations—with the exception of professional groups and unions, to which more of the male delegates belong. The women have a slight edge in membership in party organizations, while the men show a somewhat greater amount of past participation in political campaigns. Overall, then, the women and men delegates reveal fairly similar backgrounds in terms of the variables shown, though the men in this group tend to exceed the women in education and family income levels.

Because the convention delegates are part of the political elite in this country, their attitudes toward the roles women do and can play in the political system are important to understand. Women who are selected as delegates to the national nominating conventions can serve as role models for other women, particularly those in the lower echelons of party organizations. The position of convention delegate represents a level of power greater than that of voter or party worker, yet one that is more within the realistic reach of women than most state and national elective posts. Thus, the women delegates are in a good position to "show the way" to other women interested in greater political involvement. This effect may be counteracted by a tendency observed by some writers (Staines, Tavris, and Jayaratne 1973) which they called the "Queen Bee Syndrome": this is the tendency of women who have reached high positions in areas traditionally dominated by men—whether in politics, business, or the professions—to feel that they have done so on their own merits, without any special consideration because of their sex. As a result of this disassociation from the problems most women face, such queen bees may be unsympathetic to and unsupportive of the efforts of other women seeking to break into the same areas.

Equally, it is important to look at the attitudes of the male convention delegates toward the political participation of women, both in the national nominating conventions and in other areas. The 1972 conventions of both major parties had a higher proportion of women in their delegations than in any previous year: almost 40 percent of the Democratic delegates and nearly 30 percent of the Republicans were women. This increased exposure of the men in the delegations to deeply involved political women could possibly have had a softening effect: by seeing women performing effectively in roles traditionally held by males, the men working next to them might have been positively influenced in their opinions about women's political abilities. On the other hand, the male delegates, particularly the older ones who were accustomed to more traditional modes of political activity, might have seen the larger number of women as a threat and could have been negatively influenced by the emphasis on women's liberation issues among those delegates active in the National Women's Political Caucus.

The attitudes of delegates of both sexes toward women's political roles are shown in table 27. It is immediately evident that the women delegates took a more liberated stance on these questions than the men did, although for some items the difference was relatively small. Half of the women, as compared to a third of the men, felt that male party leaders try to keep women out of leadership roles. The majority of both men and women delegates said that they expect to see big changes in the role and power of women in political parties in the near future, while slightly more than half of each sex agreed that women work behind the scenes and have more political influence

Table 27. Agreement of 1972 Convention Delegates with Items on Women's Political Roles

Item	Women (n = 659)	Men (n = 677)
Most men in the party organization try to keep women out of leadership roles.	48%	33%
We can expect to see really big changes in the role and power of women in the political parties within the next ten years.	66	57
While women hold few public offices, they work behind the scenes and really have more influence in politics than they're given credit for.	58	53
Most men are better suited emotionally for politics than are most women.	17	33
It is almost impossible to be a good wife and mother and hold public office too.	17	28
To be really active in politics, men have to neglect their wives and children.	34	44
Women have just as much opportunity as men to become political leaders.	30	36

Source of Data: Center for Political Studies, Convention Delegate Study.

than they're given credit for. As would be expected, very few of the women delegates reported a belief in sex differences and role conflicts which would make women unsuited for politics; while more of the men agreed with these two questions, the majority of the male delegates seemed to see no unsuitability of women for political roles. Interestingly, though, a larger proportion of each sex—34 percent of the women and 44 percent of the men—felt that for men, serious political involvement entails neglecting their wives and children.

Without comparative data from delegates to previous conventions, we cannot measure whether change has occurred in attitudes among this group of politically active and influential people toward women's involvement in politics. It does appear, however, that the women in this sample are highly sympathetic to the increasing participation of women in politics, and that the men, though less sympathetic, are on the whole supportive as well.

Greater differences between the men and women delegates can be seen in their responses to questions concerning their aspirations to public and party office (Farah 1976). Both the aspirations of the women and men delegates and their realistic expectations of the highest public and party offices they will achieve are shown in table 28. Fully 41 percent of the women reported no interest in any public office, while only 19 percent of the men gave this response. Of those delegates aspiring to public office, the women set their sights lower than the men: nearly half of the men (49 percent) reported aspiring to the positions of president, vice-president, or member of Congress. The women's realistic expectations of the highest public office they would probably achieve lag even farther behind those of their male counterparts. Thus, only 13 percent of the women, or less than one-quarter of those with ambition to high elective office, expect to

Table 28. Aspirations and Realistic Expectations to High Office of 1972 Convention Delegates

	Women (*n* = 659)		Men (*n* = 677)	
	Aspire	*Expect*	*Aspire*	*Expect*
Public Office				
President or vice-president	2%	0%	8%	2%
Member of Congress	20	3	41	20
Governor	1	0	6	3
Member of state legislature	15	9	8	13
Mayor	1	1	1	2
No interest in any office	41	—	19	—
Party Office				
National chair or committee member	30	1	22	0
State chair or central committee member	11	10	17	12
County chair or board member	9	7	8	6
City chair	1	0	1	0
No interest in any office	26	—	23	—

Source of Data: Center for Political Studies, Convention Delegate Study.

achieve election to any of the offices listed; on the other hand, 40 percent of the men, or about half of those aspiring to high public office, reported an expectation of attaining one of these offices. Given the low political expectations of these women—who by virtue of their selection as convention delegates already constitute a politically elite group—it is not surprising that so many of them report no interest in running for high public office; and given the small proportion of women who have filled any of the elective posts listed, the low expectations of the women delegates are, unfortunately, only too accurate.

When we turn to aspirations and expectations for party office, however, the differences between the men and women delegates is slight. Interestingly enough, more of the women (30 percent as compared with 22 percent of the men) aspire to the highest party offices, those of national chair or committee member. It appears that these women are focusing their political ambitions on the party organization, an area in which they have greater experience and probably a better chance for success than in the public arena.

These differences in political ambition between the male and female delegates are also reflected, though to a lesser extent, in the reasons they gave for becoming politically active. Of the men, 22 percent cited their desire for a personal career in politics as one of their reasons for seeking political involvement, while fewer of the women (16 percent) gave this response. On the other hand, more women than men—41 percent and 34 percent respectively—mentioned an enjoyment of friendships and social contacts in response to this question. The women delegates were also somewhat more likely to indicate that their political involvement fulfilled a sense of civic responsibility, and that they became active out of a desire to see certain candidates elected. Overall, though, the patterns of response to this question are similar, with the men and women delegates differing no more than 10 percentage points on any of the reasons given. Still, the differences which do show up suggest that the motivation of the men delegates tends to be more self-serving, that of the women more public service oriented. This fits in with the roles politically active women have often played in the past, and with the low levels of political ambition expressed by this group of women delegates.

Women as Elected Office Holders

Many social observers have thought that the greater voting participation of women and their growing acceptance by the political parties, as evidenced by their roles in the 1972 nominating conventions, would soon produce more women running for and winning election to public office. The new women office holders were expected to appear first at the lower levels of the political system where competition is less keen and where minorities have traditionally begun the long climb up to national office. As the data in table 29 indicate, the number of women elected to municipal and city office almost doubled between 1975 and 1977. The striking feature of table 29, however, is the small percentage of women office holders at *any* level of

Table 29. Women Serving at Various Levels of Elected Office, by Year

	1975		1977	
Level of Office	*Number*	*Percent*	*Number*	*Percent*
U.S. House of Representatives	19	4	18	4
State Executive and Cabinet	84	10	97	11
State Legislature	610	8	696	9
County Commission	456	2	660	3
City Mayor and Council	566	4	735	8
Municipal and Township Council	5,365	—	9,195	—

Year	Number in Congress	Number in State Legislatures
1920	0	29
1925	3	126
1931	8	146
1935	8	129
1941	10	140
1945	11	234
1951	11	235
1961	19	—
1965	12	—
1971	12	—
1975	19	610

Sources of Data: Werner 1966; Johnson and Stanwick 1976; Frankovic 1977; Johnson and Carroll 1978.

government. The relatively high percentage of women at the state executive and cabinet level reflects both political appointments and election victories, but even here women constitute a clear political minority.

There are some important differences among the states that are obscured by the national figures shown in table 29. Diamond (1977) has shown that the election of women is most likely in those states where the state legislative office is less prestigious, less well paid, and therefore where there is less competition for the position. She distinguishes between citizen and professional legislatures, a distinction based upon the salary, length of session held, and size of the legislature. States paying their legislators nominal salaries to attend short sessions usually have strong state governments, and thus the role of state legislator is less powerful and less attractive. The proportion of women elected to state legislatures of this type is quite high, compared with the proportion of women in legislatures with considerable political power and remuneration. Diamond also argues that the gender of a woman candidate matters only in state political systems with moderate competition for the legislature. Where competition is minimal, the shortage of candidates leaves little room for gender discrimination; where competition is intense, only professional politicians with strong records of accomplishment, regardless of gender, win election.

A data base for testing Diamond's hypotheses is contained in Welch's (1978) analysis of the recruitment of women to state legislatures. She examined the educational and occupational characteristics of men and women legislators in twelve midwestern states using discriminant analysis, a technique we used in chapter 2. She tested whether the low representation of women seemed due more to weaker backgrounds among women in the state populations, qualifying fewer of them for election, or whether the candidate's gender appeared to be a relevant factor in successful campaigns. If education and occupation played the same roles for women and men candidates, she concluded, "these equations would predict three times as many females in these lower houses and 3.7 times as many females in the upper houses as are found in our sample" (1978, p. 378). If the twelve states were grouped according to the degree of competitiveness of legislative elections, new discriminant analyses would directly test Diamond's contention that gender is a factor only in moderately competitive elections.

Looking now at the next higher level of elective office, table 28 shows that the proportion of women in the United States Congress grew gradually from 1925, five years after suffrage was granted, until 1961, when nineteen women served in Washington, D.C. Most of the congresswomen served in the House of Representatives and up until the 1960s, the majority of them arrived through succession after the death of an officeholding husband or father (Bullock and Heys 1972). Since the early 1960s, for an increasingly large percentage of congresswomen, election to national office has been the next logical step in an established political career. That the number of women in Congress declined after 1961 and reached the same level only in 1975 may be surprising news to some readers, and this fact testifies to both the power of the media to convey erroneous impressions about women gaining strength in Congress and to the willingness of largely male political institutions to pass legislation acknowledging the rights of women.

When women do run for office, they have more difficulty raising campaign funds than do men. Their financial constraints partially account for the finding that many women candidates do not make full use of campaign techniques known to be effective. According to a survey of women candidates in 1976 conducted by Rothstein-Buckley, a campaign management firm, less than half of the state or national office-seekers based their strategies upon poll results and information allowing the targeting of probable supporters. The kinds of questions asked women candidates by campaign audiences and their opponents may constitute another disadvantage. In her nation-wide survey of women candidates and officeholders, Carroll (1979) found that one-quarter of the women initiated discussion of feminist issues; another one-quarter talked about these issues only at the instigation of their (primarily male) opponents.

A question of fundamental importance to any discussion of women and politics is whether women and men elites are different attitudinally and behaviorally, or whether there is virtually no difference between them with regard to the public policies they promote. A major goal of the current women's movement, through organizations like the National Women's Political Caucus, has been to elect women to public office. This goal is considered important for at least three reasons. First, to the extent that women and men legislators, governors, and mayors perform differently, women are thought to be more supportive of women's rights issues, and thus more likely to sponsor and secure legislation significant to the movement. Second, having women in high positions in a largely male-dominated political system encourages other women to explore political and nonpolitical opportunities afforded primarily to men. And third, it is important to remedy the clear injustice of having over half of the American electorate represented in kind by ten percent or less of the politically elite, an injustice alluded to in the title of this book.

The evidence available on differences in the political attitudes and behaviors of women and men elites is scanty and inconclusive. Although discrete studies have been done on convention delegates, as discussed earlier in this chapter, the term "elite" has also been used by Constantini and Craik (1972) to mean state party leaders. Exploration of the attitudes and voting behavior of congresswomen (Frankovic 1977) has not been matched with analysis of congressmen, and a large study of women candidates for state legislature, statewide, and congressional offices in 1976 focused solely upon women (Carroll 1979). The fundamental question—what difference would more women make—has not been answered satisfactorily yet with data either on office holders or on the electorate.

Support for Women Candidates and Feminist Positions

Given that the number of women elected to various levels of public office has been small, we could expect that the electorate would voice a distinct reluctance to support women candidates even verbally. As the data in table 30 indicates, nothing could be further from the fact. A Gallup Poll conducted in 1975 found that over 80 percent of both the women and men surveyed said they would support women candidates nominated by their party. When the question focused upon a woman presidential candidate, nearly three-quarters of the electorate said they would vote for her. In a fascinating aside on the wording of

Table 30. Support for Women Candidates at Different Levels of Public Office

	Year	Women	Men	National Sample
Mayor or top official of your city or community	1975	82%	84%	83%
Governor of your state	1975	80	81	81
Sent to Congress from your district	1975	89	88	88
President	1975	71	75	73
President	1971			66
	1969			54
	1967			57
	1955			52
	1949			48
	1937			31

Sources of Data: American Institute for Public Opinion (The Gallup Poll), and Ferree 1974.

this question down through the years, one can look at the appearance and disappearance of phrases such as "if she were qualified in all other regards" and "even if she were a woman." Positive responses to the questions have grown from 31 percent in 1937, when the Gallup Poll first included the topic, to 73 percent in 1973.

How can the difference between verbal support and electoral support be explained? There are numerous possibilities. The first explanation is that voicing support for a political minority is cost-free, whereas election support may have concrete consequences one cannot assess until presented with an actual choice between and among candidates. Another possible explanation points to the time lag between attitudinal support for a new position and changing one's behavior in a way congruent with the attitude. This is an important issue and one to which future research could well be directed.

The goal of electing more women to public office is on the agenda of the contemporary women's movement as one feminist issue among many others. One way to tap probable support for women playing more equal roles in politics, as candidates or policy advisors, is to examine public support for other feminist issues. Knoche (1978) has demonstrated that feminism is a political ideology, a set of consistent, coherent attitudes that may orient human behavior just as liberalism and conservatism may do. Four feminist issues are shown in table 31, and the support for them clearly increased between 1972 and 1976. Women's rights are more widely accepted now, and attributions for women's "self-limiting" behavior are now less likely to "blame the victim" and instead to charge the societal institutions with responsibility.

Summary and Conclusions

Participatory politics take place in town halls and the chambers of Congress, but the likelihood of finding women among the discussants is much greater in the former case than in the latter. This chapter has sought to lay out the full range of arenas within which political actions take place. In contrast to most of the chapters in this book, the focus here has been upon nonelectoral politics, their pervasiveness, their significance, and the extent to which women are or soon will be full participants. Early in the chapter, it was shown that beyond trying to influence the votes of others, women and men have not been politically active at election times, and there has been little change in their low levels of participation from 1952 to 1976. To document political activity, researchers must look both outside the temporal bounds of an election and downward to the grass roots of community involvement. At this level, women are politically active in myriad organizations, and the women who become active have

Table 31. Agreement of the United States Electorate with Feminist Items, 1972–76

Item	1972	1976
Some people feel that women should have an equal role with men in running business, industry, and government.	45%	50%
Many qualified women can't get good jobs; men with the same skills have much less trouble.	44	61
Sex discrimination keeps women from the top jobs.	27	45
Our society, not nature, teaches women to prefer homemaking to work outside the home.	29	50

Sources of Data: Knoche 1978, and Center for Political Studies, American National Election Studies, 1972–1976.

more education than their uninvolved women neighbors. In some ways, women who are knowledgeable about grass roots politics through their involvement in the political parties and the League of Women Voters are less optimistic than women who are only registered voters about the possibility of women playing full and equal political roles. If this is found to be true across a variety of communities, it suggests that some women who become involved locally choose not to take on greater responsibility because their first experience in politics is not encouraging.

Looking "up" the scale of political settings, we find that men and women convention delegates to the national nominating conventions are drawn from similar backgrounds but hold different attitudes regarding women's roles in politics. Compared with the grass roots women activists, the women delegates are better educated, older, and have more income, a difference in kind and magnitude identical to that between women delegates and congresswomen. The women who serve as convention delegates, then, are not a random sample of community activists, and instead of seeing the range of political arenas as settings activists successively experience, researchers ought to focus upon arena specialists. Support for this conclusion is drawn from an analysis of women who have served in the United States Congress. Up until fairly recently, most of these women were appointed or elected to seats previously held by their fathers or husbands. In the last ten years or so, congresswomen have increasingly resembled congressmen demographically and occupationally; whether they do so attitudinally is not conclusively known.

Although the attitudinal convergence of women and men political elites is an important question, what is most striking in this chapter is the contrast between the large numbers of women active in grass roots politics and the negligible number who win election to public office of any sort. Women have long been told that they lacked the experiences necessary for political careers in public service, and that the best training grounds were their own communities. With many years of experience in hand, however, women still find it difficult to win party endorsements, to gain financial backing, and to appear on general election ballots. Hopefully, that will not be the case much longer; realistically, there is little evidence of significant change.

chapter eight

THE COMPARATIVE PERSPECTIVE
Crossing National Boundaries and Cultures

As late as the end of the Second World War (1945), a half-century after New Zealand became the first country to enfranchise women, only 31 nations had given women the right to vote. Today, almost all of the world's population is found in the 125 countries which have extended the right to vote to women. Women's participation in politics is more widespread and more commonly accepted than ever before. At the same time traditional sex roles are being challenged around the world, and in many countries women are more independent, both economically and socially, than in the past.[1]

That is not the end of the story. Nowhere in the world is there equality between men and women in terms of the actual political power they wield. With rare exceptions, women hold no more than 10 percent of the seats in national legislative bodies, and even that figure is probably well above the average. If women are rare in national assemblies and parliaments, they have been even scarcer in higher-level appointive and elective positions and in high-level civil service posts—not to mention in the highest power positions as heads of state. When women have appeared at all at these upper levels, they have generally risen to power on the coattails of a prominent male relative, as in the cases of Eva Peron of Argentina and Indira Gandhi of India. There are, however, hints of change. In 1979, Margaret Thatcher was elected prime minister of England, the first woman to serve at that level in Western Europe. In the past decade in America two women have been elected as governors of states, and two women have been elected mayors of major cities, San Francisco and Chicago.

143

Thus far social scientists have no theory which explains adequately the failure of women to achieve political power in the nations of the world. The more common explanation is that historically the condition of women has been subordinate under male patriarchy—the "derived status," the "second sex." However, there is new interest in this intriguing question on the part of scholars who are seeking to redefine the place of women in history ("herstory") and to ask new questions about sexual asymmetry. Sociologists, psychologists, and political scientists in particular are testing a number of contradictory theories. One of these theories goes back to Mary Wollstonecraft and John Stuart Mill, and suggests that the march of history from tradition to modernization and development will inevitably lead to a more egalitarian status for women. A Finnish sociologist, Elina Haavio-Mannila (1977*a*; 1977*b*) has recently espoused this view in explaining reasons why it was easier for women from eastern Finland than from western Finland to become elected into parliament and local councils. Since women in Finland have higher representation in parliamentary halls than in other countries, some 20 percent compared to 3 percent in the United States in 1977, her comments based on statistical evidence are of interest. She concluded that the realization of equality of the sexes is a modern idea linked to modernization and development, and the concentration of capital, social services, and population in developed areas of Finland is followed by the acceptance of modern ideologies in these areas.

Margaret Mead, among others, sees a negative relationship between a nation's socioeconomic development or modernization and the economic, social and psychological development of its women. She was concerned that women have been denied access to modern agricultural techniques in part because of the belief that women cannot handle modern machinery, and following America's model, developing countries will not train women in agricultural skills (1976, Foreword). Judith Van Allen (1974) also argues that the experience of women, for example, in Africa has been that modernization can have a regressive effect on female autonomy and power. Her attack centers on the assumption that modernization and development carry within them the folk system of western ideas about male and female roles. As women in Africa (and other development areas) approximate that standard, she argues, they become more dependent on African men and more subject to economic exploitation, through the interaction of western colonial and traditional African systems of class and sex stratification (pp. 304–21).

Our concern here is to learn more about the political behavior of American women by studying women in other cultures. Can the findings for the American women be generalized to other countries where the status of women, the economic stage of development, the structure of government, and the electoral system may differ in important ways from those in the United States?

There are larger questions at issue here which cross national boundaries and cultures. Barbara Ward (1963) wrote that changes in the role and status of women in the western world in this century are as profound as in Third-World countries in Asia. Alvah Myrdal and Viola Klein (1956) observed more than twenty years ago that women now have the best opportunity for achieving equality since the Industrial Revolution. Can we follow up these statements and prove that there is a force at work in the world which is moving toward political equality for women?

We can examine a small piece of this puzzle by first summarizing the prevailing trends for women on a worldwide basis, and then pursuing in more depth a case study comparing American and British women during two national elections. We can then extend that case study to report on recent attitudes of political efficacy and involvement comparing women in Britain with women in three other Western European countries: Denmark, France, and Germany. This global review and two case studies help to reveal how the experiences of American women compare with the political status of women in other countries with similar cultures.

These are the trends which emerge from an extensive review of the comparative literature; regarding women's political behavior specifically, there are exceptions for most of these generalizations.[2]

1. With universal suffrage a virtual world phenomenon since the Second World War, women have been narrowing the gap in voting rates in comparison to men. Women still lag behind men except in stable electoral systems where women have had the vote for some

time (Britain, United States). The vote for women also lags where the influence of religious beliefs and institutions has been pervasive in effecting a continuance of traditional roles for women (Egypt, Italy, Spain). Mexico and India are exceptions which combine low social status for women with high politicization. The outlook for women in America and Western Europe is for women to vote at about the same rates as men in the 1980s.

2. Women tend to be more concerned about politics when they live in urban rather than rural settings. Urbanization seems to favor the election of women candidates.

3. Women are concentrated in the lower ranks of political party organizations in all countries. The more educated women are more often found in the activist ranks.

Perhaps the arena in which women have, so far, been most effective politically involves the type of grass roots activism discussed in chapter 7, which is outside established party politics. Women have been in the forefront of many national liberation movements, often working alongside men as near-equals, only to learn that, once such movements come into power, the women are relegated to their previous positions of powerlessness once again. The topic of activism is relatively underresearched, but there are some scattered examples of women organizing successfully at the grass roots level and exerting a strong political influence. Since women are, in most countries, concentrated in the lower ranks of political party organizations, activism outside party systems may be the only means by which they can achieve some measure of political influence.

4. When women have sought elected or appointed political posts, their efforts have been directed more often at local levels of government.

5. Social science has generally described women as being more conservative than men in their choice of candidates and political parties. It is not clear whether or not this is a continuing pattern. The younger, more activist woman in a number of countries appears to be more liberal than her masculine peers by the end of the 1970s. American women are more pacifist-minded than their men. The more traditional, conservative women are dying off in countries where religious barriers are weakening, and rigid socialization patterns are loosening.

6. The structure of government has an effect. Women occupy higher

percentages of elite political offices in one-party states than in democratic systems, as in the USSR, countries of Eastern Europe, and in some developing countries, but these are not power positions. Legislative bodies in one-party systems serve mainly to ratify policies determined by party chiefs. Thus, although in 1975 fully 35 percent of the seats in the Supreme Soviet were held by women, they comprised only 2 percent of the Central Committee and were absent from the Politburo entirely. In China and the USSR, government policy includes the involvement of women at local levels of politics, though as with national posts it is unclear how often real power is attached to offices filled by women under these conditions.

7. There is a gap between the promise and the actual realization of economic and social gains for women as mandated by governmental decision. In the United States, for example, the Equal Pay Act of 1963 languishes for lack of governmental and court enforcement. In 1980, American women still receive roughly one-third less pay than men for equal work. This is also true in England.

The outlook for change appears to lie with the younger, better-educated group of women, born since the Second World War, who have joined the paid work force in considerable numbers. As we will see in the following sections of this chapter, there is some evidence that such women are much closer to men in their political involvement and attitudes than are women of older generations. The influence of various changes such as this one, now occurring in particular in the developed industrial countries of the West, is bound to be reflected in the political roles women play in the near future. For example, in addition to the rising rates of college attendance among women, more women are working now than in the past. While women are marrying younger and at higher rates than they were twenty-five years ago, at least in European countries, more married women are remaining in the work force than at that time. Rising divorce rates and declining fertility rates in many countries are other factors of change (Blake 1974).

The increasing longevity of women, and the challenges to traditional cultures now occurring around the world, make the emerging new breed of activist women a potentially powerful political force.

On the other hand, the long-standing political inequality of the sexes in virtually every country will not disappear overnight, and so far the gains have been small in terms of the number of women who have been able to achieve positions of political power. Whether the trends we have described will continue, and what direction they will take, cannot be accurately predicted at this point, but it is clear that women, as the invisible majority of voters in many countries throughout the world, have the potential to gain a great deal more political power than they have ever had in the past. The rest of this chapter, by examining in greater detail some of the concrete evidence for change among British and other European women, will be a start in providing answers to some of these questions.

A Comparison of Voting Turnout by British and American Women

British and American women obtained suffrage at roughly the same time. British women voted in national elections in 1918, although only women thirty years of age or over who qualified as residents were enfranchised. In 1929 the vote was extended to all British women who were twenty-one years old. Gosnell, Butler, Rose, Abrams, and other political analysts in England have written that from 1929 to 1970 women voted in proportions near those of men[3]— an achievement it took American women fifty years to accomplish. But although British women still vote at significantly higher rates than American women, it appears to be a systems level difference, for men and women in Britain vote at higher rates than the American electorate. This disparity in turnout between the two nations is of long standing. The reasons for higher British turnout are not altogether clear. Butler and Stokes commented in their extensive empirical studies of the British electorate:

> Blurred ideas of popular sovereignty and universal suffrage are so interwoven in prevailing conceptions of British government that the obligation to vote becomes almost an aspect of the citizen's national identity. As a result a number of people are drawn to the polling place who would be unlikely to get there otherwise. [1969, p. 37]

Rose ends a book with the statement "England is outstanding for its durable representative institutions, and the allegiance that its citizens give to political authority" (1974*a*, p. 438).

Other reasons for a higher turnout in Britain relate to differences in electoral laws and the importance of customs. National elections in Britain usually occur during a crisis in government when the prime minister and her or his party has suffered a loss of confidence and must call an election. This type of election seems to generate more excitement and interest than the American presidential elections held every four years as required by the Constitution. Other factors which are influential include a short three-week campaign in Britain, as compared to two years or more of presidential politicking in the United States. Further, requirements for registration are more demanding in America than in Britain. Both nations have recently experienced a decline in turnout, however most of the differences in electoral habits between the British and the American electorate are clearly linked to the structural differences between the two political systems.

A major problem for any cross-national comparison is the difficulty of finding comparable equivalencies in elections and data. The problem is lessened for this particular study because of the common heritage of the United States and Great Britain. The two nations share a tradition of constitutionalism and a democratic legal system. Both countries have broadly based major political parties and a closely balanced electoral system, as well as a common language. Neither system is plagued by interference from representatives of the church or the military. Compared to almost all other political models, both England and America have had stable political systems despite major wars, depressions, and other crises. Thus although there is no British election exactly comparable to the American presidential election, we consider the vote to select local Members of Parliament similar enough to allow valid comparison. Thus we have chosen to compare the 1964 and 1970 elections in Great Britain with the 1964 and 1972 presidential elections in the United States. Our British data are taken from the surveys of parliamentary constituencies (which average about 44,000 votes) conducted by David Butler and Donald Stokes (1974). Our American survey data continue to be from the American National

Election Studies conducted by the Center for Political Studies at the University of Michigan.

The comparison of British and American women will focus on three aspects of political behavior: voting turnout, party preference, and political activism. We will examine the effects of age, education, and employment status in order to see whether the patterns of influence demonstrated for American women in chapter 2 also hold for British women.

Our data permit a close look at factors affecting the women's vote. According to the survey data collected by Butler and Stokes, the voting turnout for women in the parliamentary election of 1964 was 90 percent; for men the turnout was 92.5 percent. In 1970 the vote decreased, with 83.3 percent of women voting as compared to 87.1 percent of men. These statistics are better understood if the turnout is examined by age. Table 32 presents the percentage of voters by age category for the 1964 and 1970 British elections. British men voted at higher levels than women at all ages except thirty to fifty, with the highest turnout of all among men sixty-six years and older. Middle-aged women voted at higher rates than men of any age except sixty-six and over, while younger women voted less than any other age/sex category, 11 percent less than men of the same age cohort in 1964 and 16 percent less in 1970. In chapter 2 we commented on the significance of the increasing voting rates of young American women. However, as these data show, there is no evidence of a comparable trend among young British women in these elections.

The Relationship of Education to Voting

In chapter 2 we also saw that recent increases in the levels of education attained by American women are closely associated with their increase in voting rates. Table 33 presents voting results from the 1964 elections in both countries which illustrate that, in Great Britain as in the United States, an increase in level of education is paralleled by a corresponding increase in voter turnout for both men and women. In both countries, women who had been to college voted at rates equal to men with the same level of education, while among those with the lowest level of education, women voted at

Table 32. Relation of Age to Gender Differences in Voting in the United States and Britain

United States	1964			1972	
	Men	*Women*		*Men*	*Women*
Age					
21–29	66%	65%	(18–29)[a]	68%	65%
30–39	68	66		74	71
40–50	77	74		86	82
51–65	76	72		72	69
65–over	76	69		73	64

Britain	1964			1970	
	Men	*Women*		*Men*	*Women*
Age					
21–29	88%	77%	(18–29)[b]	88%	72%
30–50	92	97		86	88
51–65	94	91		87	84
65–over	100	89		93	79

Sources of Data: Center for Political Studies, American National Election Studies, 1952–1976 (American data), and Inter-university Consortium for Political and Social Research (British data).

a. The voting age was lowered to 18 in 1972.
b. The voting age was lowered to 18 in 1969.

lower rates than did men. British men of university education voted 10 percent more than men of low education, while for British women the difference was 14 percent. Though the effect of education level on voting behavior appears to be somewhat greater for American than for British women, this is partly a reflection of the relatively higher voting rates among the entire British electorate. With voting rates among British men and women at the *lowest* education level of 90 percent and 86 percent respectively, there is much less room for increased educational attainment to show an effect on voting rate than there is in the United States. In addition, the categories for education level are not quite comparable in the two countries, especially at the levels termed "low" and "medium." The main point to note is that in both countries, college education has the effect of

Table 33. Relation of Education to Gender Differences in Voting in National Elections

1964	Low			Medium			High		
	Men	Women	Men Minus Women	Men	Women	Men Minus Women	Men	Women	Men Minus Women
United States	64%	59%	4%	73%	70%	2%	80%	80%	0%
Britain	90	86	4	93	93	0	100	100	0

Sources of Data: Center for Political Studies, American National Election Studies, 1952–1976 (American data), and Inter-university Consortium for Political and Social Research (British data).

Note: The primary percent entries represent a simple subtraction of the proportion of women within the category voting for president from the same proportion among men. Positive percentages indicate that men turned out to vote at a higher rate than women.

United States: *Low* indicates elementary education or lower; *medium* indicates high school; *high* indicates attendance of at least one year in college.

Britain: If the respondent went to school, *low* indicates elementary, secondary modern, technical school (not college), central, higher grade, all nongrammar, denominational schools, central institute (Scotland); *medium* indicates grammar, secondary grammar, senior secondary (Scotland); *high* indicates university.

equalizing whatever differences in men's and women's voting rates exist at lower educational levels.

In America, recent years have seen women catching up to men in terms of educational attainment. By 1960, 36 percent of all people aged twenty-five to twenty-nine with a college degree were women; by 1970, the figure was 40 percent. In Great Britain the proportion of female university students is much lower, but a similar trend exists. From 1960 to 1970 the percentage of British university students who were women increased from 24 percent to 28 percent. A system level difference exists here, as well: university education is much less widespread in Great Britain than in the United States. In 1970 more than half the United States population under forty years of age had some college education, while Rose (1974*a*) reported that only about 5 percent of the British electorate has received a university education or its equivalent. Butler and Stokes estimated the figure at 4 percent in their samples. In Great Britain, more so than in the United States, higher education is the prerogative of the upper class. Only a small fraction of students attending government-funded schools go on to college, while the expensive private boarding schools, or "public schools," which educate only 3 percent of the population, prepare their students for university. And at all levels of British education, opportunities and expectations are much lower for women than for men. Approximately half of the state-supported schools and nearly all the private schools are sex segregated, often with poorer facilities in the girls' schools. Both job training opportunities and academic scholarships are more widely available to men (Ross 1976). So compared to American women, British women fall far behind in educational attainment due to both the overall lower rates of university attendance in Great Britain and the greater educational disparity for men and women in that country. Still, despite these differences, the same trend toward equalization of opportunities for women exists in both countries. Perhaps the main point here is that while increased educational attainment is correlated with increased voter turnout for women in both countries, the fact that only a small percentage of British women are highly educated makes this factor a less important one for British women in general.

Employment Status and Voting

Another factor which affects voting patterns in the United States is employment status, as we saw earlier. The increasing entry of American women into the labor force is closely paralleled by their increasing vote in federal elections. Is this an important determinant of voting behavior in Great Britain as well? The developing economic role of women has followed a similar pattern in both societies. While proportionally more British than American women work, the difference has been gradually decreasing. Thus, in 1920, American women were 20 percent of the labor force, while 30 percent of the British labor force were women. Ross reported that a 1968 survey of British industries revealed that women comprised 38 percent of the labor force; in 1968 in the United States roughly 34 percent of the labor force was female (1976, p. 167). The occupational distribution in both countries has been slow to change, with women tending to cluster in only a few of the professional and technical fields—teaching, social work, and nursing. In general, women appear to hold a similar employment role and status in both countries.

We have already seen that, in the United States, employed women vote at a somewhat higher rate than women who are not in the labor force, while there is little difference in voting rates between working women and working men. As table 34 shows, this finding can be generalized to the British population quite accurately. In 1964 self-employed women voted within 5 percentage points of men in the same category, while all other employed women voted within 1 per-

Table 34. Voter Participation by Employment Status, by Gender, 1964 National Elections

Employment Status	Voting Percentage		Gender Differences (men minus women)
	Men	Women	
United States			
Civilian labor force	73%	71%	2%
Employment	74	72	2
Agriculture	65	54	11
Nonagricultural	74	73	1
Unemployment	57	59	−2
Not in the labor force	66	64	2
Under 65 years	56	66	−10
65 and over	71	59	12
Britain			
Self-employed with employees, self-employed without employees, managers, foremen, supervisors	93	88	5
Other employees (includes all employed persons who have no direct managerial or supervisory responsibility)	90	89	1
No occupation	100	81	19

Sources of Data: U.S., Department of Commerce, Bureau of the Census, Current Population Reports, Population Characteristics, Series, P-20, no. 143 (October 25, 1965) (American data); and Inter-university Consortium for Political and Social Research (British data).

centage point of comparable men. On the other hand, working women in both categories voted 7 to 8 percentage points more than nonworking women—in other words, women who belong to the labor force have voting turnout patterns more similar to male workers than to nonemployed women. The finding that nonworking men vote substantially more than women in the same category is somewhat more difficult to interpret, but, as was found in the United States, this group of men appears to be a special category. The man who is not counted in the labor market is relatively rare in both societies, in comparison with the nonworking woman.

These findings are all the more interesting in light of the fact that, in both countries, women who work earn much less than men, due mainly to the concentration of women in lower-level occupations. Blake (1974) reported that the sex differential in hourly wages is as high as 40 percent in the United States, while a 1973 survey indicated that working women in Great Britain earned, on the average, 45 percent less than men (Ross 1976). Apparently the tendency for working women to vote at rates approaching those of men is due not simply to the equalization of income levels between these two groups, but also to other factors connected with working outside the home which are likely to enhance a woman's level of political awareness as well as her interest in personally participating in politics.

Party Preference:
Are Women More Conservative Than Men?

A recurrent theme of analysts who have studied the political behavior of women in the Western world has been an emphasis on the conservative bias of women, in their choice of political party as well as in their ideology.[4] In their five-nation comparison, Almond and Verba (1963) commented:

> Wherever the consequences of women's suffrage have been studied, it would appear that women differ from men in their political behavior only in being somewhat more frequently apathetic, parochial, conservative, and sensitive to the personality, emotional, and esthetic aspects of political life and electoral campaigns. [P. 535]

However, such studies undoubtedly reflect a class bias in the social characteristics of the women who voted in early elections. Women of higher education and income were inclined to be conservative, as were their male counterparts.

The distinctions between the parties in Britain can loosely be defined as follows: The Labour party since the period between the two world wars has stood for democratic socialism. The Liberal party represents a middle-of-the-road liberalism in the European tradition, and the Conservative party follows the conservatism of what can be described as a benevolent paternalism.

The theme that British women are conservative is recurrent in the analyses of British elections. Henry Durant, the chairman of the Gallup poll, commented on voting behavior in Britain from 1945 to 1976, "When voter preferences in Britain are analyzed in terms of sex differences, men show a consistent bias in favor of the Labour Party, and women in favor of the Conservatives" (1969, p. 168).[5]

It is easier to make the observation than to find an explanation for it. Mattei Dogan looked at political cleavage in France and Italy and made a similar comment: "In certain circumstances their (women) vote is decisive in keeping conservatives in power" (1967, p. 167). His explanation seems to center on female religious observance and attachment to religious values as well as female traditionalist tendencies in social and cultural values. Rose, writing of party differences in Britain, explained:

> Women may be expected to favour the Conservatives for a variety of different reasons: susceptibility to the appeal of leaders of high social status, a greater likelihood of having a non-manual occupation prior to marriage, or because sex correlates with such non-economic influences as age or religion. The 1970 election survey showed no significant correlation between sex and party preference among middle-class voters. A relationship appears in the working-class because it includes a disproportionate number of elderly women living on pensions: at this particular point in British political history, they favor Conservatives. [1974*b*, pp. 37–38]

There is also a prevailing impression in voting research that American women have favored the Republican Party in higher percentages than men. Berelson and Lazarsfeld took this view in 1945, entitling one article "Women: A Major Problem for the P.A.C." (Political Action Committee of the liberal trade unions). In Louis Harris's book, *Is There a Republican Majority?* (1954), he included women in that majority.

The data in chapter 3 reporting party identification for American women and men over the 1952–76 period support a different conclusion. Although women showed a slight tendency to favor the Republican party in 1952 (30 percent favored the Republicans, compared to 26 percent of the men), there was very little difference between the sexes in 1960 and 1964. In 1968, 1972, and 1976, women identified with the Democratic party in somewhat higher proportions than men. Further, if the data are stratified by age, it is apparent that women under thirty were more likely to favor the Democratic party, and women over sixty more likely to prefer the Republican party than their male counterparts. We may speculate that the increasing participation of women from wider socioeconomic backgrounds affected this shift. Certainly it is apparent that American women since 1964 have not been more conservative than men, as measured by party identification.

Stratification by age has similar results for the British data on party preference. A close examination of the age composition of the British electorate shows that the apparent conservative bias of women is largely a generational artifact.

First of all, it should be noted that the overall difference between men and women in their support of the Conservative party is very small. Looking at the breakdown by age category, shown in table 35,

Table 35. Gender Difference by Age and Party Vote in Britain's 1964 National Election

	Conservative		Labour		Liberal	
Age	*Men*	*Women*	*Men*	*Women*	*Men*	*Women*
20–29	45%	32%	46%	57%	9%	11%
30–59	36	44	49	45	15	11
60 and over	48	47	45	45	7	8

Source of Data: Inter-university Consortium for Political and Social Research.

women in the youngest age group gave less support to the Conservative party, and more support to Labour, than older women. Women over sixty were strongest in their Conservative vote. When the male vote is added to the comparison it can be seen that, in the age category twenty to twenty-nine, women were less conservative than men, while in the middle age group men were less conservative than women, though in these two age categories both men and women gave more support to the Labour party than to the Conservative party. In the sixty and over group the two sexes were nearly equal in terms of party choice, both sexes giving a slight edge to the Conservative party. To put it another way, women were most liberal in the youngest group, while men were most liberal in the middle-aged group. It is clear, then, that the apparent conservative bias of women can be at least partially explained by another variable: generation.

In commenting on the 1964 election Butler and King observed:

> The years between 1959 and 1964 witnessed a dramatic reversal in fortunes of the two major parties—the resurgence of the Labour Party. . . . The only startling fact is the extent to which those over 65 were the only age group with a decided preference for the Conservatives. [1965, p. 296]

Interestingly, the oldest age category in our British analysis—those sixty and over—was, as well as being the most conservative group, also the only group in which women significantly outnumber men. According to the 1966 census data, there are about 145 women for every 100 men in this category. In other words, a greater proportion of women than of men belongs to the sixty and over group—29 percent of women as opposed to 22 percent of men—the group of women who were most likely to vote Conservative. On the other hand, a greater proportion of men than of women belongs to the middle-aged group, and these men gave less support to the Conservative party than men in the other two groups. It becomes clear that the complex interaction of these factors—age, party preference, and proportion of each sex in each age group—gives rise to an overall appearance of conservative bias among British women. As this analysis has shown, there is a tendency in Great Britain for young women to be more liberal in voting than both young men and older women, a trend we already observed to be occurring in the United States.

The surprising victory of the Conservative Tories in 1979 was based upon the heavy conversion of Labour votes to the Conservative side: 11 percent of those who voted Labour in 1974 voted Tory this time with only 4 percent of former Conservatives switching to Labour. A survey by Gallup and the University of Essex (*The Economist*, 1979) found that men swung more strongly to the Conservatives from October, 1974, to May, 1979 (9.5 percent), than women did (3 percent). The actual vote showed a remarkable similarity among men and women (46 percent men and 45 percent women voted for the Conservative party; 38 percent of women and men voted Labour; 13 percent men, and 14 percent women voted for the Liberal party).

Political Activism

In his work on public opinion and democracy, Key (1961), described the lack of research on political activists as a "missing piece of the puzzle." He meant that the percentage of activists is small, and therefore few are captured in survey samples. Their small numbers limit the analyses researchers can do. We have already seen in chapter 7 that American women have been politically involved in a variety of activities not associated with elections and a number of organizations outside of formal political parties. Political activism is also correlated with a more general type of involvement in community and civic organizations, at least in the United States.

In earlier data, Almond and Verba found pronounced differences between British and American women on their indices of political activism. Forty-seven percent of American women reported that they belonged to a variety of organizations, of which 11 percent were designated as Civic-Political. They commented that ". . . the high level of associational membership in the United States depends to a large extent on the high level of female participation" (1963, p. 248). On the same measure, only 30 percent of British women reported belonging to the organizations. British men were 10 percent lower on this index than American men.

In the same study, they reported that 70 percent of American women discussed politics, as compared to 63 percent of British women. They found that more than two-thirds of American women belonged to voluntary organizations such as church, civic groups, etc., with fewer British women belonging to such groups. Fifty percent of American women considered participation in the local community as a duty, as against 38 percent of the British women.

The data on American women presented in chapter 7 showed that political activism in the United States has steadily increased since 1952, and that the women who are most likely to be active are those who are young and well educated. Equivalent comparable British data are not available. In part this is because there is no British scale of political activities similar to the measure used by the Michigan scholars. In order to provide statistics for rough analysis we have chosen three measures of involvement from the Butler-Stokes data (table 36): discussing the campaign, attending political meetings and doing party work. In both the 1964 and 1970 elections, political discussion among women decreased as their age increased; as in the United States younger women were more involved on this measure.

Table 36. Gender Differences in Political Activities in Britain's 1964 and 1970 National Elections, by Percentage Giving Yes Answer

Question			Age			
		17–30	31–50	51–65	66+	Total
Did you talk to	1964					
other people about	Men	72.7%	79.8%	71.1%	41.4%	72.4%
the election	Women	68.0	57.9	45.6	45.1	54.4
campaign?	1970					
	Men	90.6	82.4	71.0	40.9	76.7
	Women	71.5	67.6	60.8	52.7	64.5
Did you attend any	1964					
political meetings	Men	1.7	17.1	10.1	14.7	12.2
during the campaign?	Women	1.5	6.5	5.0	10.1	5.7
Did you do any	1970					
party work during	Men	1.7	5.7	4.7	5.1	4.4
the campaign?	Women	0.0	5.1	4.3	1.7	3.7

Source of Data: Inter-university Consortium for Political and Social Research.

However, in terms of attendance at meetings and party work this finding does not hold and the percentage of female respondents who were involved in either activity is very small.

While it is hard to generalize from the findings reported in this section, it seems that British women generally are less likely to participate in both political and civic organizations than American women, despite the fact that British women vote at higher rates. Overall, these findings suggest that British women are less active, both civically and politically, than their American counterparts; however, this may also be a reflection of class and educational differences between the two samples. As we saw earlier, a much smaller percentage of British women are university educated, and education level is strongly correlated with political participation.

If there is a connection between levels of political activism and the status of the feminist movement in Britain, the evidence is scarce and uneven. Public policy affecting women has provided de jure protection through recent legislation such as the Abortion Act of 1967, the Equal Pay Act of 1970, and the Sex Discrimination Act of 1975. However, as in the United States, the effect of these measures is greatly influenced by the Governmental guidelines on enforcement and to a large extent by public pressure. Ross (1976) wrote that Britain badly needs a redefinition of sex roles, a unifying awareness of a feminine constituency and a new self-image. The extraparliamentary militancy which led to the vote is needed again if the entrenched injustices are to be changed. The strength of tradition in the social system as well as the government, she argues, will be overcome only when a new generation of feminists begins to insist on social and political change.[6]

The last section of this chapter will extend the investigation to compare the attitudes of British women to those of women in three other Western European countries as found in a 1975 survey.

Political Attitudes among European Women

Since changes in the role and status of women in recent years are not limited to the United States but are evident worldwide, particularly in the developed countries (Blake 1974), changes in political attitudes could be anticipated. Data obtained in a recent (1975) survey of men and women in four European countries enable us to take a closer look at political attitudes as they differ between men and women and between generations. Respondents from Denmark, France, Germany, and Great Britain answered a variety of questions relating to their level of political participation, their sense of political efficacy, and their attitudes about gender role differences both in politics and in general. By breaking down the data into age cohorts we obtain a cross-sectional view of generational difference.[7]

This 1975 survey makes it possible to update the information on British women, to compare them to other women on the same continent, and to contrast European women with their American sisters. Has there been an increase in political efficacy and involvement among European women as there has been for American women? How do female attitudes about political subjects differ on the two continents? Are there similarities which exist among these countries which share so much common background? Finally, how do European women and men feel about the changing roles of women in politics and society?

Since an analysis of changes in political efficacy for American women has been a prominent theme in this work, a question on political efficacy in table 37 is of particular interest. The responses to this question, which tapped the respondents' self-perceived ability to help bring about change for the better in their country, are fairly typical of overall trends on all of the items used. Men in all countries and at all ages scored higher than women on measures of political efficacy and participation. However, for both men and women, the younger cohort in general scored higher than the older people. In addition to this, the gap between male and female scores on these measures increased with age. If the scores for the four countries are combined into a community summary (not shown), the total men's minus women's percentages increased from 7 in the youngest age group to 15, thus doubling in the oldest age group. Clearly, this supports the view that in this 1975 survey the gender differences are smaller among younger cohorts in Europe as they are in the United States. There are marked differences in nationalities, which may well reflect the impact of historical circumstances, as well as the differ-

Table 37. A Comparison by Age of Western European Men and Women on Personal Political Efficacy

Question: *Do you think that if things are not going well in ———— people like yourself can help to bring about a change for the better or not?*

	Britain				France				Germany				Denmark			
	Men		Women		Men		Women		Men		Women		Men		Women	
Age	Yes	No	Yes	No	Yes	No	Yes	No	Yes	No	Yes	No	Yes	No	Yes	No
20–29	62%	38%	58%	43%	48%	52%	43%	57%	42%	58%	41%	60%	81%	19%	64%	36%
30–39	65	35	47	53	46	54	41	59	47	53	47	53	71	29	64	37
40–49	64	36	50	50	42	58	36	64	45	55	34	66	67	33	59	41
50–59	61	39	39	61	34	66	33	67	50	50	32	68	81	19	48	53
60–69	54	46	32	69	31	69	10	90	45	55	32	68	57	43	45	55

Source of Data: Inter-university Consortium for Political and Social Research, Euro-Barometer 3, 1975.

ences in the culture and structure of government in the four nations surveyed. Men and women in Denmark and Britain scored significantly higher at all age levels on the efficacy measure. In the youngest category, in Britain 58 percent of the women aged twenty to twenty-nine said they felt they could bring about a change for the better if things were not going well in their country. British women scored 4 percentage points less than British men of the same ages. Only women in Denmark of this youngest cohort were near the score of British women. However, at all other age levels British women ranged from 15 to 22 percent less "efficacious" than British men. Younger women in France and Germany scored at considerably lower rates, but were much closer to men of similar ages.

Two questions on the extent of political participation yielded results similar to the question of efficacy (see tables 38 and 39). When asked about the frequency with which they discuss political matters with friends, more than one-third of the women (36 percent) in the survey and about one-quarter of the men (26 percent) under thirty indicated that they never participate in such discussions, while among the people over sixty one-third of the men (35 percent) and one-half of the women (50 percent) gave this response. When the data are broken down by country every one of the four countries shows the gap between men and women on this measure increasing with age. When asked about the extent to which they speak out in political discussions with friends, respondents showed little evidence of generational differences, though men still indicated a somewhat greater tendency to express their own opinions than did women at all ages. The lack of generational differences in this case indicates that although older people, particularly those over sixty, are less likely to be involved in informal political discussions, they are still as outspoken as young people when such discussions occur.

Recall the evidence in table 36 showing that among British women surveyed in 1964, the youngest cohort discussed the election campaign much more frequently than women in the oldest cohort. In the 1975 survey British men doubled the rates of women stating that they discussed politics frequently. Only the youngest female cohort reported discussing the campaign nearly as frequently as their male counterparts (women 12 percent; men 19 percent).

Table 38. A Comparison by Age of Western European Men and Women Measuring Political Discussion with Friends

Question: *When you get together with your friends, would you say you discuss political matters frequently, occasionally, or never?*

1. Frequently   2. Occasionally   3. Never

	Britain						France						Germany						Denmark					
	Men			Women			Men			Women			Men			Women			Men			Women		
Age	1	2	3	1	2	3	1	2	3	1	2	3	1	2	3	1	2	3	1	2	3	1	2	3
20	19%	45%	36%	12%	52%	37%	37%	47%	16%	24%	53%	22%	31%	55%	14%	10%	65%	25%	26%	51%	24%	21%	52%	28%
30	36	44	20	13	60	28	33	53	14	21	51	28	34	51	16	20	60	20	28	56	17	15	61	24
40	25	56	19	16	47	38	26	49	26	15	50	35	36	54	10	15	58	27	36	46	18	16	47	38
50	40	48	12	17	46	38	26	54	19	21	40	39	30	50	20	6	54	40	25	52	23	10	40	50
60	24	47	29	10	33	57	22	49	30	14	36	50	36	50	14	16	41	43	16	52	32	14	29	57

Source of Data: Inter-university Consortium for Political and Social Research, Euro-Barometer 3, 1975.

Table 39. Degree of Participation by Age of Western European Men and Women Who Discuss Politics

Question: *If respondent discusses politics, which describes your part in the discussion?*

1. Even though I have my own opinions, I usually just listen.
2. Mostly I just listen, but once in a while I express an opinion.
3. I take an equal share in the conversation.
4. I do more than just hold up my end in the conversation, I usually try to convince others that I am right.

	Britain								France								Germany								Denmark							
	Men				Women				Men				Women				Men				Women				Men				Women			
Age	1	2	3	4	1	2	3	4	1	2	3	4	1	2	3	4	1	2	3	4	1	2	3	4	1	2	3	4	1	2	3	4
20	5%	34%	43%	18%	7%	43%	40%	11%	3%	21%	50%	26%	6%	33%	50%	10%	5%	34%	41%	20%	13%	42%	37%	8%	3%	27%	60%	10%	1%	45%	43%	11%
30	6	30	47	18	4	53	32	11	8	23	51	18	13	33	48	7	6	38	35	21	19	39	30	13	2	29	40	29	3	41	42	14
40	3	38	41	19	13	31	48	8	9	26	46	19	12	38	43	8	5	25	49	20	18	52	25	5	8	23	41	28	5	48	44	3
50	6	26	48	20	2	37	49	12	9	22	47	22	13	37	32	18	2	30	57	11	15	56	29	0	4	28	52	16	3	53	33	11
60	3	30	51	16	7	46	32	16	9	23	42	26	10	42	35	13	6	39	34	21	15	36	40	8	6	30	50	14	10	45	31	14

Source of Data: Inter-university Consortium for Political and Social Research, Euro-Barometer 3, 1975.

Two other questions used in the study measured attitudes toward the participation of women in politics. Respondents were asked how much they agreed with the statement, "It is sometimes said that 'politics should be left to men.' " Percentages of "disagree" responses are shown by age and nationality in table 40. The age comparison reveals the same type of result seen in the earlier questions: young people of both sexes were more likely to indicate a tolerant attitude toward women's involvement in politics than older people, and the figures drop more sharply for women than for men as age increases. Thus, women in the youngest groups were somewhat more likely than men to disagree with the statement, while in the older groups this trend is reversed—an interaction hidden by the quite similar total figures for men and women when all age groups are combined. The recent influences of the women's liberation movement and the actual increase of women's participation in politics, the job market, and other areas of public life are no doubt factors in the attitude changes reflected in these figures.

As the comparison by nation indicates, nationality is probably a better overall indicator of response to this question than is gender. Men and women from any given country tended to respond at fairly similar rates, but there are large differences between countries located on the same continent. Still, when the data are broken down further by age within nations it becomes clear that there is no overall pattern which fits all four countries. Obviously, such patterns are hidden in the overall figures for four nations combined, and are not susceptible to easy explanation without going into a close examination of a range of social and historical differences among the countries involved. Responses to this and other questions do support, however, the general conclusion that while cross-national differences are important, the European nations under study are similar enough that the same trends tend to be visible in all of them. Thus, although the absolute response rates differ from country to country, the relative effects of gender and age operate similarly in these four nations and, as we saw in chapter 2, in the United States.

As the responses to this question indicate, the Danish and the British are generally tolerant to the idea of women's participation in politics, followed by the French and, finally, the Germans.

Table 40. A Comparison by Age of Attitudes of Western European Men and Women toward Women's Participation in Politics

Question: *It is sometimes said that "politics should be left to men." How far would you agree with that?*

1. Agree a lot   2. Agree a little   3. Disagree a little   4. Disagree a lot

	Britain								France								Germany								Denmark							
	Men				Women				Men				Women				Men				Women				Men				Women			
Age	1	2	3	4	1	2	3	4	1	2	3	4	1	2	3	4	1	2	3	4	1	2	3	4	1	2	3	4	1	2	3	4
20	10%	18	25	47%	13%	11%	19	58%	5%	16%	26%	53%	5%	12%	23%	60%	13%	21%	37%	29%	8%	23%	30%	40%	4%	9%	33%	55%	5%	9%	19%	67%
30	14	16	23	48	8	10	14	67	13	17	30	40	8	20	28	45	17	36	26	20	19	18	23	40	12	15	26	48	7	5	35	52
40	8	18	25	49	15	11	21	54	8	28	21	43	14	22	30	34	13	43	25	19	16	38	20	27	8	8	32	51	6	6	39	50
50	11	16	16	57	16	10	18	56	16	16	20	49	27	24	23	26	22	28	28	21	18	38	23	21	13	4	28	55	8	8	34	49
60	17	7	30	46	24	13	17	46	19	23	20	38	23	19	30	30	26	38	20	17	27	28	22	23	18	18	37	37	12	16	37	35

Source of Data: Inter-university Consortium for Political and Social Research, Euro-Barometer 3, 1975.

One further question on attitudes toward women in politics is worth a brief glance. Respondents were asked the question, "In general, would you have more confidence in a man or woman as your representative in parliament?" (table 41). Overall, in the combined community survey 53 percent of the men and 56 percent of the women indicated that they had no preference, while 41 percent of the men and 34 percent of the women said that they would have more confidence in a man. The latter figure increased with age while the former, in general, decreased. Thus, while a majority of both sexes indicated no preference, it is clear that women running for public office in these countries face a significant bloc of particularly older voters who are biased against them, regardless of their qualifications.

As the figures in table 41 indicate, women in Great Britain of all ages who reported that they would have more confidence in a woman scored higher than the women in the other three countries, and doubled the rates of British men. However, 77 percent of the Danish women (aged forty) reported that they would hold no difference in confidence between men and women as a parliamentary representative compared to 55 percent of the British women. The British women who were aged twenty to forty expressed the highest degree of confidence (14 percent) in comparison to women of the same ages in the other three countries.

Another pair of questions deal with more general attitudes toward gender roles in society. People were first asked whether they believed that the majority of men in their society would like to see fewer differences between the roles of men and women; the same question was then asked about the majority of women in their society. A comparison of the answers to these two questions, presented in tables 42 and 43, reveals interesting differences. While there was general agreement among both genders that most women would like to see fewer gender-role differences in society, fewer than half of either gender (except French men aged forty and fifty) felt that most men want a decrease in sex-role differences. Women respondents credit men with less desire for change than the men believe they themselves have.

British and French women of the youngest cohort were the most optimistic of any of the women in the survey, with some 33 percent

Table 41. A Comparison by Age of Western European Men and Women of Preference for a Man or Woman as Their Elected Representative

Question: *In general, would you have more confidence in a man or woman as your representative in parliament?*

1. More in a man   2. No difference   3. More in a woman

| | Britain | | | | | | France | | | | | | Germany | | | | | | Denmark | | | | | |
| | Men | | | Women | | | Men | | | Women | | | Men | | | Women | | | Men | | | Women | | |
Age	1	2	3	1	2	3	1	2	3	1	2	3	1	2	3	1	2	3	1	2	3	1	2	3
20	36%	56%	7%	18%	68%	14%	29%	66%	5%	22%	67%	11%	47%	49%	3%	31%	62%	7%	13%	85%	2%	5%	85%	10%
30	40	58	2	28	58	14	37	57	7	23	66	11	51	44	5	37	51	12	18	81	1	13	80	7
40	30	67	3	36	55	9	36	51	13	33	64	4	66	33	1	38	53	9	12	84	4	17	77	6
50	44	52	4	41	49	9	35	55	11	45	43	12	43	54	3	38	59	3	20	69	11	14	79	7
60	45	48	7	44	42	14	48	45	7	42	46	12	64	36	0	52	39	10	36	60	4	34	64	3

Source of Data: Inter-university Consortium for Political and Social Research, Euro-Barometer 3, 1975.

Table 42. A Comparison by Age of Western European Men and Women of Men's Attitudes toward Gender Roles

Question: Do you believe that the majority of men would like to see fewer differences between the respective roles of men and women in society?

	Britain				France				Germany				Denmark			
	Men		Women		Men		Women		Men		Women		Men		Women	
Age	Yes	No	Yes	No	Yes	No	Yes	No	Yes	No	Yes	No	Yes	No	Yes	No
20	45%	55%	33%	67%	44%	56%	34%	66%	46%	54%	25%	75%	46%	54%	27%	73%
30	37	63	24	76	36	64	28	72	43	58	23	77	50	50	28	72
40	31	69	25	75	61	39	31	69	25	75	25	75	51	49	29	71
50	38	62	24	76	54	46	21	79	42	59	23	77	49	51	29	71
60	31	69	21	79	48	52	20	80	36	64	17	83	43	57	33	67

Source of Data: Inter-university Consortium for Political and Social Research, Euro-Barometer 3, 1975.

Table 43. A Comparison by Age of Western European Men and Women of Women's Attitudes toward Gender Roles

Question: *Do you believe that the majority of women would like to see fewer differences between the respective roles of men and women in society?*

	Britain				France				Germany				Denmark			
	Men		Women		Men		Women		Men		Women		Men		Women	
Age	Yes	No	Yes	No	Yes	No	Yes	No	Yes	No	Yes	No	Yes	No	Yes	No
20	74%	26%	83%	17%	78%	22%	89%	11%	87%	13%	85%	15%	67%	33%	70%	30%
30	79	21	73	27	78	22	90	10	85	15	83	17	68	32	63	37
40	78	23	71	29	89	11	87	13	74	26	55	45	66	35	63	37
50	80	20	73	27	72	28	93	7	85	15	82	18	63	37	62	38
60	75	25	71	30	90	10	86	14	83	17	78	22	59	41	59	41

Source of Data: Inter-university Consortium for Political and Social Research, Euro-Barometer 3.

British and some 34 percent of the French women believing that the majority of men would like to see fewer differences between the respective roles of men and women in the society. On table 43, 83 percent of the youngest cohort of British women were favorable to seeing fewer differences between the roles of men and women in society. Women of the same years in France and Germany were equally favorable. The Danish women and men were considerably less favorable in all the age categories. Perhaps the gender roles in Denmark are less sharply defined than in the other three countries, and thus there is less support for merging them further.

Taken together, these two questions suggest that there is a general desire for the lessening of gender-role differences but that this desire is much greater among women than men. It is a bit surprising to note that even older women share in this perception of a general desire for change.

Has such change actually been occurring? Demographers tell us about worldwide increases in female education and employment levels, about changing marriage and divorce rates, and about new family patterns. The last question from the survey gives us a more direct idea of how European men and women perceive such changes, in addition to providing further evidence that change has in fact been occurring. Respondents were asked whether they thought that the position of women in their country had changed over the last ten or fifteen years, and if so, whether such change had been for the better or for the worse. As table 44 shows, in the combined four nations summary only 9 percent of the women and 7 percent of the men felt that no change was occurring, while about 80 percent of both sexes thought that there had been change for the better. For both sexes this figure dropped as age increased, suggesting that as people age, they become less comfortable with either changes in the roles of women or social change of any sort. The pattern for British women is remarkably similar to those in the other three countries. These changes over age were greater for women than for men—the same trend already observed for the diverse questions on attitudes and efficacy.

Clearly, the response to this question supports the idea that

Table 44. A Combined Summary of Comparison of Attitudes toward Gender-Role Changes by Men and Women in Britain, France, Denmark, and Germany

	Age					
	18–30	31–40	41–50	51–60	61+	Total
Men						
1. Change for better	86%	85%	84%	78%	75%	82%
2. No change	6	6	8	8	9	7
3. Change for worse	8	9	8	13	17	11
Women						
1. Change for better	85	81	82	75	69	79
2. No change	7	10	9	9	11	9
3. Change for worse	7	9	9	17	20	12

Source of Data: Inter-university Consortium for Political and Social Research, Euro-Barometer 3, 1975.

Note: Respondents were classified according to their response to the question: "Still on the subject of the position of women in society in (name of country) and judging from your own experience, do you consider that the situation has changed over the last ten or fifteen years? (If so,) has the change been for the better or for the worse?" 1. Change for better 2. No change 3. Change for worse.

gender-role definitions have changed in Western Europe over the past decade, and that the majority of both sexes, especially among the younger people, feel that such change is desirable. This evidence of a subjective awareness of change helps support the many indicators of more objective changes. In a similar study of political values and behavior Ronald Inglehart (1977) used data collected by the European Community Survey in 1970 and 1973 to analyze political party preference by gender in Britain, Germany, France, Italy, The Netherlands, Belgium, and Switzerland. In his analysis he highlighted some of the similarities and differences between European and American women.

Inglehart found that, in general, women are more likely to be conservative in their political views and voting behavior than men are, and that this trend is least marked in the United States while being most marked in countries such as France, Belgium, and Italy where religious influences are strong and traditional sex roles prevalent. In these three countries, as we noted earlier, women did not even obtain the right to vote until the end of the Second World War. Inglehart also points out that gender-role differences in political values appear to be declining over time and that these differences are smallest among the younger age groups: "If change is taking place, the pre-World War II female cohorts lag two decades behind the men; the post-war cohort is only one decade behind. In the United States, these differences disappear among the youngest cohort." Inglehart hypothesizes also that the decline in political differences between men and women reflects a more general decline in gender-role differences which is associated with increasing levels of economic and technological development (1977, pp. 89–92, 228–29).

In another relevant study, Michel (1977) presents a paradigm of changing family models which can be used to differentiate between traditional, transitional, and modern nations in terms of their prevailing attitudes toward family structures and women's roles. Michel places France and Germany among the mainly traditional European countries and Great Britain among the group of countries in transition, while the Scandinavian countries best exemplify the modern family model which sees women as persons in their own right. The data from our analysis of the 1975 survey indicate that attitudes toward women in politics follow the cross-national pattern suggested by the family-structure model, at least for the four countries surveyed here. Margaret Inglehart (1979) looked at the 1973 European Community Survey done in eight European countries (England, Germany, Ireland, Italy, Belgium, France, Denmark, and The Netherlands). In her search to explain the very low political participation of European women she examines the long-run factor of the "mark made on their societies by . . . authoritarian attitudes" (1979, p. 3). She notes that the extension of political rights took place first in Protestant countries, and occurred later in countries with powerful institutions which were hierarchical and authoritarian in nature (i.e., the Catholic church and a powerful national army). The church and the army were inherently antithetic to concepts of political equality, and both institutions were "anti-feminist as well." She hypothesizes that higher political interest would be found among women of unmixed Protestant heritage, and lower political interest would be found among women in strictly Catholic countries. Using data drawn from public opinion surveys held in the eight European countries, Ingle-hart finds support for her hypothesis.

Summary and Conclusions

The best conclusion to be drawn from the general survey of the worldwide picture is that despite striking differences between countries, the political position of women around the world is remarkably similar. In almost all countries women now have the right to vote, and in recent years female voting rates in many nations have come very close to those of men. Due to the fact that women in many countries outnumber men, there is an invisible female majority in the electorate of numerous nations. While constituting a numerical majority women are relatively powerless politically due to their absence from positions of formal power. Still, in a number of countries gains in high level political positions have been made in recent years. Factors such as rising education and employment levels for women, especially in the highly developed Western nations, are associated with higher levels of political involvement among young women in recent years. Thus though cultural differences between countries are significant and cannot be ignored, a general pattern for the political roles played by women can be traced in many countries with diverse national traditions.

Evidence from our comparison of British and American women allows us to examine in greater detail and specificity some of the differences and similarities in their political roles. Despite system level differences, such as a generally higher voting rate in Great Britain, most of the variables we examined, such as education and employment levels, operate in similar ways in both countries. In both nations, there is a tendency for the younger, better-educated women to be slightly more liberal in terms of their party preference than their peer men, and in Great Britain at least, the "conservative bias" of women is disappearing and can be seen to be due primarily to the greater longevity of women than men. Our comparison enables us to conclude that the key variables associated with political activity operate in similar ways in both of these countries.

We moved from voting patterns to measures of political attitudes and involvement in our examination of survey data from Denmark, France, Germany, and Great Britain. While our data did not allow any direct comparison with figures from the United States, it did enable us to locate trends comparable to those described for American women in chapters 3 and 4 on attitudes. Again, we obtained further evidence for the general trend documented throughout this book: that younger women tend to be much closer in their political outlook and participation to men of their own age group than older women are to older men. We were also able to present evidence indicating a general awareness of changes in gender-roles in society in recent years, and a high degree of satisfaction with these changes among both men and women, particularly in the younger groups. In terms of the outlook for the future, this certainly bodes well for the prediction of a more widespread acceptance of increasing levels of political involvement for women.

The cross-cultural data on women are, to say the least, incomplete, and this chapter has made clear that no conclusive predictions can be made at this time. The phenomena are too complex, and the factors influencing them too numerous and varied to allow us to draw any definitive conclusions. Suffice it to say, there will have to be a remarkable change in the social structure of each nation, a root cause of gender inequality, as well as change in the political behavior of women themselves for their invisibility to alter.

The outlook for the future is also linked to worldwide efforts to improve the status of women, as proclaimed by the United Nations Decade for Women, 1976–85, which followed the International Women's Year of 1975. Included in the World Plan of Action adopted at Mexico City in 1975 were wide-ranging objectives to accelerate progress toward equality and the integration of women into power politics. The evaluation of the meeting by Helvi Sipila, the first woman assistant secretary of the United Nations and the secretary general for International Women's Year, underscores the importance of the gathering.

Never before have women and men representing 133 governments, 31 intergovernmental, and 113 non-governmental organizations and seven liberation movements come together to deal with the problems of women. . . . Never before have 891 women represented 131 governments at any conference of the United Nations. [Boulding 1976, p. 763]

That women around the world constitute invisible political majorities in their homelands is clear; that women will organize and support each other's efforts to make their majority status known is a revolutionary idea.

chapter nine

THE GENDER GAP
Women Voters and Candidates in
a Time of Change

The 1980 election marked a milestone: women voters were recognized for their political independence for the first time in American politics. Women supported candidates in different proportions on election day and responded differently to the campaign issues than did men. These differences were termed the "gender gap." Many of these differences were the outcome of trends apparent in the electoral behavior of men and women—trends beginning in 1952 and documented in earlier chapters of this book. Yet the magnitude of the differences surprised many observers. Some interpreted the election as prima facie evidence that women now constitute a voting bloc that will have power in the voting booth. Other analysts claimed that the election reflected a coincidental convergence between the issues debated by the candidates and the concerns of women. The 1980 election was, they argued, an anomaly.

As the 1982 elections neared, candidates and party officials became increasingly concerned about polls showing gender gaps in the campaigns of candidates in a number of states. Women were showing a distinct preference for Democratic candidates. When asked on election eve in 1982 how he would change the election to benefit his party, a Republican party official remarked that he would like to repeal the Nineteenth Amendment.

The 1982 election results demonstrated the value of the gender gap concept. Women voters constituted the winning margin in numerous congressional and gubernatorial races and in contests for state legislature seats. The term is widely used to describe the difference between the percentage of votes a candidate received from women voters and the percentage received from men. The search for the gender gap is now part of standard political analyses in the United States.

In this chapter, we update our study of women's electoral activities and investigate empirically some assertions regarding women's roles in the 1980 and 1982 elections. We continue to rely on data for 1980 from the American National Election Study collected by the Center for Political Studies (CPS) at the University of Michigan.[1] Their data on the 1982 elections were not available as this book went to press. We also rely on the findings of other surveys, notably the CBS News/*New York Times*, National Opinion Research Center, and Gallup and Harris polls, especially for the 1982 elections.[2]

In the first section we explore whether the demographic variables historically related to voting turnout continued to be important. Why did women cast their vote differently from men? Although a majority of men and women cast their ballots for Ronald Reagan, he received a lower proportion of votes from women. How can this difference be explained? Was it due to his party, his personality, his campaign communications, the issues debated, or his ideology? Which of the issues debated in 1980 triggered the difference in voting response by men and women? Why were some issues particularly important to women? Were there differences as well in choice of political party? Did 1980 mark a turning point in electoral history with a basic realignment of party identification giving the Republican party majority status for the first time since the New Deal election in 1932? If there were a turn to the conservative right in 1980, did women contribute to this drift in the same proportions as men? How did women react to peace issues? Economic issues? Environmental issues? Nuclear issues? Did black women voters, victims of the double whammy, continue to show their remarkable growth in electoral participation apparent in earlier elections?

Shifting attention away from the presidential race, we then look at women as activists and candidates. What change has occurred with activists? Did women run for and win election to national and state offices at increasing rates in 1980 and 1982? The final section discusses the well-documented gender gap and whether it marked the appearance of the long-awaited bloc vote.

The majority vote won by Ronald Reagan, which multiplied into an electoral college landslide, was achieved from an apathetic electorate. National attitude polls agreed that the election was held amid massive voter discontent and that the outcome primarily reflected the unpopularity of the incumbent, President Jimmy Carter.

There was one premier issue, however, and that was the state of the economy. Reagan's prescription for the ailing economy, although radical and untested, offered more hope for recovery than the ineffective measures which President Carter had already administered. Voters were drawn to the polls by other factors as well, including an opportunity to express their position on other major issues, a sense of citizen duty or habit, or perhaps the desire to respond to the referenda on state and local ballots.

The divergence in men's and women's votes in 1980 was larger than it had been in the past. Statistics on the turnout rate for the electorate vary from source to source. There are complicated reasons for this disparity, as described in chapter 2. Further, many voters overreport, that is, they tell interviewers that they voted when actually they did not. In the CPS 1980 study, 70 percent of the women and 73 percent of the men surveyed claimed to have voted. When their official voting records were checked at city halls and county buildings, only 57 percent (55 percent of the women and 58 percent of the men) were found to be actual voters.[3] These numbers represent an increase of only 1 percent in the turnout rate of women between 1976 and 1980, but a decrease of 4 percent for men, as shown in figure 8. More importantly, they indicate that the gender gap in voting narrowed to 3 percent in 1980.

The turnout rates calculated by the Bureau of the Census showed 59 percent of each sex to have voted in 1980. Since women outnumber men, this meant that 53 percent of the 93 million people voting were women (U.S., Department of Commerce, 1981). Women voters outnumbered men by nearly 6 million, the largest majority women have ever enjoyed in a presidential election. Other polls showed slightly higher rates for both genders, but there was consensus that women and men voted at nearly identical rates.

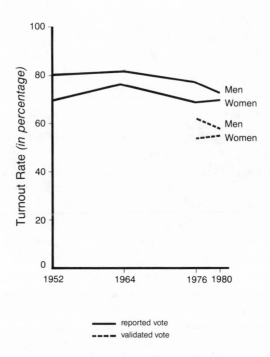

reported vote
validated vote

Fig 8. Voter turnout rates of women and men, by election. (*Source of Data: Center for Political Studies, American National Election Studies, 1952–1980*)

Education

In chapter 2, we discussed in some detail how social characteristics such as education, age, and employment status influence the likelihood of people going to the polls on election day. Figures 2 through 5 and 7 in chapter 2 show the turnout levels of various subgroups of women in the electorate. Those comparisons are extended by the data in table 45. For example, figure 2 in chapter 2 shows that college-educated women have voted at higher rates than two groups of their less well-educated sisters since the 1952 presidential election. Over recent elections, the turnout gap between women who have attended college and those who ended their education following graduation from high school has increased slightly, and it continued to increase in 1980, as shown in table 45. Women with less than a high school diploma historically have turned out at a much lower level than the two other groups; that pattern continued in 1980 as well.

Income and Employment Status

The historically higher voting rates of women from high income families (see fig. 4) continued unchanged in 1980, but there were several significant changes among subgroups stratified by other variables. For example, housewives surpassed clerical and sales women

Table 45. Turnout Rates of Women Voters in 1980, by Stratification Variable

Variable	Turnout Rate
Education	
Some college	81%
High school graduate	71
Less than high school	53
Occupation	
Professional	74
Clerical, sales	64
Housewife (not working at all)	66
Blue collar	42
Income Level	
High	80
Medium	70
Low	63
Region	
Non-South	69
Border state	73
South	70
Age	
61 and above	63
51–60	65
41–50	68
31–40	65
18–30	48

Source of Data: Center for Political Studies, American National Election Studies, 1980.

(see fig. 3 and table 45) in their voting rate for the first time, although professional women continued to turn out at the highest rate and blue collar, working women at the lowest rate. One interpretation of this finding is that housewives, largely dependent on someone else's income, felt a greater stake in determining the economic policies for the nation's next four years than did employed clerical and sales women.

Region

Another change is apparent in the turnout rates of women grouped by region. Women living in southern states (listed in fig. 5) have increased their voting rate in each presidential election since 1952. In 1980, they voted at a rate slightly higher than women living in nonsouthern states, but continued to be surpassed by women from border states. This change may reflect the growing urbanization and industrialization of the American South and the influx of better-educated women from northern states. It also reflects Reagan's campaign strategy of neutralizing Carter's home region advantage by spending considerable time and money encouraging conservative voters to go to the polls. It also reflects an increasing vote by black men and women.

Age

The final change in relative turnout rates stems from women grouped by age. As figure 7 and table 45 show, the youngest age group (women eighteen through thirty) has had the lowest voting rate in every election between 1952 and 1980. The group historically showing the next lowest rate is women aged sixty-one and above. As of 1976, many of these women had grown up when there was a lingering ambivalence about the propriety of women voting. By 1980, a portion of these women had died and been replaced in the age group by women who, four years earlier, had helped to make up the cohort with the highest turnout rate. In the 1980 election, the four subgroups of women aged thirty-one and over turned out at very similar rates. These rates represented a reduction from the 1976 levels, however.

All in all, the profile of the woman who was most likely to vote in 1980 had not changed much from her 1976 sister. She continued to be college educated, employed as a professional, and living in a family in the top third of the national income distribution. She was, for the first time, from a border state and age thirty-one years or older. This multivariate profile predicts a higher level of voting than any other combination of social stratification characteristics.

As discussed in chapter 2, we can employ a statistical technique known as discriminant analysis to discover the relative importance of social factors which are not completely independent of each other. Discriminant analysis makes it possible to determine statistically which variable from a set of variables serves to separate most distinctly a group of people already known to differ in some way (Nie et al. 1975). Women and men respondents in the 1952, 1964, and 1976 national election studies were classified as voters or nonvoters in these elections. Discriminant analyses were conducted on the three data sets to find out which variable (gender, education, income, employment status, region, or age) best predicted their voting or nonvoting. Education emerged each time as the most important predictor of voting. Age was the second most important predictor in the 1964 and 1976 analyses, and the fourth in 1952. Gender was the second most important predictor in 1952, fifth in 1964, and third in 1976.

In an analysis of the 1980 data, age and employment status emerged as the leading powerful predictors, followed by education and region. Gender and income failed to generate coefficients, signifying that they cannot serve as single-factor explanations of the 1980 election (see table 58 in the Appendix). Political analysts must look at voters in a multivariate fashion. The voters who produced the gender gaps in 1980 and 1982 were not simply women, but were likely to have been professional working women over the age of thirty. A recognition of the multiple characteristics of women (and men) voters leads to an understanding of why the gender gap will be part of American political reality in the future. The following sections examine the attitudes and activities of the electorate in the 1980 election, the first election which produced a gender gap in the voting for president.

Candidate Choices

Newspaper columnists have observed that the biggest story in the 1980 election was not the landslide for Reagan, but the fact that women contributed significantly less to his victory than did men. (What is more interesting is that various polls have continued to show lagging support for Reagan among women during his first two years in the White House and also a lag in support of his party in the 1982 election.) In the final vote cast in November, 1980, 47 percent of the women compared to 55 percent of the men voted for Reagan. Forty-two percent of the women supported Carter compared to 36 percent of the men. Men and women supported Anderson similarly at 8 percent, and some 2 percent reported voting for other candidates.

Our analysis is more easily interpreted if it is linked to two alternative models which describe electoral change. The first model follows from traditional democratic theory in which dissatisfaction with the current state of governmental affairs leads to changes in the policy preferences of the electorate. This leads in turn to the election of leaders who pursue these desired policy directions (Schattschneider 1960). The second model posits that dissatisfaction with incumbents leads directly to votes for their opponents, regardless of their policy positions. Genuine shifts in policy may or may not result, depending on the ideology and success of the new government leaders (Downs 1957; Key 1964). Researchers at the Center for Political Studies contend that this "ratification" model better fits the 1980 election (Miller and Wattenberg 1981). Voters' decisions stemmed from a negative assessment of the incumbent, they argue, and not from a positive endorsement of the policy alternatives espoused by his challenger.

Miller and Wattenberg's choice of the ratification model was widely supported by other studies of the 1980 election. Sundquist and Scammon (1981) wrote that the central circumstance of the 1980 election was the unpopularity of Jimmy Carter. They noted that in the summer of 1979 Carter's approval rating by the Gallup poll was under 30 percent. It was boosted temporarily by the rallying around the president that took place in reaction to the seizure of United States hostages in Iran and the Soviet invasion of Afghanistan. But by the following summer (July, 1980), Carter's approval rating had fallen to 21 percent, the lowest in the four decades of the Gallup poll. Patrick Caddell, chief of surveys for Carter, also felt that the 1980 campaign was essentially a negative one focused on the widespread disappointment with Carter's performance, competence, and vision (Caddell 1981).

Three measures drawn from the 1980 study show the different evaluation given Carter by women and men. In the spring (April-May wave), the question was asked: "Do you approve or disapprove of the way Jimmy Carter is handling the job as president?" Men indicated 41 percent approval with 59 percent disapproval. Women, in contrast, gave Carter 6 percentage points more approval (47 percent), and were six points lower in their disapproval than men (53 percent), although this measure showed varying support during the campaign. The data are presented in table 46.

Lake (1982) made a careful analysis of attitudes toward Carter's handling a number of other issues using the same data, and she found that across these issues women tended to feel less disapproving of Carter than did men. The smallest difference in disapproval rate was over Carter's handling of unemployment and the hostage situation in Iran. Men's disapproval of Carter's actions to stem unemployment and inflation increased during the course of the campaign. Disapproval of Carter among women was highest in regard to energy, inflation, and unemployment. She concluded that Carter was not perceived as a good leader by either men or women, and faith in his leadership abilities declined during the campaign.

The relatively abstract issues of inflation and unemployment did not reveal major differences between women and men. One question which especially captured the electorate's turn to Reagan, particularly the late deciders, asked whether the respondent felt her or his family

Table 46.   Evaluation of Carter's Handling of the Presidency

	Strongly Approve	Approve	Disapprove	Strongly Disapprove
Women	21%	26%	20%	33%
Men	15	26	18	41

Source of Data: Center for Political Studies, American National Election Studies, 1980.

was better or worse off financially compared to a year earlier. Forty-one percent of the men said they were worse off, but 49 percent of the women felt that way, as indicated in table 47. It is instructive to note that almost half (45 percent) of the population felt themselves to be worse off. On this response women were eight percentage points more pessimistic than men.

In 1980 women appeared to look at the economic issues differently from men. We noted in chapter 4 that women in previous elections were somewhat more liberal on social welfare issues than men. This distinction, however, has not been obviously associated with women's voting preferences. Lake's analysis found women more liberal than men in 1980 on social welfare measures, that is, being more in favor of continuing government services and not cutting spending, and of federal guarantee of jobs. She found further that in comparing their individual attitudes on federal policies related to reducing inflation, government spending, and defense spending, men were more inclined than women to distance themselves from current Carter policy. Since there is a marked difference when race is introduced into this discussion, we will pursue these questions when we look at the attitudes and voting by black women.

A third measure of candidate evaluation is a "feeling thermometer" which allows a respondent to indicate the degree of warmth or coolness felt toward candidates or social issues. On this scale too, women in the pre-election survey showed their greater support for Jimmy Carter (65 percent of the women were classified as positive versus 56 percent of the men). The tilt by women toward Carter continued through to election day, although there was a slight defection in June.

A fourth measure of attitude toward the presidential contenders involves an assessment of candidate traits. Markus and Converse

Table 47.   Financial Condition Now Compared to a Year Ago, 1980

	Better	Same	Worse
Women	27%	24%	49%
Men	33	26	41

Source of Data: Center for Political Studies, American National Election Studies, 1980.

(1979) have observed that perceptions of a candidate's personal traits are increasingly important in helping the voter to come to a decision. Survey respondents in 1980 were asked to indicate whether seven adjectives—moral, dishonest, weak, knowledgeable, power hungry, inspiring, and providing strong leadership—described each of the major political figures. Markus (1981) used a statistical technique known as factor analysis to construct competence and integrity indices for Carter and Reagan in 1980. He depicted the public's perception of Carter in February as "one of a basically good man, but one whose leadership skills were in doubt. This assessment did not change dramatically over the year, but whatever change did occur was negative" (1981, p. 5).

This negative image of Carter was not linked with a correspondingly positive image of Reagan. As late as mid-June, a considerable percentage of voters were simply unable to describe Reagan's personal qualities with the seven adjectives provided. Further, equally large proportions of women and men had reservations about Reagan's competence and integrity: 36 percent placed him at the low end of the competence index, and 26 percent placed him at the low end of the integrity index.

The 1980 election was remarkable not only for the public's lack of enthusiasm toward the two major candidates but also for the activity of credible third party candidates. John Anderson's Independent campaign received support from nearly 25 percent of the electorate in mid-June, only five months before the election. He suffered the fate of most minor party candidates, however, and lost support as voters perceived he had no real chance to win. Credible presidential campaigns were also run by the Libertarian party's Ed Clark and the Citizen's party's Barry Commoner. LaDonna Harris, a feminist activist and leader in American Indian politics, ran as vice-presidential candidate on the Commoner ticket. However, minor party candidates traditionally lose badly in presidential elections.

Party Identification

Party identification has been generally stable over thirty years as a major determinant of vote choice. The 1976 and 1980 elections have been characterized as reflecting a new era of electoral dealignment and instability. The electorate, observers contend, was less tied to parties, ideologies, and candidates than ever before. One indicator of this is the high proportion of voters who did not decide on a presidential candidate until very late in the election. Another indicator is the drop in the percentage of citizens willing to call themselves Democrats or Republicans.

Did women differ from men in their party allegiance in the 1980 election? A remarkable similarity between women and men in their self-designation of party preference has existed in the data of the Center for Political Studies from 1952 to 1976, as noted in chapter 4. The first real break in this pattern of similarity in party preference was revealed in 1976 when 5 percent (p. 67) more women than men were likely to describe themselves as Democrats (53 percent as compared to 48 percent). Although party identification as designated by the respondent does not necessarily coincide with actual vote choice, it was more influential for women than for men in 1980.

As table 48 shows, women expressed a 4 percent higher preference for the Democratic party than did men and 2 percent less identification with the Republican party (combining percentages). Women were 4 percent less inclined to select the independent choice. It is significant also that the same small percentage of men and women (2 percent) identified themselves as "apolitical." We noted in chapter 4 that the oldest generation in the electorate contained women who

Table 48.   Gender Differences in the Distribution of Party Identification, 1980

Party Identification	Men	Women
Strong Democrat	20%	16%
Weak Democrat	18	27
Independent Democrat	12	11
Independent	15	11
Independent Republican	12	9
Weak Republican	14	14
Strong Republican	8	9
Apolitical	2	2

Source of Data: Center for Political Studies, American National Election Studies, 1980.

were more inclined than comparable men to describe themselves as "apolitical" (12 percent in 1952; 16 percent in 1956). Their disappearance has benefited the overall statistics reporting the increasing politicization of women.

The results in 1980 have additional meaning if we apply a statistical technique called normal vote analysis which distinguishes the effects of long-term historical voting patterns from short-term fluctuations due to the influences in a current election. This theory argues that party identification is a long-term force in influencing partisan choice. In 1980, the expected Democratic vote was 54 percent by women and 53 percent by men. In fact, deviations from the normal vote produced an 11 percent gap in the vote for Reagan between men and women. This was the celebrated gender gap. The relationship between vote and party self-identification is shown in table 49. Women who identified with the Democratic party, however weakly, voted in higher percentages for Carter than did men. The most revealing category in the table presents the votes of independents. Seventy-seven percent of the independent men compared to 49 percent of the independent women voted for Reagan. Thirty percent of the independent women voted for Carter as compared to 5 percent of the independent men. The number of people who identify themselves as independents has increased over recent years but varies considerably from survey to survey. The commercial polls found as many as one-third of the voters and nonvoters in this category in 1980.

Did the disparity between men and women in party allegiance continue into the election in 1982? Among pollsters who have examined this question, Harris commented:

For President Reagan and the Republicans, the single and most formidable obstacle to their becoming a majority party in the 1980s is the vote of women. . . . Below the surface, the concerns of women about the Reagan Administration are more evident in two principle areas. One is the traditionally greater worry among women about the nation getting into war, while the other is the widespread view among all adults that women are not treated equally to men in economic and financial matters. [Press release, August 3, 1981]

Table 49. Vote by Men and Women by Self-Identified Political Party Preference, 1980

Party Preference	Reagan	Carter	Anderson	Other
Strong Democrats				
Men	8%	89%	3%	0%
Women	5	91	4	0
Weak Democrats				
Men	37	53	10	0
Women	32	58	10	0
Independent Democrats				
Men	39	45	15	0
Women	17	58	17	8
Independents				
Men	77	5	14	4
Women	49	30	15	6
Independent Republicans				
Men	80	6	14	0
Women	65	18	15	3
Weak Republicans				
Men	88	3	7	1
Women	84	6	8	1
Strong Republicans				
Men	97	0	3	0
Women	98	2	0	0

Source of Data: Center for Political Studies, American National Election Studies, 1980.

The split between men and women in party preference continued into the 1982 election. Women favored Democratic over Republican candidates by twenty-one points in congressional races according to the ABC exit polls, and they provided margins of victory for Democratic candidates in congressional and state legislative races in many states. The women's vote was given credit in particular for electing Democratic governors in the key states of New York, Texas, and Michigan.

Are Women More Conservative than Men?

One of the most interesting questions raised by the 1980 election is whether Reagan received a mandate to move the country in a conservative direction. If so, we might expect that women contributed to that drift. As we pointed out in chapter 8, a recurrent theme in Western European political analyses has been that women are more conservative than men. This tendency has been particularly notice-able in Catholic countries and in environments where traditional social roles dominate. We saw some changes underway, however. In Italy, for example, women have moved away from conservatism in their support of parties on the Left, and in supporting measures such as divorce and abortion. We presented evidence that in a recent election in Great Britain, women and men supported the Conserva-tive party in similar proportions.

Are American women in fact more conservative than men, and did they contribute to a genuine conservative shift in the 1980 elec-tion? One way to examine this question is to look for gender differ-ences in self-designation along a continuum ranging from conserva-tive to liberal. The CPS surveys have traditionally included such an item, which makes it possible to detect change over time. According to Converse (1964), however, most voters did not use ideological terms such as liberalism and conservatism to evaluate political parties and candidates in the early Michigan surveys. The change appears to have occurred in the 1964 election (Nie, Verba, and Petrocik 1976).

Contrary to popular journalism which has suggested that a conser-vative trend has been evident for some years, the Michigan data reveal only a slight variance in self-designated ideological outlook of the electorate from 1972 to 1978. The proportion of respondents who identified themselves as conservatives, out of the subset of respon-dents who were willing to choose any ideological position, rose from 37 percent in 1978 to 44 percent in 1980. If these figures also include the nearly one-third of respondents (32 percent of the women and 26 percent of the men) who stated after the election that they had not thought much about categorizing themselves as conservatives or lib-erals, the percent of conservative self-identifiers drops to 31 percent (26 percent of the women and 38 percent of the men).

The self-report of respondents as liberals, moderates, or conserva-tives in the 1972, 1976, and 1980 studies are shown in table 50. The percent of liberals fell six points from 1972 to 1980 and the percent of conservatives increased seven points. As presented in table 51, men

Table 50.   Ideological Orientation by Men and Women, 1972–80

Orientation	1972	1976	1980
Liberal	26%	24%	20%
Moderate	37	38	36
Conservative	37	38	44

Source of Data: Center for Political Studies, American National Election Studies, 1972, 1976, 1980.

Table 51.   Self-Placement on Seven-Point Liberal/Conservative Scale, 1980

Self-Placement	Men	Women
Extremely Liberal	2%	1%
Liberal	7	5
Slightly Liberal	9	8
Moderate	17	20
Slightly Conservative	16	11
Conservative	14	11
Extremely Conservative	2	2

Source of Data: Center for Political Studies, American National Election Studies, 1980.

were more likely to call themselves conservatives in 1980 than were women (32 percent and 24 percent, respectively). Men were also more likely to call themselves liberals (18 percent versus 14 percent). It is significant that 33 percent of the men and 42 percent of the women chose not to label themselves.

We also looked at liberal-conservative self-designation by level of education. The greatest contrast was among respondents with less than a high school education. Sixty-three percent of men in that category designated themselves as conservative, contrasted with 38 percent of women. Only 18 percent of the men declared themselves liberal while 27 percent of the women did. Among high school graduates, 52 percent of both women and men labeled themselves conservative. Similarly, 40 percent of college-educated women and men declared themselves conservative. There is no simple explanation for the finding that at the lowest level of education, half as many women as men considered themselves conservative. It can be argued that poorly educated women were particularly disadvantaged by the economic hard times of the late 1970s and began to favor more liberal political solutions. The less well-educated women also voted for Reagan at a lower rate than did their male counterparts.

The connection generally among the citizen's expression of ideological outlook, attitude toward issues, and vote decision is not easily determined. As we have declared previously, voting is a complex form of behavior which does not lend itself to simple analysis. The meaning of an election is not always clear. Other analysts have made assessments of the long-run implications of 1980, and have found interesting emphases. Frankovic looked at CBS/*New York Times* post-election polls and concluded:

> Overall, there is no reason to accept the election outcome in 1980 as indicating a conservative tide in this country, even though the elected candidate was clearly known and perceived by a majority of the electorate as a conservative. Movements on specific issues were minor, and while some of the issues were related to candidate preference in 1980, these issues have historically separated Democratic and Republican voters. [1981, p. 115]

Two leading experts, Warren E. Miller and Merrill Shanks, concluded from Michigan data:

> . . . although partisan and ideological predispositions plus performance evaluations were the decisive factors in explaining the variation between voters in their final [1980] choices, dominant preferences for a change in the direction of federal policy must be given at least parity in explaining the Reagan victory. [1982, p. 352]

Other experts, Arthur H. Miller and Martin P. Wattenberg, looking at the same data were in agreement, but with a slightly different perspective:

> The electorate as a whole did not enthusiastically support Reagan's proposed programs. In fact, defecting Democrats, the group that gave Reagan his margin of victory, did not consider themselves conservatives; nor were they in total agreement with him on the critical issues. [1981, p. 19]

Their key emphasis was that issues were salient in the 1980 election, and that ideology had less impact in 1980 than it did in 1976. Carter lost his constituency, thus weakening the correlation between ideology and the vote.

Interestingly, Gallup found no evidence that a conservative tide was sweeping the electorate. When his interviewers asked Americans in late November, 1980, to place themselves along a Left-Right continuum, the proportion who said they were "right of center" was virtually identical to the proportion documented in 1976 (Gallup, November 20, 1980, p. 16). In the exit polls conducted by CBS/New York Times on election day, only one of ten voters cited his or her conservatism as a major reason for their support of Reagan.

In conclusion, women in 1980 were somewhat less inclined to call themselves conservatives and supported the conservative candidate, Ronald Reagan, in fewer numbers than did men. Further, the 1980 election did not signal a major turn to the ideological right. However, the results are sufficiently complex to permit President Reagan to declare his victory a mandate.

The Campaign Issues

Peace/War Policy

Although women do not recognize it, they have voted together at times on one crucial issue: opposition to war. As we described in chapter 4, foreign policy since 1950 far more than any other issue has divided men and women. This tendency, reflected in the women's vote, results from shared personal attitudes and not from political organization. Public opinion polls have repeatedly described women as more opposed than men to American military involvement in Korea, Southeast Asia, and in other areas of the world. Women continue to be more peace-minded than men in survey findings.

The peace/war issue was a prominent one in 1980 for two reasons. First, Reagan's support for significantly increased defense spending and his Cold War view of contemporary international relations were perceived by many voters as his most distinctive policy positions. Second, these issues are exactly the ones which have historically divided women and men the most. It is our speculation that the gender gap in 1980 (an 8 percent lower vote for Reagan by women) had its origins in this issue.

A major difficulty in predicting how the antiwar sentiments of women translate into candidate support or opposition lies in specifying which position on an issue is the peace-oriented one and which is relatively war-oriented. The CPS study did not contain many items on the war/peace issue, but it does offer some insights into the attitudes of women and men on defense spending and détente with the Soviet Union. Further, we can show how voters with more "peaceful" attitudes were more likely to support Carter than Reagan.

A number of social scientists have suggested that the Democratic party had the advantage in 1980 on the peace issue. Gallup (1980) found, in the fall of the election year, that almost half of the electorate (42 percent) thought that the Democrats were more likely to keep the country out of World War Three. He found further that only 25 percent felt that the Republicans were more apt to avoid war.

When asked in the Michigan survey whether defense spending should be increased or decreased, similarly low percentages of women and men replied that spending should decrease (11 and 9 percent, respectively) as shown in table 52. Men significantly surpassed women in support of a spending increase for defense (72 percent of men compared to 54 percent of women). These interviews were taken at a time when the international environment was profoundly disturbing. United States hostages were being held in Iran. The Soviet Union had invaded Afghanistan. The evident decline of American power overseas became a hotly debated topic in the campaign.

Carter's effort to establish stable relations with the Soviet Union and Reagan's long-standing hostility toward the Russians made détente an important campaign issue. The interviewees were asked whether they felt it important for the United States to try to get along with Russia or whether trying would be a mistake. As table 52 shows, 32 percent of the women but 37 percent of the men gave prodétente responses. Women also gave less support than men to an antidétente position (29 percent versus 36 percent). Women were more likely to indicate a neutral position or to say that they hadn't thought much about it.

Table 52. Attitudes toward Defense Spending, Détente, and Candidate Support, 1980

Question:	Some people believe that we should spend much less money for defense. Others feel that defense spending should be greatly increased. Where would you place yourself on this scale, or haven't you thought much about this?

	Women	Men
Decrease spending	11%	9%
Neutral	18	12
Increase spending	54	72
Haven't thought about it	17	7

Question:	Some people feel it is important for us to try very hard to get along with Russia. Others feel it is a big mistake to try too hard to get along with Russia. Where do you place yourself on this scale, or haven't you thought much about this?

	Women	Men
Prodétente	32%	37%
Neutral	22	20
Antidétente	29	36
Haven't thought about it	17	7

Attitude toward Détente	Candidate Supported	
	Reagan	*Carter*
Women		
Prodétente	29%	50%
Neutral	28	24
Antidétente	43	26
Men		
Prodétente	36	50
Neutral	21	23
Antidétente	43	27

Source of Data: Center for Political Studies, American National Election Studies, 1980.

In an effort to shake his "warmonger" image, Reagan contended throughout the campaign that the chances for peace would increase with a tougher stance toward the Soviet Union. The data presented above indicate that women did not accept this as the most likely means to secure world peace.

When the respondents are classified by the pro- or antidétente attitude and the candidate they supported, as shown in table 52, it is clear that women and men who supported détente were more likely to vote for Carter than for Reagan. Among women who said they voted for Reagan, only 29 percent held a prodétente attitude; among women voting for Carter, 50 percent were prodétente. The percentages switch when we look at antidétente women and their candidates. Here, 43 percent of Reagan's supporters but only 26 percent of Carter's had antidétente attitudes. The same patterns hold for men. While we cannot conclude that a respondent's attitude on the détente issue determined her or his vote, we can say that voters clearly perceived and supported the candidate who shared their view of international politics.

Analysts working with different data sets from the 1980 campaign generally agreed with these conclusions. Schneider stated:

> Both the CBS/*New York Times* poll and the NBC/AP poll asked people whether they felt that if Reagan were elected president he would get us into a war. Between 32 and 39 percent of the public answered yes in eight different polls. Significantly, women indicated greater concern on this point than men. That appears to be one reason why, throughout the campaign and on election day, Reagan did notably worse among women than among men. Men tend to give greater emphasis to defense, and women tend to give more to peace, in forming opinions on foreign policy. Reagan's toughness on foreign policy had a good deal to do with the differentiation of the candidates in this area. But so did Jimmy Carter's record. Preserving peace was Carter's one substantial accomplishment, and the voters seemed to be aware of it. [1981, p. 234]

Clymer examined a CBS/*New York Times* poll of 12,782 voters as they left the voting booth on election day, and concluded:

Mr. Reagan's long-standing difficulties in persuading women to vote for him held down his percentage again Tuesday. These problems were strongest among women at either end of the educational scale, those with less than a high school education and those who had graduated from college. The poll suggested that both fear about war and his opposition to the ERA handicapped Mr. Reagan's bid for their support. [*New York Times*, November 9, 1980, p. 28]

Smith, Director of the National Opinion Research Center, was quoted as follows:

In the last election we had the largest sex difference in history, a 10 percent edge for Carter among women. . . . The principal election factor among men and women was economic performance under Carter. After that, war and peace was the biggest concern among women, followed by ERA and possibly abortion. On social women's issues—abortion, ERA, would you vote for a woman president—there is traditionally no difference between men and women, or men even are a little more liberal. On anything to do with war or violence—capital punishment, gun control—there is a 10 percent to 20 percent difference, with women the more cautious. [Quoted by Cattani, *Christian Science Monitor*, July 9, 1981, p. 6.]

And finally we quote Elizabeth Drew, who monitored the campaign on a day-to-day basis. Her comments give us one explanation for Reagan's view on foreign policy:

Wirthlin's [Reagan's chief survey consultant] polling also has indicated that a percentage of people—about 44 percent—considered Reagan "dangerous." They respond affirmatively when they are asked whether Reagan is best described by the phrase. "He is most likely to get us into an unnecessary war." [1981, p. 313]

She wrote further:

In part, the Reagan people think, this is related to the fact that Reagan comes across as the stronger leader. . . . They concede it has to do with the statements that Reagan has made in the past about areas in which he might intervene with military force, including his suggestion, in January, 1980, that one option for reacting to Soviet invasion of Afghanistan was a blockade of Cuba—a suggestion to which George Bush, among others, took great exception—and his recent comment about the SALT treaty and arms race. Some people around Reagan have suggested to me that one of the factors at work here is that many of the people who are supposed to advise Reagan on foreign policy have their roots in the world of defense and strategic planning, and that when Reagan himself is dealing with foreign policy issues he tends to think in terms of strategic weaponry—the B-1 bomber and so on. And in part it has been because Carter's attacks have taken hold. [1981, p. 313]

Thus our conclusion that the peace/war issue had more influence on women than on men in 1980 is supported in a range of surveys during the course of the campaign. Its ranking and relationship in regard to other issues is not altogether clear, but our surmise is that the gender gap had its origins in women's perception of Reagan as more likely than Carter to involve the country in war.

Race

Black voters provided the only major element of the old Democratic coalition that stayed with President Carter in customary proportions. Blacks divided 82 percent for Carter, 14 percent for Reagan, and 3 percent for Anderson (CBS/*New York Times* election day poll).

We can look with interest at 1980 to update the behavior of black women.[4] In chapters 5 and 6, we noted their unique record of having voted at higher rates than black men and at rates higher than their socioeconomic status would predict. Overall, 53 percent of black women voted in 1980, as compared to 48 percent of black men (U.S., Department of Commerce, 1980). The higher voting rate of black women was evident at all age levels except for the oldest cohort (seventy-five years and older). This is a continuation of a pattern since 1952 showing that black women have increased their voting at higher rates than black men. White women also voted at slightly higher rates than men until the age of fifty-five, as found in the Census Bureau survey.

Since the Reagan campaign appeared to make very little effort to attract the black voter, it is reasonable to understand why blacks carried over their support of Carter from 1976. We can look at the black vote on three particular dimensions which suggest the tone of the environment for blacks during the campaign. First, we can return to the scale of political efficacy, designed as a measure of subjective sense of involvement by an individual in the political system, as discussed at some length in chapter 3. The main significance of the scale is that a high sense of political efficacy has been shown to be correlated with voting. However, in 1980 all voters seemed to have a negative view of the campaign. One would expect to find a decline in sense of efficacy, and this is the case for men and women of both races. Efficacy declined more for women than for men. On every measure of the scale the decline is higher for women of both races, doubling for black women and with white women ranging about 10 percent lower in efficacy than men. Table 53 presents the data for one efficacy item to show the differentiation between men and women.

Trust in government officials was also very low in the 1980 campaign. As discussed in chapter 6, trust is one aspect of political involvement and is closely linked to participation. Both races evidenced considerable lack of trust and at remarkably similar levels on two questions relating to trust in governmental officials (see table 54). White men appeared to have the most faith in the intelligence of government leaders; white women had the least faith that Washington officials are honest.

A related issue is faith in the judgment of civil rights leaders. When asked about the speed of civil rights leaders in pushing for

Table 53. Responses by Race and Gender to Item Measuring Sense of Political Efficacy, 1980

Question:	*Sometimes politics seems so complicated that a person like me can't understand what's going on.*	
	Agree	Disagree
Black women	85%	15%
Black men	75	25
White women	77	23
White men	61	39

Source of Data: Center for Political Studies, American National Election Studies, 1980.

Table 54. Responses by Race and Gender to Items about Government Officials and Civil Rights Leaders, 1980

Question: *Do you feel that almost all of the people running the government are smart people, or do you think that quite a few of them don't seem to know what they are doing?*

	Are Smart People	Don't Know What They Are Doing
Black women	27%	68%
Black men	28	69
White women	32	64
White men	37	59

Question: *Do you think that quite a few of the people running the government are crooked, not very many are, or do you think hardly any of them are crooked?*

	Not Many/Hardly Any Crooked	Quite a Few Crooked
Black women	52%	49%
Black men	52	48
White women	49	51
White men	55	45

Question: *Do you think that civil rights leaders are trying to push too fast, are going too slowly, or are they moving at about the right speed?*

	Too Fast	About Right	Too Slowly
Black women	7%	47%	32%
Black men	5	42	52
White women	34	51	7
White men	36	45	10

Source of Data: Center for Political Studies, American National Election Studies, 1980.

blacks' rights, black women showed greater patience with their leaders than did black men. Thirty-two percent and 52 percent, respectively, replied that civil rights leaders are going "too slowly." The comparable figures among white women and men are 7 and 10 percent, as shown in table 54.

On a related issue focusing on busing, 94 percent of the white sample favored keeping children in their own neighborhoods. Blacks were generally less favorable, with women twelve percentage points more favorable than black men.

The disillusionment found among black voters continued into the 1982 election. The Joint Center for Political Studies, which monitors issues of concern to blacks, reported that the ferment among black voters, particularly in the South, helped reverse a twenty-year trend of declining participation in midterm elections. The Center (1980) found black turnout to be a crucial factor in several southern Democratic victories. Three black men were newly elected to Congress, and the number of blacks elected to state legislatures increased by seventeen.

Religion and the Moral Majority

There is a general feeling in popular journalism that women are disproportionately represented in the following of the "Christian right." Some members formed special interest groups in the late 1970s, and became very active in the 1980 election. The most visible of these, the Moral Majority, was organized partially by television preachers, including the Reverend Jerry Falwell. These groups seemed motivated primarily by social issues because in their view, a moral and spiritual decline was endangering the health of the nation. This movement built large television audiences, raised millions of dollars for political action, and claimed victories in supporting conservative candidates, mostly running under the Republican label. Key issues for the evangelical leaders and activists were opposition to abortion, equal rights for women, homosexuality.

Many feminists viewed the political rise of these ultraconservative evangelicals as a response to the success of the women's movement in changing American attitudes toward equality for women. The well-financed political action committees of the Moral Majority targeted a number of prominent liberals in Congress, most of whom had championed women's rights. Many of these politicians lost, but by margins significantly smaller than those by which Carter lost their home states. The Moral Majority also threw their support behind the Reagan candidacy. Although the group garnered extensive media coverage, they received little empathetic support among the electorate surveyed in the 1980 study. Respondents were asked whether they felt particularly close to each of eighteen groups, such as middle-class people, whites, conservatives, labor unions, and "evangelical groups active in politics, such as the Moral Majority." The latter group ranked fourteenth and was mentioned by only 1 percent of the respondents. Among those who did identify with the Moral Majority, however, women outnumbered men.

There is a growing literature looking at the effects of religion on the role and status of women. The general impression is that women are found in greater numbers than men in supporting religious beliefs and in church attendance. We looked briefly at the influence of the church on black women in chapter 6 and quoted Stone (1979, p. 581) as saying that the church was the most important social institution in the black community, and the one in which the black woman spent most of her time and energy. One would expect, therefore, that women would have been prominent in following the leadership of the conservative evangelicals.

These questions can only be partially answered from the existing data. As we noted in chapter 8, extensive cross-cultural research has been conducted on the correlates of religious orientation. Women living in countries where religious influences were strong and authoritarian, and where traditional sex roles were prevalent, were slower in achieving the right to vote and to participate in politics.

In the 1980 American data, women declared themselves considerably more religious-minded and influenced by religion than did men. Eighty-one percent of the women versus 67 percent of the men considered religion to be a very important part of their lives. Further, religion did influence voting behavior. Women who identified themselves with the Moral Majority or indicated that they were very religious were much more likely to vote for Reagan than were their less religious sisters. This was the only demographic segment of women in 1980 that defected from their normal voting preference (based on education, region, party identification, and several other variables) to support Reagan in the same magnitude as did comparable men (Lake 1982). In other words, religious women and men who would have been expected to support Carter were more likely to support Reagan instead. In other segments of the electorate, as shown earlier, men were more likely than women to abandon their presumed support for Carter and to vote for Reagan.

Gallup conducted a national survey in August, 1980, to measure the level of public awareness of the Moral Majority and to investigate the attitudes of individuals following that fundamentalist political movement. He found that less than half the sample (40 percent) had heard or read about the Moral Majority, and only 26 percent were familiar with its objectives. Among the latter group, disapproval of the Moral Majority outweighed approval (13 percent to 8 percent, with 5 percent undecided). However, in his descriptive profile of evangelicals he found more women than men (62 percent of the women versus 38 percent of the men, Gallup 1981). These observations would suggest that more women than men may be found in the evangelical following. However, that is probably true because the evangelicals draw much of their support from the older groups and women outnumber men in those cohorts.

Environmental Issues

Women differ from men on federal policy regarding the use of nuclear energy, as we noted in chapter 4. This pattern continued in the 1980 election survey with only half as many women as men favoring the construction of more nuclear plants, as shown in table 55. Twenty-one percent of the women, as compared with 14 percent of the men, favored closing all nuclear plants.

There is also a gender gap in regard to governmental regulation of the environment. As table 55 indicates, 23 percent of the men compared to 14 percent of the women favored relaxing governmental standards. We looked at this question by age and found that the oldest male cohort was considerably more inclined to relax governmental standards (33 percent) than were comparable women (15 percent).

Women's Issues

Women's policy preferences can become national policy through a variety of means. Some activists advocate the emergence of a power-

Table 55. Responses by Gender to Items about Environmental Issues, 1980

Question: *Some people say that the nation needs to develop new power sources from nuclear energy in order to meet our needs for the future. Other people say that the danger to the environment and the possibility of accident are too great. What do you think?*

	Build More Nuclear Plants	Operate Only Those Built	Close Down All Plants
Women	24%	55%	21%
Men	50	36	14

Question: *Present government regulations with regard to pollution and other environmental problems limit full use of some energy sources. Do you think the government should relax environmental protection regulations to increase the use of these energy sources, or should the government keep environmental protection regulations unchanged even though this may delay the production of more energy? Should the government relax government regulations on environment a lot, some, or just a little?*

	A Little	Some	A Lot
Women	19%	67%	14%
Men	17	60	23

Source of Data: Center for Political Studies, American National Election Studies, 1980.

ful women's voting bloc which will become forceful enough in politics to enact the women's agenda. Another avenue is for the American electorate to come to agree with women's positions and then act politically to make public policy consonant with them. We showed in chapter 7 that support for four feminist issues had clearly increased between 1972 and 1976. Responses in 1980 to the first item, the belief that women should play an equal role with men, have already been discussed in terms of a seven-point continuum. Sixty-two percent of both women and men placed themselves within the first three points, indicating support for the equal role position. This represents an increase of 16 percent from their 1976 levels.

Table 56 presents the extent of support for three other feminist

Table 56.   Support for Feminist Issues, 1980

	Women	Men
Do you approve or disapprove of the proposed Equal Rights Amendment to the Constitution, sometimes called the ERA Amendment? (Approve)	63%	60%
In general, do you agree or disagree with the following statement: Our society discriminates against women? (Agree)	56	55
There's been some discussion about abortion during recent years. Which of these opinions best agrees with your view?		
Abortion should never be permitted.	10	9
Abortion should be permitted only if the life and health of the woman is in danger	44	44
Abortion should be permitted if, due to personal reasons, the woman would have difficulty in caring for the child.	16	20
Abortion should never be forbidden, since one should not require a woman to have a child she doesn't want.	29	24

Source of Data: Center for Political Studies, American National Election Studies, 1980.

issues. When asked whether they support the Equal Rights Amendment, about 60 percent of both women and men stated that they did; when asked whether society discriminates against women, about 55 percent of all respondents agreed. Presented with four statements about abortion, almost half of the people surveyed agreed that abortion should never be forbidden or that it should be allowed if, due to personal reasons, the women would have difficulty caring for the child. On all of these questions, the proportions of women and men agreeing with the feminist position are quite high and strikingly similar.

These findings suggest there is a growing coalition of proequality voters, to use Gloria Steinem's term, which captures the larger constituency in regard to political issues. After acknowledging that analysts often look no further than classic women's issues for signs of bloc voting, she contends that

> There are also unique issues of reproductive, economic and social equality for which women of all races are both the natural support and the natural constituency. If we don't take our lessons seriously, who will? Even if, as individuals, we care more about the issues of war and peace, we still must be powerful enough as women to make our cultural values felt. [1980, p. 103]

The term also implies that future analyses should move beyond the search for significant differences between women's and men's political attitudes and behavior to look for commonalities and self-aware alliances. These may provide the best opportunity for women's rights to become the human rights agenda. When that happens, the gender gap will close and disappear.

Activists and Candidates

The political status of women is not entirely determined by voting turnout. As we argued in chapter 7, there are other forms of political participation that take place outside the voting booth and beyond the temporal bounds of an election. Table 22 in chapter 7 compares the level of participation of men and women in a variety of electoral and nonelectoral activities. Nonvoting activities, such as attending political meetings and rallies, have involved less than 10 percent of the respondents on the key measures across the twenty-eight years examined in this analysis. The pattern of low involvement continued into the 1980 election. Only 7 percent of the women and 8 percent of the men interviewed had attended a meeting or rally. Even for the most popular activity, only 33 percent of the women and 40 percent of the men reported trying to influence the vote of others.

Curbstone observation of the increasing grass roots activism raises a question as to the validity of this measure. As V. O. Key, Jr., observed years ago, national surveys may not sample many people who meet the standard definition of political activists. Even so, it is clear that political activity remains a low priority for women and men. However, the number of women who attended the national nominating convention increased between 1976 and 1980. Further, women at the Democratic National Convention had sufficient clout to pass a resolution limiting support in the states for candidates who did not support the Equal Rights Amendment. Republican women suffered a loss when their party rejected support of this amendment.

The major women's political organizations such as NOW, the National Women's Political Caucus, the National Women's Education Fund, and the Women's Campaign Fund were very successful in 1980. They raised more money for women and feminist candidates, sent out more mailings, and spent more effort emphasizing the records of the major national candidates on women's issues than ever before.

The major grass roots effort in recent years has been the extraordinary organized energy of women who identified with the campaign to ratify the Equal Rights Amendment in the states. This campaign cut across partisan lines and brought organizations such as the League of Women Voters and the National Federation of Business and Professional Women into the forefront of lobbying as never before. The campaign for ERA served to educate and unify many women who had not previously been knowledgeable or caring about the legal and economic discriminations against women in American society. The ERA effort served to encourage women to vote and think differently from men in the 1980 and 1982 elections.

We also showed in chapter 7 that the percentage of women elected to high public offices had risen only incrementally between 1975 and 1977. The small but steady increase continued through the 1980 election. According to figures compiled by the National Women's Education Fund, women increased their presence in the state legislatures by about 1 percent each election, from 9 percent in 1977 to 10 percent in 1979, and 12 percent in 1981.

In 1982, NOW had targeted both the Illinois and the Florida legislatures where the fight to ratify the ERA had been finally lost in

June of that year. NOW support helped to elect nine women to the Florida Senate, and enough women's rights legislators to the Florida and Illinois houses to secure ratification in those states.

Women broke new ground by fielding more candidates for state office in 1982 than in previous years. Two major-party women candidates ran, though unsuccessfully, for governor. However, there were seven major-party candidates for lieutenant governor, with three elected in 1982, making a total of seven women holding this post.

At the national level, the change has been even slower. In 1975, there were nineteen women in the United States Congress; in 1980, there were only twenty (or 4 percent of the two chambers). Eleanor Smeal, president of NOW, calculated that at this rate, it would take women "217 years to reach parity, a prospect which does not give you solace." In 1982 three major-party candidates ran and lost senate seats. More women than before ran for the House of Representatives with thirty-three losing and twenty-one winning. Although 1982 did not mark the year when women candidates won more contests than ever before, there were a number of important victories which may affect elections in the future.

The organization NOW participated in elections in 1982 more seriously than before, and claimed in some months to be raising more funds than the Democratic National Committee. Although women did not win as many contests as they had hoped, it was apparent that in a number of races there was an advantage for the first time in American politics for the candidate to be a woman. An example of this phenomenon was found in a state legislative race in Washtenaw County, Michigan. Lana Pollack defeated by a two-to-one margin, two men career-candidates in the primary and won the election by defeating a male candidate who had served sixteen years in the Michigan House of Representatives.

The outlook for women as candidates is not altogether clear. Women have made remarkable advances in breaking down the barriers which limit admission to the professions that have historically led to careers in politics. Actually sharing the power held by political elites may be the most difficult goal to achieve. A hopeful sign is found in the research of Welch and Sigelman (1982) who looked at public attitudes toward women in 1972, 1974, and 1978. They found modest increases in public support for women being politically active. Solid support was found among young people and those with more education. As the American population becomes both older and better educated, some of this support should help break down the remaining barriers to full political equality.

Summary and Conclusions

The 1980 presidential election was a milestone for women: for the first time their vote was a recognizable force in American politics. Voting in roughly the same proportions as men, women exceeded men by almost six million votes. The new visibility of this majority group was a result of women in the electorate evaluating candidates and policies differently from men, and in voting for major candidates in different proportions.

The term gender gap, meaning the difference in percentage points in votes cast by women and men, became part of the political vernacular during the 1982 election. The women's vote made the difference in a number of close races. Although four women running for major offices lost, the election clearly demonstrated that candidates patently ignoring women's concerns would probably lose. Women favored Democrats over Republicans by twenty-one points in congressional races according to network exit polls. Women provided margins for victory in the selection of governor in the three major states of Michigan, New York, and Texas. Altogether, the women's vote made the difference in a number of races, thus marking a change from their record in previous elections.

New developments in 1980 included a higher voting rate by housewives than by clerical and sales women for the first time. Professional women continued to turn out at the highest rate and blue collar, working women at the lowest rate. Women in the southern states have increased their voting rate impressively since 1952, and in 1980 they voted at a rate slightly higher than women living in nonsouthern states, but continued to be surpassed by women from border states. The profile of the woman most likely to vote in 1980 had not changed much from her 1976 sister. However, education was no longer the primary determinant of turnout in 1980 as it had been in earlier elections. Age and employment status emerged as the most powerful predictors, followed by education and region.

Although women gave Republican candidate Ronald Reagan the majority of their votes, they were much less supportive of his candidacy than were men. Women were much closer to their level of predicted support for the Democratic candidate than were men. Women expressed a 6 percent higher preference than men for the Democratic party and a 4 percent lower preference for the Republican party. If a realignment of political parties is taking place, it was not reflected in the measurement of partisan loyalties made in 1980.

Religion influenced voting behavior. Women who identified themselves with the Moral Majority or who indicated that they were very religious were more likely to vote for Reagan than were their less religious sisters.

Black women voters stayed with President Carter in customary proportions in 1980, and continued to vote at higher rates than black men, as indicated by the validated vote turnout. Black men and women differed markedly from whites on a number of economic issues, with the black voter favoring the maintenance of high levels of services provided by the federal government.

On environmental issues, women continued to be less favorable than men to a federal policy to build more nuclear plants. Women were also less likely than men to favor relaxing governmental regulations concerning the environment.

On the women's issues the proportions of men and women agreeing with the feminist position are quite high and strikingly similar. The peace question and women's issues clearly influenced the women voters in the 1980 election. There also were gender differences in attitudes regarding many of the economic issues prominent in the campaign.

A single election does not make a long-run trend, but it may offer clues to future events. Voting by men has continued a long-run decline, while women have increased their turnout rate after years of comparable declines. The 1980 election is significant because gender explained much more of the variation in vote than did political party identification and other traditional determinants.

The number of votes cast by women surpassed those cast by men in 1980 and 1982 by ever increasing margins, and their votes often supported different candidates. Is a trend developing? Voting turnout by women is anchored in long-run variables, such as employment experience, a low birthrate, and higher education, which are not subject to short-run reversals. If candidates in a race offer contrasting positions on issues of concern to women, as they often did in 1980 and 1982, the gender gap is likely to continue. On the other hand, if a coalition of "proequality" voters, including women and men, succeeds in ushering in a more egalitarian and peaceful society, gender differences in political attitudes and behaviors will decrease or disappear entirely.

chapter ten

THE OUTLOOK

The presidential election in 1980 emerged as the year of the women's vote. For the first time in a major election, women gained public recognition as having political attitudes and candidate preferences different from men. Their independent voting behavior generated the "gender gap." Because of the greater number of adult women in the population and their tendency to vote in similar proportions as men, women constituted a large electoral majority. About six million more women than men cast ballots in 1980. Until then, women had been an invisible political majority with little influence over governmental policy and the selection and election of candidates. The gender gap was widely discussed during campaigns preceding the 1982 election. Once the votes were counted, they were credited with providing the margin of victory in a number of congressional and state races.

At the same time, issues of particular interest to women gained remarkable acceptance across the country. According to various public opinion surveys, every major issue supported by the women's movement had found majority support from men and women by 1982. These issues included the Equal Rights Amendment, equal pay, equal access to education, women's rights to abortion, acceptance of women in political office, and world peace.

The explanation for this new visibility of women as voters and as issue activists is found in the profound changes taking place in the roles of women in contemporary American society. The significant increase in women's socioeconomic status has given them the background, resources, and interest in playing a more influential political role. With their strength in numbers, leadership experience, and organizational skills, women now have the best opportunity in the sixty years since suffrage to exercise political clout. Their clout is especially powerful in the closely balanced electoral system of the United States. When winning margins are smaller, a well-organized voting bloc can often determine election outcomes, as women demonstrated in 1982.

The social and demographic changes in women's roles make it possible for women in the 1980s to carry the egalitarian thrust of the 1960s and 1970s to its logical conclusion: to elect women to positions of influence in congress, in the administrative bureaucracies, in governor's mansions, in state legislatures, in city halls, and in the federal and state courts.

Another critical issue is whether gender would make a difference if women held political power. The 1982 election suggested a new mystique about the woman candidate. Since women have not been involved in policy fiascos and Washington scandals, and since there are so few in high office, women have not been held accountable for the failures of government. The woman candidate in 1982 was at times perceived as apt to have more integrity and compassion than her male rivals. This advantage was backed by better financed and better organized campaigns than ever before. Although victory was elusive, these developments promise more women in public office in the years ahead.

Many questions are only partially answered here, and their review has been an attempt to provide a status report. Our other purpose in analyzing the interaction of gender with key stratification variables has been to raise issues for investigation in the next round of research on the role of women in American politics. A theme that emerges in this analysis is constancy and change. As we see it, the weakening of traditional gender-role definitions that relegated women to domestic duties at home, and the change in the norms which saw politics as a man's world, have been crucial to the increasing political participation of women. The shift by women to more citizen participation is a reflection of the growing egalitarianism in gender roles. The changes for women are well known. The profound demographic changes, such as the drop in fertility rate, women's continuing entry into the paid work force, and their enrollments in colleges and universities are major developments. The change in the fabric of society associated with the social movements of the 1960s and 1970s are undoubtedly linked to the goal of egalitarianism. The women's movement has encouraged consciousness raising for their sisters to become more assertive in public life, and to organize to upgrade their economic and social status through political action.

What does the future hold? We think the future may well bring women into visible political roles, but the timing of this development is uncertain for a number of reasons. One significant fact is that the women's movement and other similar groups which have been underrepresented in the political system have come upon the hard times of the 1980s. The drift of worldwide events such as the energy shortage and the scarcity of other economic resources at home, coupled with inflation, do not augur well for women to become full partners with men in economics and politics—two areas which are inextricably linked to one another. Yet despite the uncertain economic forecast for the 1980s, our assessment of survey data over thirty years makes it clear that the disparity between the voting turnout of men and women has essentially disappeared. The variables which we have presented as related to women's increasing politicization are anchored in long-run trends. A brief review of the earlier chapters will underscore this point.

The analyses in chapter 2 showed that the difference in voting rates between women and men have narrowed since 1952 to the point where it was negligible in 1976 and even smaller in 1980. College-educated women have long turned out on election days at rates similar to college-educated men. As women have achieved higher education, more income, and greater labor force participation, they have voted at rates increasingly similar to men. These correlates of political participation must be looked at simultaneously because they serve to reinforce each other and to boost collectively the voting rate of women. As we have said, another demographic change of great importance is the decline in fertility rate to the point where, in the 1980s, proportionately fewer women will bear children in the United States than ever before and women who choose to have children will have fewer of them. Many social scientists see changes in the fertility rate with its effects on women's life-styles as the most significant development in the past decade. Shifts in family structure, including living arrangements and the sharing of responsibility for raising children, have important implications for women's increasing entry into mainstream politics. All of these demographic changes, however, will take years to have the impact they promise, and one impact is greater political participation of women.

In chapters 3 and 4, the growing politicization of women between 1952 and 1976 was documented. In terms of the attitudes known to be predictive of political behavior, women and men show little difference in their interest in political campaigns and in their concern over which party wins the presidency. College-educated women hold attitudes very similar to their peer men, while women with only a high school diploma have a lower sense of political efficacy than high school graduate men. Women with little education who regarded themselves as "apolitical" are disappearing from the statistics, as their generation dies off. Across a variety of public policy issues, women have shown a long-term tendency to be more pacifist and less supportive of violent solutions than men, to support the rights of blacks, and to support social welfare policies. Surveys also show that women are more concerned about the safety of nuclear plants and the protection of the environment. Women choose solutions which are not potentially violent.

Deep divisions have split men and women on foreign policy since the Second World War. Women were more opposed than men to American involvement in Korea and Southeast Asia, and by 1972 more women than men still gave ending the war first priority. It is this dove-hawk issue which may have propelled women voters to become the visible majority in the 1980s. It should also be noted that men often join women on this issue, and thus there may well be a pacifist bloc in the electorate. Women were prominent in the nuclear freeze movements in 1980 and 1982. Men also join women in support of many key feminist issues, such as the Equal Rights Amendment and abortion, so that a distinction should be made between a women's vote and a feminist vote.

It should also be noted that women have differed from men in supporting candidates, ranging from Dwight Eisenhower to George Wallace and George McGovern. The difference was especially apparent in the 1980 election of Ronald Reagan. Foreign policy was an important factor in securing women's support or antipathy in these campaigns. In future elections it will be necessary for an organized women's bloc to secure public recognition for its support of one candidate or another. The political environment has changed over the last three decades, and the increasing politicization of women has taken place at a time when the political system is open to new influences. As the hold of the parties over their faithful weakens, groups formerly excluded from the centers of political power now have the best opportunity to play significant roles.

Black women are political minorities on two accounts, and their political behavior and attitudes were investigated in chapters 5 and 6. As recently as 1952, only a third of the eligible black women voted in presidential elections. By 1964, they were arriving at the polls at the same rates as black men; in 1976 and 1980, they surpassed the men. This tremendous increase in electoral participation has taken place while turnout has been generally declining (since 1960) among white women and men, and while the educational, income, and employment levels of black women have remained the lowest in society. Age and education boost the turnout of black and white women in similar ways, so that younger and college-educated black women vote at higher rates than comparable black men. And surprisingly, black women with the least education vote at higher rates than similar white women.

Support for the heightened participation of black women does not lie in the political attitudes correlated with political participation among whites. Contrary to the attitudes found among whites and black men, black women show less trust in government, less satisfaction with and control over the quality of their lives, and a weak sense of political efficacy. Perhaps black women share an interest group identity which both acknowledges their low socioeconomic status and mobilizes them to seek redress through the political system. Part of that identity is based upon gender, and the greater turnout among black women giving feminist responses to a series of questions suggests that the perception of discrimination based upon both their gender and race serves as a motivating factor. In fact, the period of great racial consciousness and the growth of racial pride among blacks coincided with the remarkable increase in black women's political participation in the United States. Black Americans have formed one of the most powerful voting blocs in history, a bloc that has obtained important legislation and visible clout because of its unity. This is the sort of voting bloc that women may be able to organize on some political issues in the near future.

In chapter 7, the discussion of political behavior moved beyond the voting booth to focus upon other electoral and nonelectoral forms of participation. Women have long played significant roles in local volunteer associations and have acquired political skills that may or may not be transferred to formal political settings by their running for public office. Few women have won election to elite positions, but there is a trend for increasing proportions of local office holders to be women. Just as there is now the largest cohort of women in the professions traditionally leading to political careers, the record-setting numbers of women in local offices should result in larger numbers of women joining the political elite in the years ahead. Much of the impetus for women pursuing professional careers and testing their political skills in partisan campaigns has come from the women's movement, ascendant again in 1960 through 1980. Through a nationwide network of organizations and consciousness-raising groups, the movement solidified efforts to obtain important legislation for women.

The portrait of American women sketched in the first seven chapters was compared to that of British and other European women in chapter 8. Attention was first directed to the correlates of turnout documented in chapters 2 through 4 for American women, and their usefulness in explaining the higher turnout of British women. Education leads to higher participation among women in both nations, but British women as a whole are not as well educated as American women. The continuing puzzle was finally solved through recognition of the structural and historical differences between the political systems which make electoral participation easier and less frequently required in Great Britain than in the United States. An examination of the responses of European women and men to a series of questions about gender roles underscored the importance of the cultural differences among the countries. The great support of women and men for changes in gender role definitions across the four European societies bodes well for the future of European women becoming more visible politically.

Chapter 9 updated the preceding chapters through an analysis of the enormously significant 1980 presidential election. The gender gap in the voting rate of women and men disappeared in that election; a new gap emerged in the candidate preferences of women and men voters. The election is best understood, we argued, as a unique convergence of the issues raised by the candidates and the economic and pacifist concerns most deeply held by women. The victory of Ronald Reagan stemmed more from a rejection of the incumbent president, Jimmy Carter, than from a massive shift of voters to a conservative political ideology or identification with the Republican party. In fact, polls conducted since November, 1980, have shown that the slight increase in men and women calling themselves Republicans during the course of the election has been dramatically reversed among women. If this trend continues, the 1984 presidential election will generate an even larger gender gap.

Readers looking for the "theory" tested in this book will be disappointed, for there is little. The topic of women and politics is too new for much theory-building and theory-testing research to have been done. In principle, the development of social science theory and the collection of data go hand in hand. Studies should be conducted on the basis of deductive hypotheses or in a conscious effort to generate theory. Research findings should be interpreted in light of the original hypotheses, and the theoretical model should be revised accordingly. This description of the interactive nature of research and theory describes only a small portion of the studies on women and politics published today.

Most topics studied by social scientists are first pursued through exploratory investigations attempting to discern the major concepts and themes important in understanding the topic. As researchers gain a sense of the primary concepts, descriptive studies are undertaken to document the pervasiveness of the themes and their variation across social and historical settings. Only after the empirical groundwork has been laid can the formal hypothesis-testing characteristic of explanatory research begin. This is the epistemological point at which theory construction begins. Research on women and politics is just approaching the explanatory stage, and the years ahead should be full of exciting attempts to fit data to theoretical models. But what category of models is best suited to this topic? Models of majority-minority relations do not seem appropriate, for although women are the statistical majority, they are treated, by themselves as well as social institutions, as a social minority. Models focusing upon class conflict are unsatisfactory also because women occupy the same range of socioeconomic statuses as men do. Even simple models about social change always weakening traditional gender role definitions do not fit the experience of women in the developing nations. Perhaps the set of models that best illuminates women and politics issues focus upon the different expressions of political power in societies where social minorities are excluded from full political participation.

Aside from the issue of which models seem most appropriate to study women and politics is the less challenging but still important set of research questions needing to be asked and answered. Throughout the book, topics have been pointed out that need exploration. The intensity of political involvement among black women, who collectively evidence attitudes not conducive to participation, remains puzzling. Perhaps their church participation has encouraged their unusually high trust in institutions which are perceived at the same time as being unresponsive; perhaps other variables are more important. Most of the early descriptive analyses of politically elite women in America came from large cities, which are the strongholds of working-class, ethnic, unionized Democrats. How can the hypothesis that the number of viable women candidates depends on the competitiveness of the parties be adequately tested in one-party settings? Taking this argument to the national level, how can the causal relationships among demographic changes and the status of women be determined by looking at the comparative data available primarily from other postindustrialized, capitalist nations? The efforts to disentangle within-culture and across-culture patterns must involve both the construction of appropriate new data sets and the testing of good comparative hypotheses.

The delegate selection processes instituted for the 1972 nominating conventions were described in chapter 7, and in chapter 8 brief mention was made of differences between two-party and multiparty political systems. More research needs to be done on the effects of weakening party identity and party strength on women's prospects for more equitable political roles. Does the growing tendency for voters to identify themselves as independents mean more or fewer successful women candidates?

Men and women did not differ in their preference for political parties until the 1980 election. Although women gave the Republican candidate the majority of their votes, they were less supportive of his candidacy and his party than were men. As we noted in chapter 9, if a realignment of parties is taking place it was not reflected in the measurement of political party loyalties in 1980, nor was it apparent in self-designated ideology, since women were more apt than men to identify themselves as moderates on a liberal-conservative continuum in the 1980 election.

We also found in 1980 that religion influenced voting behavior. Women who identified themselves with the Moral Majority or indicated that they were very religious were more likely to vote for Reagan than were their less religious sisters.

Another major issue for future research is the importance of a woman's voting bloc. Women, the numerical majority but political minority, are "integrated" into society to a degree not experienced by any other minority group. Women visibly share little beyond their gender. Yet compared to men of their own rank, most women are resource poor, and this status inequity exists across the social classes. Women's tendency to support less militaristic and more humane solutions to social problems has led them to vote as a bloc in recent elections; their unity has been more fortuitous than intentional. Female doves can influence elections. What types of leadership and issues could serve as lightning rods for women's votes, and how the prospect of a bloc could change the standard American political equations are issues well worth further investigation.

There are insufficient hard data at the present time to make a strong case that if women were in positions of political power, they would make a difference in policy outcome. The studies of women's roles in state legislatures suggest that they do take a more humanitarian line. The scanty research on women in Congress make the same argument. There have been so few women in elite positions, however, that the researcher is limited even in observation. Individual women leaders both in politics and in the women's movement generally make an assumption that politics would benefit from the feminist factor. Women who attend the rap sessions at national meetings of the National Organization of Women and the National Women's Political Caucus make a case that women in the new politics would be different, equal, and better.

In addition to this research agenda is an action agenda. For most researchers dealing with women and politics, the inspiration is both personal and professional. As social scientists, they cannot help perceiving the systematic and unjust exclusion of more than half the world's population from a voice in their own fate; as feminists, they cannot help perceiving the terrible consequences of such exclusion for the quality of human lives. The idea that research on women's issues and research on social action should and do sustain each other is apparent in the remarks of Robert L. Kahn, former director of the Institute for Social Research at the University of Michigan.

> The new emphasis on research about women . . . is part of a movement—a far-reaching process of social change. It is particularly appropriate, therefore, to ask how that research can help bring about changes that represent solutions to some persistent problems of women . . . and men. To put the question more generally: how can we insure that these accumulating social facts are leading to appropriate social action? [1973, p. 263]

The need for valid and reliable research and concrete action is as great today as it was ten years ago, during the flurry of activity for women's rights. Although the women's movement appears quiescent today, the lack of headline-grabbing events should not be interpreted to mean that support for gender equality has disappeared. Heilbrun has termed the current low profile of the movement as "inevitable" because of three factors: the failure of women to bond together, the failure of women to imagine themselves as autonomous, and the failure of "achieving women to resist, sooner or later, the protection to be obtained by entering the male mainstream" (1979, p. 26). While her analysis may be apt for the women's movement in the 1920s, it does not apply to the second wave of the movement apparent today. Social movements grow, spread, and appear to fade away in predictable stages (Dowse and Hughes 1972), but the lack of visibility does not imply powerlessness. A truly successful movement will have gained institutionalized policy changes which accomplish quietly and routinely the goals worth taking to the streets for a few years earlier. And the contemporary women's movement has done just that. Along with the demographic changes of recent years, fostered in part by the movement, the looser definitions of gender roles have brought American women into a new era, and there is no going back to a *status quo ante* (Bernard in Boulding 1976, p. 762).

The political maturing of women who fought for the Equal Rights Amendment insures that the past will not overtake the future. The 1982 defeat of the drive for ratification produced a tremendous increase in the campaign funds and membership of the major women's political organizations. More importantly, the defeat taught women that lobbying is an inherently less effective means to securing women's rights than electing women to public office. The multitude of women who acquired political skills, forged networks, and raised money on behalf of the ERA will now be focused on a wide range of economic and social issues important to women. With this increased activism and effectiveness, the 1980s promise to be the decade when women move from political invisibility to political visibility and equality.

It is more likely that the women's movement in America is entering what can be described as a third wave. This development had its origins in the historical struggles of women in the nineteenth and early twentieth century to secure the rights of suffrage for the second sex. Along with temperance fights, the drive for suffrage was a single-issue campaign, and once temperance and suffrage were achieved, the first women's movement disintegrated. There was no sustaining ideology to motivate or organize women from the 1920s to the 1960s. Women in those years tended to rally around good causes, but they were not involved in direct political action except as volunteers in political parties.

The women's movement of the 1960s was the second wave. It rose as a protest movement in a world of rapid, large-scale changes in societies, technologies, cultures, and politics. The overwhelming fact of our time is change, especially in the life-styles of women. Women have recognized change, coped with it, and would appear now to constitute a force in America that is comparable to the organized labor movement of the twentieth century. What began as a special interest protest has emerged into a cohesive group, loosely organized, highly individualistic, and composed of women bearing left and right ideologies. The third wave of the women's movement will attempt to secure equal human rights, including full participation in the political system.

APPENDIX

Table 57. Standardized Discriminant Function Coefficients Distinguishing between Voters and Nonvoters in Four Presidential Elections

Step Entered	1952		1964		1976		1980	
1	Education	0.756	Education	0.666	Education	−0.765	Age	0.981
2	Gender	−0.419	Age	0.696	Age	−0.678	Employment Status	−0.551
3	Region	−0.311	Region	−0.326	Gender	0.260	Education	0.295
4	Age	0.261	Income	0.250	Region	0.174	Region	−0.181
5	Income	0.226	Gender	−0.157	Income	−0.150	—	
6	—		Employment Status	−0.114	Employment Status	0.164	—	

Source of Data: Center for Political Studies, American National Election Studies, 1952–1980.

Note: When the sign is ignored, the coefficients can be interpreted as the relative contributions of each variable to the discriminant function which best distinguishes between voters and nonvoters in each election study (Nie et al. 1975).

Table 58. The Relationship between Education and High Interest in Political Campaigns for Women and Men, by Election Year

Level of Education	1952		1956		1960		1964		1968		1972		1976	
	Men	Women	Men	Women	Men	Women	Men	Women	Men	Women	Men	Women	Men	Women
Grade school	29%	20%	32%	16%	40%	18%	26%	23%	33%	27%	31%	20%	39%	29%
High school	38	34	33	25	37	28	38	30	41	39	31	25	32	28
College	63	56	38	38	50	50	53	55	61	47	49	40	49	45

Source of Data: Center for Political Studies, American National Election Studies, 1952–1976.

Note: Respondents were classified according to the degree of their interest in the campaign from their responses to the following question: "Some people don't pay much attention to the political campaigns. How about you? Would you say that you have been very much interested, somewhat interested, or not much interested in following the political campaigns so far this year?" This table reports respondents, measured by level of education, who were very much interested in following the campaigns by election years.

Table 59. The Relationship between Education and High Level of Concern about Outcome of Presidential Elections for Women and Men, by Election Year

Level of Education	1952		1956		1960		1964		1968		1972		1976	
	Men	Women	Men	Women	Men	Women	Men	Women	Men	Women	Men	Women	Men	Women
Grade school	23%	19%	21%	17%	23%	17%	24%	23%	66%	60%	57%	57%	59%	52%
High school	27	27	28	23	26	29	29	29	65	64	58	61	50	54
College	44	38	35	35	29	41	34	40	70	70	79	72	62	61

Source of Data: Center for Political Studies, American National Election Studies, 1952–1976.

Note: Respondents were classified according to the degree of their concern over the election outcome from their response to the following question: "Generally speaking, would you say that you personally care a good deal which party wins the presidential election this fall, or that you don't care very much which party wins?" Respondents saying they cared "very much" and "pretty much" in the 1952–68 studies are categorized as having a high level of concern. In the 1972 and 1976 studies, respondents saying they "care a good deal" were so categorized.

Table 60. Gender Differences in the Distribution of Party Identification, by Election Year

Party Identification	1952 Men	1952 Women	1956 Men	1956 Women	1960 Men	1960 Women	1964 Men	1964 Women	1968 Men	1968 Women	1972 Men	1972 Women	1976 Men	1976 Women
Strong Democrat	24%	20%	23%	20%	23%	24%	27%	27%	20%	20%	16%	15%	13%	15%
Weak Democrat	22	26	23	24	23	26	23	27	23	27	22	29	22	27
Independent Democrat	11	8	9	5	9	3	11	8	11	9	—	—	14	11
Independent	6	4	10	9	10	8	8	8	9	11	34	31	16	13
Independent Republican	8	7	9	8	7	7	6	5	11	8	—	—	14	8
Weak Republican	12	14	13	16	14	15	12	15	17	14	13	13	14	15
Strong Republican	13	14	13	18	14	17	12	11	9	11	10	11	18	11
Percent strongly attached to either party (strong Democrat plus strong Republican)	37% >	34%	36% <	38%	37% <	41%	39% >	38%	29% <	31%	26% =	26%	31% >	26%

Source of Data: Center for Political Studies, American National Election Studies, 1952–1976.

NOTES

Chapter One

1. The American National Election Studies conducted by the Survey Research Center/Center for Political Studies of the Institute for Social Research at the University of Michigan from 1952 through 1976 provide the principal data analyzed in this book.

    The data and tabulations utilized were made available by the Interuniversity Consortium for Political and Social Research. The principal investigators in 1952 were Angus Campbell, Gerald Gurin, and Warren E. Miller. The principal investigators in 1956 and 1960 were Angus Campbell, Philip E. Converse, Warren E. Miller, and Donald E. Stokes. The principal investigator in 1964 and 1968 was the Political Behavior Program. The principal investigators in 1972 were Warren E. Miller, Arthur H. Miller, Richard Brody, David Kovenock, Jack Dennis, and Merrill Shanks. The principal investigators in 1976 were Warren E. Miller and Arthur H. Miller.

2. In an effort to pinpoint the source of the different voting rates produced by the CPS and the Census Bureau surveys, Traugott and Katosh (1979) first looked to see whether the samples of people interviewed were similar in 1976. The discussion in chapter 2 concerns how and why various background characteristics, such as level of education and age, are related to the likelihood that a person votes in national elections. If the CPS and Census Bureau samples in 1976 contained different proportions of college graduates, for instance, then the discrepancy between the voting rates would be partially accounted for because college graduates cast votes at a higher rate than do people without a college degree. The cross sections of the American population interviewed in the two surveys *were* comparable in 1976; however, the research designs were not. Respondents in the CPS survey were interviewed both before and after the November election in 1976, while the people interviewed by the Census Bureau were contacted only after the election.

The higher voting rate of people who had been interviewed before the election raises the possibility that the interview experience was a stimulus to voting. In other words, being questioned about your perceptions of the political system, the candidates, and your intention to vote may increase the likelihood that you *will* vote. A portion of the respondents in the CPS survey had been interviewed from one to three times before the 1976 study was done. Traugott and Katosh reasoned that if being interviewed was a stimulus to vote, a more accurate estimate of the national turnout rate could be obtained if the people repeatedly interviewed were dropped from the calculation. With this group excluded, the voting rate turned out to be 54 percent, which is lower than the Census Bureau rate of 59 percent but *identical* with the official estimate based upon actual election returns. Being interviewed about your intention to vote apparently increases your likelihood to do so; it may also increase your likelihood of reporting inaccurately.

The tendency to overreport is not uniform across the American electorate, but appears to be greater among nonwhites (20 percent misreported having voted) than whites (12 percent did), and only slightly greater among men (15 percent misreported) than women (12 percent). More significantly for our analysis, people who are not interested in politics, who do not follow elections, and who do not claim either political party as their own are more likely to misreport having voted than people more involved in politics. Perhaps the emphasis in this society on democratic participation leads people feeling politically apathetic to claim some minimal involvement, such as voting. The design of the CPS studies, with interviews conducted both before and after the election, may underscore the civic duty of their respondents—political participation must be important because of the attention it receives from researchers. Persons interviewed only after an election, then, should be less likely to misrepresent their behavior.

The following table shows the different calculations of turnout in 1976:

Source	Men	Women	Difference
U.S., Census Bureau	60%	59%	1%
Center for Political Studies, American National Election Studies, 1952–1976	77	68	9
Revised after validation check (Traugott and Katosh 1979)	62	56	6

3. Neither the original collectors of the data nor the Inter-university Consortium for Political and Social Research bear any responsibility for the analyses or interpretations presented in the book.
4. The data found in chapter 8 are from the *Study of Political Change in Britain, 1963–1970* (2 vols), by David E. Butler and Donald E. Stokes. The second set of data in chapter 8 are from Euro-Barometer 3: European Men and Women, May, 1975. The principal investigators were Jacques-Rene Rabier and Ronald Inglehart.

Chapter Two

1. The reader is reminded of the discussion in chapter 1 concerning the overestimate of turnout contained in the 1952, 1964, and 1976 CPS figures. The tendency for men to overreport their vote more frequently than women means that the gender differences shown in figure 1 are actually less than they appear in the figure.
2. The standardized discriminant function coefficients for the six variables, coefficients which can be read as the relative predictive power of each variable vis-à-vis the others, are presented in table 44 in the appendix.

Chapter Five

1. For an extensive bibliography see Stone and Brown (1978).
2. See section on the rise of black voting since 1944, pp. 17–20, and section on gender and political participation, pp. 65–70, in Matthews and Prothro (1966). The South in their study was defined as the former Confederate states: Alabama, Arkansas, Florida, Georgia, Louisiana, Mississippi, North Carolina, South Carolina, Tennessee, Texas, and Virginia.

Chapter Six

1. Earlier research on this topic was reported by Marjorie Lansing at the Annual Meeting of the American Political Science Association, Washington D.C., 1973, and in a chapter entitled "The Voting Patterns of American Black Women" found in *A Portrait of Marginality*, edited by Marianne Githens and Jewel L. Prestage (New York: David McKay, 1977), pp. 379–94.

Chapter Eight

1. Earlier research on this topic was reported by Baxter and Lansing at the Eighth World Congress of Sociology, Toronto, Canada, August, 1974; in a paper presented by Lansing at the annual meeting of the American Political Science Association, August, 1976; and by Lansing at a workshop on Women in Politics at the European Consortium for Political Research, Berlin, West Germany, April, 1977.

2. There is a burgeoning literature. See especially Iglitzin and Ross (1976), Giele and Smock (1977), Newland (1979), and Boulding (1976a; 1977).

3. There has been little investigation of the role of women in British politics. The studies of female roles by Tingsten (1937) and Duverger (1955) did not include British data. Both Alford's four-nation study (1963) and the *International Guide to Electoral Statistics*, edited by Rokkan (1969), have few statistics on women. Butler and Stokes (1969; 1974) similarly have few references to British women. Converse (1964) excluded sex from his list of priority variables in electoral research. Only Lipset in earlier work (1963) and Almond and Verba (1963) included data on British women. These sources are helpful: Abrams and Little (1965), Bonham (1954), Butler (1952; 1955; 1959; 1963), Butler and King (1965; 1966), Butler and Pinto-Duschinsky (1971), Butler and Rose (1960), Butler and Stokes (1969; 1974), Craig (1969), Currell (1974), Freeman (1969), Gosnell (1930), Kinnear (1968), Lipset and Rokkan (1971), Rose (1964; 1965; 1966; 1968a; 1968b; 1969; 1970a; 1970b), Stone (1972), Verba, Nie, and Kim (1978).

4. For a review of the literature, see Goot and Reid (1975), pp. 21–25.

5. Durant commented further: ". . . quantitatively the bias is much smaller than the bias of the middle class towards the Conservatives and the working-class voters toward Labour. . . . It is important to note, however, that while sex differences in voting persists, and may be found in a number of other Western Countries, the differences are so small proportionately that sex has little accuracy as a predictor of the vote of an individual." Butler and Stokes (1974, chaps. 7–11) saw the emergence of the Labour party as a "strong and explicitly class-based party." They commented further: "The class alignments supplied British politics its dominant motif for half a century. Much of the electoral history of this period can be presented in terms of a process of realignment on class lines that is in some respects still underway. It may therefore seem paradoxical to suggest that the class basis of party allegiance was becom-

ing weaker in the 1960s. After all class was at least as heavily Labour in the youngest age group as in the older cohorts. Indeed, the 1960s continued a long process of evolution" (p. 193).
6. See also Rasmussen (1977), Rendel (1977), and Hills (1977).
7. Euro-Barometer 3: European Men and Women, May, 1975, a survey made available by the Inter-university Consortium for Political Research.

Chapter Nine

1. The 1980 election study involved eight integrated survey data collections undertaken at strategically chosen periods in 1980. This design allows researchers to measure changes in public sentiment toward the issues, candidates, and parties salient during the campaign period. The data reported in this chapter are taken from the pre-election interviews conducted in September and October and the follow-up interviews with the same respondents (if they could be located) in November and December after the election. These data parallel the pre- and postelection survey data from 1952 through 1976 presented in the earlier chapters. The principal investigator in 1980 was Warren E. Miller.
2. The 1982 data, especially those derived from exit polls, are subject to higher margins of sampling error than either national telephone polls or face-to-face interviews conducted with the same number of respondents. The overall agreement among exit polls and more reliable surveys in 1980 and 1982 suggests that general conclusions based on exit polls can be carefully drawn.
3. Both the 1976 and 1980 National Election Studies included an effort to validate respondents' claims to have voted through a check of local voting records. As indicated in note 2 to chapter 1, the validation check in 1976 reduced the self-reported turnout rate of men by 11 percent and of women by 8 percent, producing a gender gap in voting of 6 percent. The validation in 1980 lowered both men and women's self-reported turnout rate by 15 percent, to 58 percent and 55 percent, respectively.

As also indicated in the chapter 1 footnote, the CPS turnout rates have traditionally varied from those published by the United States Census Bureau. For the 1980 election, the Census Bureau's data indicate that 59 percent of eligible women and men voters cast ballots. These are slightly higher rates than the CPS data indicate, but the Census Bureau makes no effort to validate the self-reports.

Most researchers relying on the 1980 Michigan data have limited their analyses to validated voters. We have chosen not to do so for two reasons. First, we wish to keep the data comparable across the eight presidential elections analyzed in this book. Second, the bulk of analyses reported in this chapter are correlational, and a check on results revealed very similar patterns of relationship whether the sample of voters was defined as self-reported or validated interviewees.

4. The pre- and postelection waves of the 1980 election study contained only 187 blacks, which constituted 12 percent of the sample. Their frequency is too small to support rigorous analysis. We have generated the findings reported in this section only to provide continuity with the data in chapters 5 and 6. We caution the reader, however, about the tentativeness of the results. Researchers interested in more reliable analyses of the black vote in 1980 should consult the tabulations produced by the Census Bureau or by national polling firms.

BIBLIOGRAPHY

Aarons, Leroy. "To TV Viewers, It's Been a Dull Show." *Washington Post*, August 13, 1972, p. A–14.

Abrams, Philip, and Little, Alan. "The Young Activist in British Politics." *British Journal of Sociology* 16 (1965):315–33.

Adams, Mildred. *The Right to Be People*. Philadelphia: J. P. Lippincott, 1967.

Alford, Robert R. *Party and Society*. Chicago: Rand McNally, 1963.

Almond, Gabriel L., and Verba, Sidney. *The Civic Culture: Political Attitudes and Democracy in Five Nations*. Princeton: Princeton University Press, 1963.

Almquist, Elizabeth M. "Untangling the Effects of Race and Sex: The Disadvantaged Status of Black Women." *Social Science Quarterly* 55 (June 1975):129–42.

Amundsen, Kirsten. *The Silenced Majority: Women and American Democracy*. Englewood Cliffs, N.J.: Prentice-Hall, 1971.

————. *A New Look at the Silenced Majority*. Englewood Cliffs, N.J.: Prentice-Hall, 1977.

Andersen, Kristi. "Working Women and Political Participation, 1952–1972." *American Journal of Political Science* 19 (August 1975):439–53.

Asher, Herbert B. "The Reliability of the Political Efficacy Items." *Political Methodology* 1 (Spring 1974):45–72.

Bardwick, Judith M. *Psychology of Women: A Study of Bio-Cultural Conflicts*. New York: Harper and Row, 1971.

Baxter, Sandra. "Women and Politics: The Parties, the League of Women Voters and the Electorate." Ph.D. dissertation, University of Michigan, 1977.

Baxter, Sandra, and Lansing, Marjorie. "Women Voters: The Misunderstood Majority." *Washington Post*, November 2, 1980, p. C–1.

Bennetts, Leslie. "Record Number of Women to Hold Seats in Congress." *New York Times*, November 6, 1980, p. A–30.

Berelson, Bernard R., and Lazarsfeld, Paul F. "Women: A Major Problem for the P.A.C." *Public Opinion Quarterly* 9 (Spring 1945):79–82.

Berelson, Bernard R.; Lazarsfeld, Paul F.; and McPhee, William N. *Voting.* Chicago: University of Chicago Press, 1954.

Bers, Trudy H. "Local Political Elites: Men and Women on Boards of Education." *Western Political Quarterly* 31 (September 1978):381–91.

Blair, Emily N. "Women in the Political Parties." *Annals of the American Academy of Political and Social Science* 143 (May 1929):217–29.

Blake, Judith. "The Changing Status of Women in Developed Countries." *Scientific American* 231, no. 3 (1974):136–47.

Blood, Robert O., and Wolfe, Donald M. *Husbands and Wives. The Dynamics of Married Life.* Glencoe, Ill.: Free Press, 1960.

Bonham, John. *The Middle-Class Vote.* London: Faber, 1954.

Boserup, Ester. *Women's Role in Economic Development.* New York: St. Martin's Press, 1970.

Boulding, Elise. *Handbook of International Data on Women.* New York: John Wiley and Sons, 1976a.

———. *The Underside of History: A View of Women Through Time.* Boulder: Westview Press, 1976b.

———. *Women in the Twentieth Century World.* Beverly Hills: Russell Sage Publications, 1977.

Bourque, Susan, and Grossholtz, Jean. "Politics as an Unnatural Practice: Political Science Looks at Female Participation." *Politics and Society* 4 (Winter 1974):255–66.

Bressler, Tobia, and McKenney, Napeo D. R. "Negro Women in the United States." Unpublished paper for Population Association of America, U.S., Bureau of the Census. Washington D.C., 1968.

Broder, David. *The Party Is Over.* New York: Harper and Row, 1972.

Bullock, Charles S., III, and Heys, Patricia L. F. "Recruitment of Women for Congress: A Research Note." *Western Political Quarterly* 25 (September 1972):416–23.

Burlew, Ann K. "Career and Educational Choices among Black Females." *Journal of Black Psychology* 3 (February 1977):88–106.

Butler, David E. *The British General Election of 1951.* London: Macmillan & Co., 1952.

———. *The British General Election of 1955.* London: Macmillan & Co., 1955.

———. *The Electoral System in Britain Since 1918.* 2d ed. Oxford: Clarendon Press, 1963.

———, ed. *Elections Abroad.* London: Macmillan & Co., 1959.

Butler, David E., and King, A. S. *The British General Election of 1964.* London: Macmillan & Co., 1965.

———. *The British General Election of 1966.* London: Macmillan & Co., 1966.

Butler, David E., and Pinto-Duschinsky, M. *The British General Election of 1970.* London: Macmillan & Co., 1971.

Butler, David E., and Rose, Richard. *The British General Election of 1959.* London: Macmillan & Co., 1960.

Butler, David E., and Stokes, Donald E. *Political Change in Britain.* London: Macmillan & Co., 1969.

———. *Political Change in Britain.* 2d ed. London: Macmillan & Co., 1974.

Caddell, Patrick, as quoted in "Face Off: A Conversation with the Presidents' Pollsters." *Public Opinion* 3 (December/January 1981):2–12, 63–64.

Campbell, Angus. "Surge and Decline: A Study of Electoral Change." In Angus Campbell, Philip E. Converse, Warren E. Miller, and Donald E. Stokes, *Elections and the Political Order.* New York: John Wiley and Sons, 1966.

Campbell, Angus, and Converse, Philip E. *The Human Meaning of Social Change.* New York: Russell Sage Foundation, 1972.

Campbell, Angus; Converse, Philip E.; Miller, Warren E.; and Stokes, Donald E. *The American Voter.* New York: John Wiley and Sons, 1960.

———. *Elections and the Politcal Order.* New York: John Wiley and Sons, 1966.

Campbell, Angus; Converse, Philip E.; and Rodgers, Willard L. *The Quality of American Life.* New York: Russell Sage Foundation, 1976.

Campbell, Angus; Gurin, Gerald; and Miller, Warren E. *The Voter Decides.* Evanston, Ill.: Row Peterson, 1954.

Carden, Maren L. *The New Feminist Movement.* New York: Russell Sage Foundation, 1974.

Carroll, Susan. "Women Candidates and Support for Women's Issues: Closet Feminists." Paper delivered at the Annual Meeting of the Midwest Political Science Association, Chicago, Ill., 1979.

Catt, Carrie Chapman. "Woman Suffrage: Only an Episode in Age-Old Movement." *Current History* 27 (October 1927):1–6.

CBS News/*New York Times*, Post-Election Poll, November, 1980, released November 15–16, 1980.

Chafe, William H. *The American Woman: Her Changing Social, Economic, and Political Roles, 1920–1970.* New York: Oxford University Press, 1972.

————. *Women and Equality*. New York: Oxford University Press, 1977.

Chamberlain, Hope. *A Minority of Members: Women in the U.S. Congress*. New York: Praeger, 1973.

Chassler, Sey. Keynote Address delivered at the National Women's Political Caucus Convention, Cincinnati, Ohio, July 14, 1979.

Clymer, Adam. "Displeasure with Carter Turned Many to Reagan." *New York Times*, November 9, 1980, p. 1–28.

Conference Board. *Women: A Demographic, Social and Economic Presentation*. New York: Conference Board, 1973.

Constantini, Edmund, and Craik, Kenneth. "Women as Politicians: The Social Background, Personality, and Political Careers of Female Party Leaders." *Journal of Social Issues* 28 (1972):217–36.

Converse, Philip E. "The Nature of Belief Systems in Mass Publics." In *Ideology and Discontent*, edited by David E. Apter. Glencoe, Ill.: Free Press, 1964.

————. "The Concept of a Normal Vote." In Angus Campbell, Philip E. Converse, Warren E. Miller, and Donald E. Stokes, *Elections and the Political Order*. New York: John Wiley and Sons, 1966.

Converse, Philip E.; Clausen, Aage R.; and Miller, Warren E. "Electoral Myth and Reality: The 1964 Election." *American Political Science Review* 59 (June 1965):321–36.

Converse, Philip E., and Markus, Gregory B. "Plus ça change. . .: The New CPS Election Study Panel." *American Political Science Review* 73 (March 1979):32–49.

Craig, F. W. S. *British Parliamentary Election Results, 1918–1949*. Glasgow: Political Reference Publications, 1969.

Currell, Melville. *Political Woman*. London: Croom Helm, 1974.

Darcy, R., and Schramm, Sarah S. "When Women Run Against Men." *Public Opinion Quarterly* 41 (Spring 1977):1–12.

de Beauvoir, Simone. *The Second Sex*. Translated and edited by H. M. Parshely. London: Jonathan Cape, 1953.

Diamond, Irene. *Sex Roles in the State House*. New Haven: Yale University Press, 1977.

Dogan, Mattei. "Political Cleavage and Social Stratification in France and Italy." In *Party Systems and Voter Alignments: Cross-National Perspectives*, edited by Seymour M. Lipset and Stein Rokkan. New York: Free Press, 1967.

Downs, Anthony. *An Economic Theory of Democracy*. New York: Harper and Row, 1957.

Drew, Elizabeth. *Portrait of an Election: The 1980 Presidential Campaign.* New York: Simon and Schuster, 1981.

Dubeck, Paula J. "Women and Access to Political Office: A Comparison of Female and Male State Legislators." *Sociological Quarterly* 17 (Winter 1976):45–52.

Durant, Henry. "Voting Behavior in Britain, 1945–66." In *Studies in British Politics: A Reading in Political Sociology,* edited by Richard Rose. 2d rev. ed. London: Macmillan & Co., 1969.

Dutton, Frederick. *Changing Sources of Power: American Politics in the 1970's.* New York: McGraw-Hill, 1971.

———. *National Journal,* September 23, 1972, p. 1512.

Duverger, Maurice. *The Political Role of Women.* Paris: UNESCO, 1955.

Epstein, Cynthia Fuchs. "Black and Female: The Double Whammy." *Psychology Today* 7 (August 1973):57–61.

Erbe, William. "Social Involvement and Political Activity: A Replication and Elaboration." *American Sociological Review* 29 (April 1964):198–215.

Evans, Sara. *Personal Politics: The Roots of Women's Liberation in the Civil Rights Movement and the New Left.* New York: Alfred A. Knopf, 1979.

Farah, Barbara G. "Climbing the Political Ladder: The Aspirations and Expectations of Partisan Elites." In *New Research on Women and Sex Roles at the University of Michigan,* edited by Dorothy G. McGuigan. Ann Arbor: Center for the Continuing Education of Women, University of Michigan, 1976.

Farah, Barbara G., and Jennings, M. Kent. *A Social and Political Profile of the Michigan Delegation to the 1964 and 1976 National Conventions.* Ann Arbor: Center for Political Studies, 1977.

Farris, D. "Selected Attitudes on Foreign Affairs as Correlates of Authoritarianism and Political Anomie." *Journal of Politics* 22 (February 1960):50–57.

Ferree, Myra Marx. "A Woman for President? Changing Responses 1958–1972." *Public Opinion Quarterly* 37 (Fall 1974):390–99.

Finifter, Ada W., ed. *Alienation and the Social System.* New York: John Wiley and Sons, 1972.

Flanigan, William H., and Zingale, Nancy H. *Political Behavior of the American Electorate.* Boston: Allyn and Bacon, 1979.

Flexner, Eleanor. *Century of Struggle: The Woman's Rights Movement in the United States.* Cambridge, Mass.: Belknap Press, 1959.

Forthal, Sonya. *Cogwheels of Democracy: A Study of a Precinct Captain.* New York: William-Frederick Press, 1946.

Frankovic, Kathleen A. "Sex and Voting in the U.S. House of Representatives, 1961–1975. *American Politics Quarterly* 5 (July 1977):315–30.

———. "Public Opinion Trends." In *The Election of 1980: Reports and Interpretations*, edited by Gerald Pomper. Chatham, N.J.: Chatham House Publishers, 1981.

Freeman, J. *British Political Facts, 1900–1968*. London: Macmillan & Co., 1969.

Freeman, Jo. *Women: A Feminist Perspective*. Palo Alto, California: Mayfield Publishing Co., 1975.

Gallup, George. *The Political Almanac*. New York: Forbes, 1952.

———. "Divining the Devout: The Polls and Religious Beliefs." *Public Opinion*, 1980, pp. 20–41.

Gallup Opinion Index, Political, Social and Economic Trends, Report no. 183, December, 1980. Princeton, N.J.: The Gallup Poll, 1980.

Gallup Report, The. "Religion in America," Report nos. 201–2, Princeton, N.J.: Princeton Religion Research Center, June-July, 1982.

Gehlen, Frieda L. "Women Members of Congress: A Distinctive Role." In *A Portrait of Marginality*, edited by Marianne Githens and Jewel L. Prestage. New York: David McKay, 1977.

Giele, Janet Z., and Smock, Audrey C., eds. *Women: Roles and Status in Eight Countries*. New York: John Wiley and Sons, 1977.

Gilman, Charlotte Perkins. "Woman's Achievements since the Franchise." *Current History* 27 (October 1927):7–14.

Goot, Murray, and Reid, Elizabeth. *Women and Voting Studies: Mindless Matrons or Sexist Scientism?* Contemporary Political Sociology Series, no. 06–008. Beverly Hills: Russell Sage Publications, 1975.

Gosnell, Harold F. *Why Europe Votes*. Chicago: University of Chicago Press, 1930.

———. *Democracy: The Threshold of Freedom*. New York: Ronald Press, 1948.

Griffiths, Martha W. "Requisites for Equality." In *Women and the American Economy: A Look to the 1980's*, edited by Juanita M. Kreps. Englewood Cliffs, N.J.: Prentice-Hall, 1976.

Haavio-Mannila, Elina. "Changes in Sex Roles in Politics as an Indicator of Structural Change in Society." Paper delivered at Workshop on Women in Politics, at the European Consortium for Political Research, West Berlin, Germany, April 2, 1977*a*.

———. *Women in the Economic, Political and Cultural Elite in Finland*. Research Reports, Department of Sociology, University of Helsinki, no. 209, 1977*b*.

Hacker, Helen. "Women As a Minority Group." *Social Forces* 30 (October 1951):60–69.

Hansen, Susan B.; Franz, Linda M.; and Netemeyer-Mays, Margaret. "Women's Political Participation and Policy Preferences." *Social Science Quarterly* 56 (March 1976):576–90.

Hare, Julia, and Hare, Nathan. "Black Women, 1970." *Transaction* 8 (November-December 1970):65–68.

Harris, Fred R. "The 1980 Elections: The Voters Turn Toward Reagan and the Republicans." 1981 supplement to *America's Democracy*. 2d ed. Glenview, Ill.: Scott, Foresman and Co., 1981.

Harris, Louis. *Is There a Republican Majority? Political Trends 1952–1956*. New York: Harper and Brothers, 1954.

————. "The Harris Survey: Democrats' Session Got High Marks." *Washington Post*, August 20, 1972, p. A–7.

————. *The Harris Survey*. Press Release, August 3, 1981.

Harris, Louis, and Associates. *The 1972 Virginia Slims American Women's Opinion Poll: A Survey of the Attitudes of Women on Their Roles in Politics and the Economy*, 1972.

Hero, Alfred. "Public Reaction to Government Policy." In *Measures of Political Attitudes*, edited John P. Robinson, Jerrold G. Rusk, and Kendra B. Head. Ann Arbor: Survey Research Center, Institute for Social Research, 1968.

Hills, Jill. "Women in the Labour Party." Paper delivered at Workshop on Women in Politics, at the European Consortium for Political Research, West Berlin, Germany, April, 1977.

Hirschfield, Robert S.; Swanson, Bert E.; and Blank, Blanche D. "A Profile of Political Activists in Manhattan." *Western Political Quarterly* 15 (September 1962):489–506.

Hodge, Robert W., and Treiman, Donald J. "Social Participation and Social Status." *American Sociological Review* 33 (October 1968):722–40.

Horner, Matina S. "Why Women Fail." *Psychology Today* 3, no. 6 (November 1969): 37–39.

————. "The Motive to Avoid Success and Changing Aspirations of College Women." In *Readings on the Psychology of Women*, edited by Judith M. Bardwick. New York: Harper and Row, 1972.

Huber, Joan; Rexroat, Cynthia; and Spitze, Glenna. "A Crucible of Opinion on Women's Status: ERA in Illinois." *Social Forces* 57 (December 1978):549–65.

Iglitzin, Lynne E., and Ross, Ruth, eds. *Women in the World: A Comparative Study*. Santa Barbara: Clio Books, 1976.

Inglehart, Margaret L. "Political Interest in West European Women: An Historical and Empirical Comparative Analysis." Paper delivered at the Midwest Conference of Political Scientists, Chicago, Ill., March 23, 1979.

Inglehart, Ronald. *The Silent Revolution.* Princeton: Princeton University Press, 1977.

Janeway, Elizabeth. "The Weak are the Second Sex." *Atlantic Monthly,* December 1973, pp. 91–104.

Janowitz, Morris, and Marvick, Dwaine. *Competitive Pressure and Democratic Consent.* Ann Arbor: Bureau of Government, University of Michigan, 1956.

Jennings, M. Kent, and Thomas, Norman. "Men and Women in Party Elites: Social Roles and Political Resources." *Midwest Journal of Political Science* 12 (November 1968):469–92.

Johnson, Haynes. "A Portrait of Democrats' New Delegate." *Washington Post,* July 8, 1972, p. A–1.

Johnson, Marilyn, and Carroll, Susan. "Statistical Report: Profile of Women Holding Public Office, 1977." In *Women in Public Office.* Compiled by the Center for the American Woman and Politics, Eagleton Institute of Politics, Rutgers, the State University of New Jersey. 2d ed. Metuchen, N.J.: Scarecrow Press, 1978.

Johnson, Marilyn, and Stanwick, Kathy. "Statistical Essay: Profile of Women Holding Public Office." In *Women in Public Office: A Biographical Directory and Statistical Analysis.* Compiled by the Center for the American Woman and Politics, Eagleton Institute of Politics, Rutgers, the State University of New Jersey. New York: R. R. Bowker, 1976.

Karnig, Albert K., and Walter, Oliver B. "Election of Women to City Councils." *Social Science Quarterly* 56 (March 1976):605–13.

Kelley, Stanley, Jr.; Ayres, Richard E.; and Bowen, William G. "Registration and Voting: Putting First Things First." *American Political Science Review* 61 (June 1967):359–79.

Key, V. O., Jr. *Public Opinion and Democracy.* New York: Alfred A. Knopf, 1961.

———. *Politics, Parties, and Pressure Groups.* New York: Crowell, 1964.

Key, V. O., Jr., and Munger, Frank. "Social Determinism and Electoral Decision: The Case for Indiana." In *American Voting Behavior,* edited by Eugene Burdick and Arthur J. Brodbeck. Glencoe, Ill.: Free Press, 1959.

Kilberg, Bobbie G. "Republican Women Assessing Their Gains and Losses." *Washington Post,* September 2, 1972, p. A–18.

Kinnear, Michael. *The British Voter: An Atlas and Survey Since 1885.* London: Batsford, 1968.

Kirkpatrick, Jeane J. *Political Woman.* New York: Basic Books, 1964.

———. *The New Presidential Elite.* New York: Russell Sage Foundation and the Twentieth Century Fund, 1976.

Knoche, Claire F. "Feminism and Political Participation: The Role of Ideology, 1972–76." Ph.D. dissertation, University of Wisconsin, 1978.

Kornhauser, Arthur; Sheppard, Harold L.; Mayer, Albert J. *When Labour Votes.* New York: University Books, 1956.

Kraditor, Aileen S. *The Ideas of the Woman Suffrage Movement, 1890–1920.* New York: Columbia University Press, 1965.

Krauss, Wilma Rule. "U.S. State Environments and Women's Recruitment to Legislatures and Congress: An Organizational Theory Approach." Paper delivered at the Annual Meeting of the American Political Science Association, San Francisco, Calif., 1975.

Kreps, Juanita M., and Leaper, R. John. "Home Work, Market Work, and the Allocation of Time." In *Women and the American Economy: A Look to the 1980's,* edited by Juanita M. Kreps. Englewood Cliffs, N.J.: Prentice-Hall, 1976.

Kruschke, Earl R. "Female Politicals and Apoliticals." Ph.D. dissertation, University of Wisconsin, 1963.

Ladner, Joyce A. *Tomorrow's Tomorrow: The Black Woman.* New York: Doubleday, 1972.

Lake, Celinda C. "Guns, Butter and Equality: The Women's Vote in 1980." Paper delivered at the Annual Meeting of the Midwest Political Science Association, Milwaukee, Wisc., 1982.

Lamphere, Louise, and Rosaldo, Michelle, eds. *Women, Culture, and Society.* Stanford: Stanford University Press, 1974.

Lane, Robert E. *Political Life: Why People Get Involved in Politics.* Glencoe, Ill.: Free Press, 1959.

Lansing, Marjorie. "Sex Differences in Political Participation." Ph.D. dissertation, University of Michigan, 1970.

———. "Women: The New Political Class." In *A Sampler of Women's Studies,* edited by Dorothy G. McGuigan. Ann Arbor: University of Michigan, Center for the Continuing Education of Women, 1973.

———. "The American Woman: Voter and Activist." In *Women in Politics,* edited by Jane S. Jaquette. New York: John Wiley and Sons, 1974.

———. "Political Change for the American Woman." In *Women in the World,* edited by Lynne B. Iglitzin and Ruth Ross. Santa Barbara: Clio Books, 1976.

————. "Voting Patterns of American Black Women." In A *Portrait of Marginality*, edited by Marianne Githens and Jewel L. Prestage. New York: David McKay, 1977.

————. "Women in American Politics." In *The Contemporary American Woman: Her Past, Her Present, Her Future Prospects*, edited by Marie Richmond-Abbott. New York: Holt, Rinehart and Winston, 1979.

————. "Women's Power." *New York Times*, September 25, 1980, p. A–27.

Lazarsfeld, Paul F.; Berelson, Bernard; and Gaudet, Hazel. *The People's Choice*. New York: Duell, Sloan and Pearce, 1944.

League of Women Voters of the United States. *Reports I, II, III, IV, and V*. Ann Arbor: Survey Research Center, Institute for Social Research, University of Michigan, 1956–58.

Lee, Marcia Manning. "Toward Understanding Why Few Women Hold Public Office: Factors Affecting the Participation of Women in Local Politics." In A *Portrait of Marginality*, edited by Marianne Githens and Jewel L. Prestage. New York: David McKay, 1977.

Lemons, J. Stanley. *The Woman Citizen: Social Feminism in the 1920's*. Urbana, Ill.: University of Illinois Press, 1973.

Lerner, Gerda. "Placing Women in History: Definitions and Challenges." *Feminist Studies* 3 (Fall 1975):5–14.

Lewis, Diane K. "A Response to Inequality: Black Women, Racism, and Sexism." *Signs* 3 (Winter 1977):339–61.

Lipset, Seymour M. *Political Man*. New York: Anchor Books, 1963.

Lipset, Seymour M., and Rokkan, Stein, eds. *Party Systems and Voter Alignments*. New York: Free Press, 1971.

Ludovici, Anthony. "Woman's Encroachment on Man's Domain." *Current History* 27 (October 1927):21–5.

Maccoby, Eleanor, and Jacklin, Carol. *The Psychology of Sex Differences*. Stanford: Stanford University Press, 1974.

Markus, Gregory B. "Political Attitudes during an Election Year: A Report on the 1980 NES Panel Study." Paper delivered at the Annual Meeting of the Social Science History Association, Nashville, Tenn., 1981.

Markus, Gregory B., and Converse, Philip E. "A Dynamic Simultaneous Equation Model of Electoral Choice." *American Political Science Review* 73 (December 1979):1055–1070.

Mason, Karen O.; Czajka, John L.; and Arber, Sara. "Change in U.S. Women's Sex-Role Attitudes, 1964–1974." *American Sociological Review* 41 (August 1976):573–96.

Matthews, Donald R., and Prothro, James W. *Negroes and the New Southern Politics*. New York: Harcourt, Brace and World, 1966.

McCourt, Kathleen. *Working-Class Women and Grass Roots Politics.* Bloomington, Ind.: Indiana University Press, 1977.

McMenamin, Reverend Hugh L. "Evils of Woman's Revolt Against the Old Standards." *Current History* 27 (October 1927):30–32.

Mead, Margaret. "A Comment on the Role of Women in Agriculture." In *Women and World Development,* edited by Irene Tinker and Michelle Bo Bransen. Overseas Development Council. New York: Praeger, 1976.

Merriam, Charles E., and Gosnell, Harold F. *Non-Voting: Causes and Methods of Control.* Chicago: University of Chicago Press, 1924.

Michel, Andree. "Family Models of the Future." In *Becoming Visible: Women in European History,* edited by Renate Bridenthal and Claudia Koonz. Boston: Houghton Mifflin Co., 1977.

Milbrath, Lester W. *Political Participation.* Chicago: Rand McNally, 1965.

Milbrath, Lester W., and Goel, M. L. *Political Participation.* Chicago: Rand McNally, 1977.

Miller, Arthur H. "Political Issues and Trust in Government: 1964–1970." *American Political Science Review* 68 (September 1974):951–72.

Miller, Arthur H.; Brown, Thad A.; and Raine, Alden S. "Social Conflict and Political Estrangement, 1958–1972." Paper delivered at the Annual Meeting of the Midwest Political Science Association, 1973.

Miller, Arthur H., and Miller, Warren E. "Partisanship and Performance: 'Rational' Choice in the 1976 Presidential Election." Paper delivered at the Annual Meeting of the American Political Science Association, Washington, D.C. 1977.

Miller, Arthur H.; Miller, Warren E.; Raine, Alden S.; and Brown, Thad A. "A Majority Party in Disarray: Policy Polarization in the 1972 Election." *American Political Science Review* 70 (September 1976): 753–78.

Miller, Arthur H., and Wattenberg, Martin P. "Policy and Performance Voting in the 1980 Election." Paper delivered at the Annual Meeting of the American Political Science Association, New York City, New York, 1981.

Miller, Warren E., and Levitin, Theresa. *Leadership and Change.* Cambridge, Mass.: Winthrop Publishers, 1976.

Miller, Warren E., and Shanks, J. Merrill. "Policy Directions and Presidential Leadership; Alternative Interpretations of the 1980 Presidential Election," *British Journal of Political Science,* July 1982, pp. 299–356.

Millett, Kate. *Sexual Politics.* New York: Avon, 1971.

Moore, Joan W. "Social Deprivation and Advantage as Sources of Political Values." *Western Political Quarterly* 15 (June 1962):217–26.

Myrdal, Alvah, and Klein, Viola. *Women's Two Roles: Home and Work.* London: Routledge and Kegan Paul, 1956.

Myrdal, Gunnar. *An American Dilemma.* New York: Harper and Row, 1962.

National Roster of Black Elected Officials, The, vol. 10. Washington, D.C.: Joint Center for Political Studies, 1980.

Newland, Kathleen. *The Sisterhood of Man: The Impact of Women's Changing Roles on Social and Economic Life Around the World.* New York: W. W. Norton, 1979.

Nie, Norman H., and Andersen, Kristi. "Mass Belief Systems Revisited: Political Change and Attitude Structure." *Journal of Politics* 36 (August 1974):540–91.

Nie, Norman H.; Hull, C. Hadlai; Jenkins, Jean G.; Steinbrenner, Karin; and Bent, Dale H. *SPSS: Statistical Package for the Social Sciences.* New York: McGraw-Hill, 1975.

Nie, Norman H.; Verba, Sidney; and Petrocik, John R. *The Changing American Voter.* Cambridge, Mass.: Harvard University Press, 1976.

O'Neill, William L. *Everyone Was Brave: The Rise and Fall of Feminism in America.* Chicago: Quadrangle Books, 1969.

Page, Benjamin, and Brody, Richard. "Policy Voting and the Electoral Process: The Vietnam War Issue." *American Political Science Review* 66 (September 1972):979–95.

Pisciotti, Joseph P., and Hjelm, Victor. "Profiles and Careers of Colorado State Legislators." *Western Political Quarterly* 21 (December 1968):698–722.

Pomper, Gerald M. *Voter's Choice: Varieties of American Electoral Behavior.* New York: Dodd, Mead and Company, 1975.

Pomper, Gerald M. "The Presidential Election." In *The Election of 1976,* edited by Marlene Pomper. New York: David McKay, 1977.

Pool, Ithiel de Sola; Abelson, Robert P.; and Popkin, Samuel. *A Computer Simulation of the 1960 and 1964 Presidential Elections.* Cambridge, Mass.: M.I.T. Press, 1964–65.

Prewitt, Kenneth. "Political Ambitions, Volunteerism, and Electoral Accountability." *American Political Science Review* 64 (March 1970):5–17.

Quinn, Sally. "The Republican Women's Attempt at Semi-Activism." *Washington Post,* August 24, 1972, p. A–18.

Rasmussen, Jorgen S. "The Role of Women in British Parliamentary Elections." *Journal of Politics* 39 (1977):1044–54.

Rendel, Margherita. "Women and Feminist Issues in Parliament." Paper delivered at Workshop on Women in Politics, at the European Consortium for Political Research, West Berlin, Germany, April, 1977.

Rice, Stuart A., and Willey, Malcolm M. "American Women's Ineffective Use of the Vote." *Current History* 20 (July 1924):641–47.

Rokkan, Stein, ed. *Comparative Research Across Cultures and Nations.* Paris and The Hague: Mouton, 1968.

Rokkan, Stein, and Meyriat, Jean, eds. *International Guide to Electoral Statistics.* Paris: Mouton, 1969.

Rose, Richard. "England: A Traditionally Modern Culture." In *Political Culture and Political Development,* edited by Lucien W. Pye and Sidney Verba. Princeton: Princeton University Press, 1965.

———. "The Nuffield Election Studies Come of Age." *Times* (London), October 2, 1966.

———. "Class and Party Divisions: Britain as a Test Case." *Sociology* 11 (1968*a*):2.

———. "Party Systems, Social Structure, and Voter Alignments in Britain." In *Party Systems, Party Organizations and the Politics of New Masses,* edited by Otto Stammer. Berlin: Institute fur politische Wissenschaft, Free University, 1968*b*.

———. *The Polls and the 1970 Election.* Occasional Paper No. 7. Glasgow: University of Strathclyde Survey Research Centre, 1970*a*.

———. *The United Kingdom as a Multi-National State.* Occasional Paper No. 6. Glasgow: University of Strathclyde Survey Research Centre, 1970*b*.

———. *Electoral Behavior: A Comparative Handbook.* New York: Free Press, 1973.

———. *Politics in England: An Interpretation.* Boston: Little, Brown and Co., 1974*a*.

———. *The Problem of Party Government.* London: Macmillan & Co., 1974*b*.

———, ed. *Studies in British Politics: A Reading in Political Sociology.* 2d rev. ed. London: Macmillan & Co., 1969.

Ross, Ruth. "Tradition and the Role of Women in Great Britain." In *Women in the World: A Comparative Study,* edited by Lynne Iglitzin and Ruth Ross. Santa Barbara: Clio Books, 1976.

Rossi, Alice S. "Inequality Between the Sexes." In *The Woman in America,* edited by R. V. Lifton. Boston: Houghton Mifflin Co., 1964.

Sanders, Marion K. *The Lady and the Vote.* Boston: Houghton Mifflin Co., 1956.

Schattschneider, E. E. *The Semisovereign People*. New York: Holt, Rinehart and Winston, 1960.

Schneider, William. "The November 4 Vote for President: What Did It Mean?" In *The American Elections of 1980*, edited by Austin Ranney. Washington, D.C.: The American Enterprise Institute for Public Policy Research, 1981, pp. 212–62.

Scott, Ann. *The Southern Lady: From Pedestal to Politics, 1830–1930*. Chicago: University of Chicago Press, 1970.

Shabad, Goldie, and Andersen, Kristi. "Candidate Evaluations by Men and Women." *Public Opinion Quarterly* 43 (Spring 1979):18–35.

Sigelman, Lee. "The Curious Case of Women in State and Local Government." *Social Science Quarterly* 56 (March 1976):591–604.

Silbey, Joel; Bogue, Allan; and Flanigan, William, eds. *The History of American Electoral Behavior*. Princeton: Princeton University Press, 1978.

Smith, Tom as quoted by Richard J. Cattani, in *Christian Science Monitor*, July 9, 1981.

Sonquist, John A., and Dunkelberg, William C. *Survey and Opinion Research*. Englewood Cliffs, N.J.: Prentice-Hall, 1977.

Soule, John W., and McGrath, Wilma E. "A Comparative Study of Male-Female Political Attitudes of Citizen and Elite Levels." In *A Portrait of Marginality*, edited by Marianne Githens and Jewel L. Prestage. New York: David McKay, 1977.

Staines, Graham, L.; Tavris, Carol; and Jayaratne, Toby E. "The Queen Bee Syndrome." In *The Female Experience*, edited by Carol Tavris. Del Mar, Calif.: Communications Research Machines, 1973.

Stanton, Theodore, and Blatch, Harriet Stanton, eds. *Elizabeth Cady Stanton 1815–1920, as Revealed in Her Letters, Diary, and Reminescences*. New York: Harper and Brothers, 1922.

Steinem, Gloria. "Can Half of America be Single-Issue Politics? The Problems of Taking 1980 Lying Down." *Ms. Magazine*, September 1980, p. 98.

Stone, Olive M. "The Status of Women in Great Britain." *American Journal of Comparative Law*, Spring 1972.

Stone, Pauline T. "The Black Woman in Transition." *Newsletter*, Center for the Continuing Education of Women, University of Michigan, 2, no. 1 (1978).

———. "Feminine Consciousness and Black Women." In *Women: A Feminist Perspective*, edited by Jo Freeman. 2d ed. Palo Alto, Calif.: Mayfield Publishing Company, 1979.

Stone, Pauline T., and Brown, Cheryl L. "The Black American Woman in the Social Science Literature." Department of Political Science, University of Michigan, Michigan Occasional Papers in Women's Studies, vol. 2 (Fall 1978).

Stouffer, Samuel, and Lazarsfeld, Paul F. Foreword. In Louis Harris, *Is There a Republican Majority? Political Trends 1952–1956*, New York: Harper and Brothers, 1954.

Sundquist, James L., and Scammon, Richard M. "The 1980 Election: Profile and Historical Perspective." *Congressional Quarterly*, edited by Ellis Sandoz and Cecil V. Crabb, Jr. Washington, D.C.: Congressional Quarterly, 1981, pp. 19–44.

Taeuber, Karl E., and Sweet, James A. "Family and Work: The Social Life Cycle of Women." In *Women and the American Economy: A Look to the 1980's*, edited by Juanita M. Kreps. Englewood Cliffs, N.J.: Prentice-Hall, 1976.

Tingsten, Herbert. *Political Behavior: Studies in Election Statistics*. London: P. S. King and Son, 1937.

Tolchin, Susan and Tolchin, Martin. *Clout: Woman Power and Politics*. New York: Coward, McCann and Geoghegan, 1974.

Traugott, Michael W., and Katosh, John P. "Response Validity in Surveys of Voting Behavior." *Public Opinion Quarterly* 43 (Fall 1979):359–77.

Twentieth Century Fund. Task Force on Women and Employment. *Exploitation from 9 to 5*. New York: Twentieth Century Fund, 1975.

U.S., Department of Commerce, Bureau of the Census. *Female Family Heads*. Current Population Reports, Population Characteristics. Series P-23, no. 50. Washington, D.C.: Government Printing Office, 1974.

———. *Statistical Abstract of the United States*. Washington, D.C.: Government Printing Office, 1977.

———. *The Social and Economic Status of the Black Population in the United States, 1974*. Current Population Reports, Population Characteristics. Series P-23, no. 80. Washington, D.C.: Government Printing Office, 1974.

———. *Voting and Registration in the Election of November 1964*. Current Population Reports, Population Characteristics. Series P-20, no. 143. Washington, D.C.: Government Printing Office, October, 1965.

———. *Voting and Registration in the Election of November 1968*. Current Population Reports, Population Characteristics. Series P-20, no. 192. Washington, D.C.: Government Printing Office, December, 1969.

———. *Voting and Registration in the Election of November 1976*. Current Population Reports, Population Characteristics. Series P-20, no. 322. Washington, D.C.: Government Printing Office, March, 1978.

————. *Voting and Registration in the Election of November 1980 (Advance Report)*. Current Population Reports, Population Characteristics, Series P–20, no. 359. Washington, D.C.: Government Printing Office, January, 1981.

U.S., Commission on Civil Rights. *Report of the Commission on Civil Rights*. Washington, D.C.: Government Printing Office, 1959, 1961, 1964.

Van Allen, Judith. "Memsahib, Militante, Femme Libre: Political and Apolitical Styles of Modern African Women." In *Women in Politics*, edited by Jane S. Jaquette. New York: John Wiley and Sons, 1974.

Verba, Sidney, and Nie, Norman H. *Participation in America: Political Democracy and Social Equality*. New York: Harper and Row, 1972.

Verba, Sidney; Nie, Norman H.; and Kim, Jae-On. *Participation and Political Equality*. Cambridge: Cambridge University Press, 1978.

Walum, Laurel R. *The Dynamics of Sex and Gender: A Sociological Perspective*. Chicago: Rand McNally, 1977.

Ward, Barbara E., ed. *Women in the New Asia*. Netherlands: UNESCO, 1963.

Welch, Susan. "Recruitment of Women to Public Office: A Discriminant Analysis." *Western Political Quarterly* 31 (September 1978):372–80.

Welch, Susan, and Sigelman, Lee. "Changes in Public Attitudes Toward Women in Politics." *Social Science Quarterly* 6, no. 2 (June 1982):312–322.

Wells, Audrey S., and Smeal, Eleanor C. "Women's Attitudes toward Women in Politics: A Survey of Urban Registered Voters and Party Committee Women." In *Women in Politics*, edited by Jane S. Jaquette. New York: John Wiley and Sons, 1974.

Werner, Emmy E. "Women in Congress: 1917–1964." *Western Political Quarterly* 19 (March 1966):16–30.

————. "Women in the State Legislatures." *Western Political Quarterly* 21 (March 1968):40–50.

Wirthlin, Richard as quoted in "Face Off: A Conversation with the Presidents' Pollsters." *Public Opinion* 3 (December/January 1981):2–12, 63–64.

Woodhouse, Chase Going. "The Status of Women." *American Journal of Sociology* 35 (May 1930):1091–96.

INDEX

Abrams, Philip, 148
Abelson, Robert P., 63
Activism, political, 116–42; and world perspective, 146–47; British, 159–61, 209–14
Addams, Jane, 119
Age; and voter turnout, 33–35, 184–85; distribution of women, 34; and race and turnout, 80; of 1972 convention delegates, 130; of women members of Congress, 130; of British women voters, 151
Alienation, political, 91–93, 100
Almond, Gabriel, 8, 45, 155, 159
Almquist, Elizabeth M., 101–2
American Dilemma, An, 76
American Voter, The, 2, 14, 48, 65
American Woman, The, 27
Andersen, Kristi, 27, 55, 61
Anthony, Susan B., 19
Apolitical women, 6, 67–69, 116–25
Attitudes: and behavioral correlates, 41; and party identification, 56; and women's welfare, 57; pacifism, 57–59; racial strife, 59; social welfare, 60; social indicators for black women, 97–100; feminism for black women, 106–10; Eurpean men and women, 161–78

Ayres, Richard E., 22

Bardwick, Judith M., 49
Baxter, Sandra, 116, 118, 121, 123–25
Berelson, Bernard R., 43, 66, 157
Bers, Trudy H., 126
Black power, 88
Black women; and low socioeconomic status of, 73; voting history of, 74; effects of race and gender on voting of, 75–76, 201; as never voters, 78; generational differences of, 79; and age, 80; sit-in participation of, 81; regional voting of, 82–84; effects of education and, 84–86; labor force participation of, 86–89; and trust in Congress, 94; political efficacy of, 94, 202–4; and social indicators, 97–100; and attitudes on seriousness of problems, 99–100; and church influence, 101; and race and sex, 102; and gender roles, 103; heads of households and wives voting, 104; fear of success of, 105; and feminism and voting, 106–10; and self-interest, 111–12
Blair, Emily N., 119
Blake, Judith, 147, 161

253